LS

KIERKEGAARD

and the

LEV SHESTOV

OHIO UNIVERSITY PRESS

Existential Philosophy

TRANSLATED BY ELINOR HEWITT

Athens

English Translation from Russian
Copyright © 1969 by Ohio University Press
Library of Congress Catalog Card Number: 68–29656
Manufactured in the United States of America.
Kierkegaard and the Existential Philosophy was
published in German in 1949 under the title *Kierkegaard und die
Existenzphilosophie*

SBN 8214–0060–6

TO NATHALIE BARANOFF
AND TATIANA RAGEOT

Contents

Kierkegaard and Dostoyevsky

INSTEAD OF A PREFACE

Kierkegaard and Dostoyevsky[*]

INSTEAD OF A PREFACE

You do not, of course, expect me to exhaust the complicated and difficult subject of the work of Kierkegaard and Dostoyevsky during the hour allotted to me. I shall therefore limit myself to speaking of how Dostoyevsky and Kierkegaard understood original sin; in other words, my subject will be speculative and revealed truth. But I must say first that in so short a time I shall hardly be able to give as complete an explanation as you might like of what Dostoyevsky and Kierkegaard thought and told us about the Fall of Man. At best I shall be able to indicate—and schematically, at that—why original sin caught the attention of these men, two of the most remarkable thinkers of the nineteenth century. I might mention here that even Nietzsche, usually thought to be so far removed from biblical themes, considered the problem of the Fall to be the axis or pivot of his whole complex of philosophical questions. His principal, essential theme is Socrates, whom he saw as a decadent man, that is, as the fallen man par excellence.

[*] A paper read at the Academy of Religion and Philosophy in Paris, May 5, 1935.

Moreover, he saw Socrates' fall in that quality which history and the history of philosophy in particular had always found, and taught us to find, most praiseworthy: in his boundless confidence in reason and the knowledge obtained by reason. When you read Nietzsche's thoughts on Socrates, you cannot avoid being reminded constantly of the biblical story of the forbidden tree and those enticing words of the tempter: ye shall be knowing. Kierkegaard tells us more about Socrates than Nietzsche does, and he speaks with greater urgency. What is more surprising is that Kierkegaard considers Socrates the most remarkable phenomenon in the history of humanity before the appearance on Europe's horizon of that mysterious book known as the Book, i.e., the Bible.

The Fall of Man has troubled human thought since earliest times. Men have always felt that all is not right with the world, and even that much is wrong: "Something is rotten in the state of Denmark," to use Shakespeare's words; and they have made tremendous and intense efforts to explain how this evil originated. I must say at this point that Greek philosophy, just like the philosophy of other peoples, including those of the Far East, replied to this question with an answer directly opposed to what we find in the story of the Book of Genesis. One of the first great Greek philosophers, Anaximander, says in a passage that has come down to us: "From that source whence came birth to individual creatures, thence also, by necessity, shall come their destruction. At the appointed time they do penance and accept retribution, one from the other, for their iniquity." This thought of Anaximander's pervades all ancient philosophy: the appearance of individual things (mainly, of course, living creatures, and primarily human beings) is considered wicked effrontery, for which their death and destruction is fit punishment. The idea of γένεσις and φθορά ("birth" and "destruction") is the starting point of ancient philosophy (this same idea, I repeat, was persistently in the minds of the founders of the Far Eastern religions and philosophies). Man's natural thought, at all times and among all peoples, has stopped helplessly, as if bewitched, before fatal necessity which brought into the world the terrible law of death, inseparably bound up with man's birth, and the law of destruction, which waits for everything that has appeared and will appear. In being itself human thought has discovered something wrong, a defect, a sickness, a sin, and accordingly wisdom has demanded the vanquishing of that sin at its roots; in other words, a renunciation of being which, since it has a beginning, is fated inevitably to end. The Greek catharsis, or purification, has as its source the conviction that the immediate data of consciousness, which attest to the inevitable destruction of all that is born, reveal to us a truth that is primordial, eternal, inflexible, and forever invincible. True being, real being (ὄντως ὄν) is not to be found among ourselves or for ourselves; it is to be found where the power of the law of birth and destruction ends, that is, where there is no birth and where therefore there is no destruction. This is the point of origin of speculative philosophy. The law, discovered by intellectual vision, of the inevitable destruction of all that has arisen and been created seems to us to be a law eternally inherent in being itself. Greek philosophy was as firmly convinced of this as was the Hindu wisdom, and we, who are separated from the Greeks and the Hindus by thousands of years, are just as incapable

3

of breaking free from the power of this most self-evident truth as those who first discovered it and showed it to us.

In this respect the Book of books alone constitutes a mysterious exception.

What is said in it directly contradicts what men have found out through their intellectual vision. Everything, as we read in the very beginning of the Book of Genesis, was made by the Creator, everything had a beginning. But this not only is not seen as a precondition of the decay, imperfection, corruption, and sinfulness of being; on the contrary, it is an assurance of all possible good in the universe. To put it another way, God's act of creation was the source, and moreover the only source, of all good. On the evening of each day of creation the Lord said, as he surveyed what He had made: "It is good," and on the last day, looking around at everything that He had created, God saw that it was all very good. Both the world and its people (whom God had blessed) were made by the Creator, and it is for the very reason of their creation by Him that they were made perfect, without any defects. There was no evil in the world created by God, nor was there any sin from which evil could proceed. Evil and sin arose later. Whence came they? Scripture gives a definite answer to this question. God planted among the other trees in the Garden of Eden the tree of life and the tree of knowledge of good and evil. And He said to the first man: "Of every tree of the garden thou mayest freely eat: but of the tree of the knowledge of good and evil, thou shalt not eat of it: for in the day that thou eatest thereof thou shalt surely die." But the tempter (in the Bible he is called the serpent, the most cunning of all God's creatures) said: "No, ye shall not die; your eyes shall be opened, and ye shall be as gods, knowing." Man succumbed to temptation, ate of the forbidden fruit; his eyes were opened and he became knowing. What was revealed to him? What did he find out? He learned the same thing that the Greek philosophers and Hindu sages had learned: the "it is good" uttered by God was not justified—all is not good in the created world. There must be evil and, what is more, much evil, intolerable evil, in the created world, precisely because it is created. Everything around us—the immediate data of consciousness—testifies to this with unquestionable evidence; he who looks at the world with "open eyes," he who "knows," can draw no other conclusion. At the very moment when man became "knowing," sin entered the world; in other words, it entered together with "knowledge"—and after sin came evil. This is what the Bible tells us.

The question is put to us, the men of the twentieth century, just as it was put to the ancients: whence comes sin, whence come the horrors of life which are linked with sin? Is there a defect in being itself, which, since it is created, albeit by God, since it has a beginning, must inescapably, by virtue of that eternal law that is subject to no one and nothing, be burdened down by its imperfections, which doom it ahead of time to destruction? Or do sin and evil arise from "knowledge," from "open eyes," from "intellectual vision," that is, from the fruit of the forbidden tree? One of the most notable philosophers of the last century, Hegel, who had absorbed the whole of European thought covering twenty-five hundred years (and in this lies his significance and his importance),

5

Kierkegaard

maintains without any hesitation that the serpent did not deceive man, that the fruit of the tree of knowledge became the source of philosophy for all time to come. And I must say immediately that historically Hegel is right. The fruit of the tree of knowledge has truly become the source of philosophy, the source of thought for all time to come. Philosophers—and not just the pagan ones, those foreign to Holy Scripture, but also the Jewish and Christian philosophers who recognized Scripture as a divinely inspired book—have all wanted to be knowing and have not been persuaded to renounce the fruit of the forbidden tree. For Clement of Alexandria at the beginning of the third century, Greek philosophy was the second Old Testament. He asserted that if it were possible to separate gnosis (that is, knowledge) from eternal salvation and if he had to make a choice, he would choose, not eternal salvation, but gnosis. All medieval philosophy tended in the same direction. Even the mystics offer no exception in this respect. The unknown author of the celebrated *Theologia deutsch* maintained that Adam could have eaten twenty apples and no harm would have resulted. Sin did not come from the fruit of the tree of knowledge, for nothing bad can come from knowledge. Where did the author of *Theologia deutsch* get this conviction that no evil can come of knowledge? He does not raise this question; evidently it did not occur to him that one may seek and find the truth in Scripture. One must seek the truth only in one's own reason, and only that which reason recognizes as truth is truth. The serpent did not deceive man.

Kierkegaard and Dostoyevsky were both born in the first quarter of the nineteenth century (however, Kierke-

6

gaard, who died at forty-four * and was ten years older than Dostoyevsky, had already concluded his literary career when Dostoyevsky was just beginning to write) and they both lived during the period when Hegel dominated European thought; they could not, of course, have failed to feel that they were wholly in the power of Hegelian philosophy. It is true that Dostoyevsky is supposed never to have read a single line by Hegel (in contrast to Kierkegaard, who knew Hegel through and through), but during the time that he belonged to Belinsky's circle he became familiar enough with the basic statements of Hegel's philosophy. Dostoyevsky had an extraordinary flair for philosophical ideas, and what Belinsky's friends had brought back from Germany sufficed to give him a clear picture of the problems posed and resolved by Hegelian philosophy. However, not only Dostoyevsky but also Belinsky himself, a "perpetual student" and certainly a man whose philosophical insight was far behind Dostoyevsky's, truly felt, and not only felt but found the necessary words to express, all that he found unacceptable in the doctrines of Hegel, which then seemed just as unacceptable to Dostoyevsky. Let me remind you of the passage from Belinsky's famous letter: "If I should succeed in ascending to the highest rung of the ladder of development, even there I would ask you to render me an account of all the victims of circumstance in life and history, of all the victims of chance, of superstition, of the Inquisition of Philip II, etc., etc.: otherwise I would fling myself headfirst from the highest rung. I do

* Kierkegaard (1813–1855) actually died at forty-two. [This footnote and the two that follow are adapted from those written by James M. Edie and James P. Scanlan for their translation of the Preface. Tr.]

7

not wish happiness even as a gift, if my mind is not at rest regarding each one of my blood brothers." * Needless to say, if Hegel could have read these lines by Belinsky, he would merely have shrugged his shoulders contemptuously and called Belinsky a barbarian, a savage, an ignoramus, who obviously had not tasted the fruit of the tree of knowledge and consequently did not even suspect the existence of the immutable law by virtue of which everything that has a beginning (that is, those very human beings for whom he interceded so passionately) must have an end; and that therefore there is absolutely no one to whom one can reasonably turn with such demands for an account of creatures which, being finite, are not subject to any protection or defense. These defenseless ones are not just those victims of chance who first come to mind, but even such as Socrates, Giordano Bruno, and many other great, very great men, wise and just; the wheel of the historical process crushes them all mercilessly and takes as little notice of them as if they were inanimate objects. The philosophy of the spirit is the philosophy of the spirit precisely because it is able to rise above all that is finite and transitory. And conversely, all finite and transitory things can participate in the philosophy of the spirit only when they cease to be concerned with their own interests, which are insignificant and therefore not deserving of any concern. This is what Hegel would have said, and he would have cited the chapter in his *History of Philosophy* which explains that it was quite proper for Socrates to have been poisoned and that this was no great misfortune: an old Greek died—is such a trifle worth making a fuss over? All that is real is rational; in other

* [From Belinsky's letter to Botkin, March 1, 1841. Tr.]

8

words, it cannot and must not be other than it is. Anyone who does not understand this is not a philosopher and has not been given the intellectual vision to penetrate to the essential nature of things. Furthermore, the man who has not found this out cannot truly consider himself to be a religious person (all this according to Hegel). For any religion, and especially the absolute religion (that is what Hegel called Christianity) reveals to men through images (that is, less perfectly) what the thinking spirit itself sees in the nature of existence. "The true content of the Christian faith is therefore justified by philosophy, but not by history" (that is, by what is told in Holy Scripture), says Hegel in his *Philosophy of Religion.* This means that the Scriptures are acceptable only insofar as the thinking spirit admits that they are in agreement with those truths that it acquires itself, or, as Hegel puts it, that it draws from itself. All the rest ought to be discarded. We already know that the thinking spirit of Hegel drew from itself the idea that in spite of what Scripture says, the serpent did not deceive man and the fruit of the forbidden tree has brought us the very best thing that life holds—knowledge. In a like manner the thinking spirit discards as impossible the miracles described in Scripture. We can see how thoroughly Hegel despised Scripture from the following words written by him: "Whether there was more than enough or not enough wine for the guests at the wedding at Cana in Galilee is a matter of complete indifference. In the same way, it is purely accidental that a certain man was cured of a paralyzed hand: millions of people go about with paralyzed hands and other deformities, and no one heals them. Also, it is related in the Old Testament that at the time of the Exodus from Egypt the doors of the houses of the Jews were marked with red so that the angel of the Lord could identify them. Such a faith has no meaning for the spirit. Voltaire's most venomous gibes are directed against this sort of faith. He says that it would have been better if God had taught the Jews about the immortal soul, instead of teaching them how to relieve the call of nature (*aller à la selle*). In this way, privies become the content of faith." Hegel's "philosophy of the spirit" treats Scripture with derision and contempt and accepts from the Bible only what can be "justified" before rational consciousness. Hegel had no need of "revealed" truth; to be more exact, he does not accept it, or rather he considers revealed truth to be what his own mind reveals to him. Certain Protestant theologians arrived at this idea without the help of Hegel; in order not to confuse themselves and others with the mysterious quality of biblical revelation, they declared that all truths are revealed truths. The Greek word for truth is ἀλήθεια; by deriving this word from the verb ἀ-λανθάνω ("un-veil"), the theologians freed themselves from the obligation, so burdensome to a cultivated man, of acknowledging the privileged position of Scriptural truths. Every truth, precisely because it is a truth, reveals something formerly concealed. Seen in this way, Biblical truth offers no exception and has no advantage over other truths. It is acceptable to us only when it can justify itself before our reason and be viewed with our "open eyes." It goes without saying that under these circumstances we must reject three-quarters of what is told in Scripture and interpret what remains in such a way that reason will not yet find something offensive in it. For Hegel (as for the medieval philosophers) Aristotle is the greatest authority. Hegel's

Encyclopedia of the Philosophical Sciences concludes with a long passage (in Greek in the original) from Aristotle's *Metaphysics* on the subject ἡ θεωρία τὸ ἥδιστον καὶ τὸ ἥδιστον, which means: "Contemplation is the best and sweetest." And also in the *Encyclopedia,* he writes at the beginning of the third part, in the sections that head "The Philosophy of the Spirit": "Aristotle's books on the soul are even today the best work and the only one of a speculative sort on this subject. The essential goal of the philosophy of the spirit must be simply to introduce the idea of the concept into the knowledge of the spirit, and thus to open the way to the books of Aristotle." Dante had reason to call Aristotle *il maestro di coloro, chi sanno* ("the master of those who know"). He who wants to "know" must follow Aristotle, and must regard his works —*De Anima,* the *Metaphysics,* the *Ethics*—not only as a second Old Testament, as Clement of Alexandria said, but also as a second New Testament; he must regard them as a Bible. Aristotle is the only master of those who want to know, those who do know. Further inspired by him, Hegel solemnly proclaims in his *Philosophy of Religion:* "The fundamental idea [of Christianity] is the unity of the divine and the human natures: God has become man." And in another passage, in the chapter on "The Kingdom of the Spirit," he says: "The individual must be imbued with the truth about the primary unity of the divine and the human natures, and this truth is to be grasped through faith in Christ. For him, God no longer seems a being part." This is all that the "absolute religion" brought Hegel. He joyfully quotes the words of Meister Eckhard (from his sermons) and the same words of Angelus Silesius: "If God were not, I would not be: if I were not, God would not be." The content of the absolute religion is thus interpreted and put on a level with the thought of Aristotle or of the Biblical serpent who promised our forefather that "knowledge" would make him equal to God. And it never for a moment entered into Hegel's mind that in this lies the terrible, fatal Fall, that "knowledge" does not make a man equal to God, but tears him away from God, putting him in the clutches of a dead and deadening "truth." The "miracles" of Scripture (i.e., the omnipotence of God) were, as we recall, contemptuously rejected by Hegel, for as he explains in another passage: "It is impossible to require of men that they believe in things in which they cannot believe past a certain degree of education: such a faith is faith in a content which is finite and fortuitous, that is, which is not true: for true faith has no fortuitous content." According to this, "a miracle is a violation of the natural connection of phenomena, and is therefore a violation of the spirit."

II

I have had to dwell somewhat on Hegel's speculative philosophy, for the reason that both Dostoyevsky and Kierkegaard (the first without realizing it, the second fully aware of it) saw their life work as a struggle with, and victory over, that system of ideas embodied in Hegelian philosophy, the culmination of the development of European thought. For Hegel, a break in the natural connection of phenomena, a break that shows the power of the Creator over the world, and his omnipotence, is an unbearable and most dreadful thought: for him, this is a "violation of the spirit." He ridicules the Biblical stories— they all pertain to "history," they speak only of the "finite," which a man who wishes to live in the spirit and the truth must shake off. He calls this the "reconciliation" of religion and reason; in this way religion is justified by philosophy, which finds a "necessary truth" in the diversity of religious systems, and in this necessary truth discovers an "eternal idea." There is no doubt that reason is thus fully satisfied. But what is left of the religion which has been justified in this manner before reason? There is also no doubt that in reducing the content of the "absolute religion" to the unity of the divine and the human natures, Hegel and all his followers became "knowing," as the tempter promised Adam when he lured him with the fruit from the forbidden tree. In other words, Hegel discovered in the Creator the same nature which had been revealed to him in his own being. But do we turn to religion in order to acquire knowledge? Belinsky sought an account of all the victims of chance, of the Inquisition, etc. But is such an account the concern of knowledge? Would knowledge be able to render such an account? On the contrary, one who knows, and particularly one who knows the truth about the unity of the natures of God and man, is certain that what Belinsky demands is impossible. To demand the impossible means to reveal weakmindedness, as Aristotle said; where the realm of the impossible begins, there must human seeking end; there, to express it in Hegel's words, all the interests of the spirit must cease.

And now we come to Kierkegaard, who was brought up on Hegel and in fact venerated him in his youth; who, having run aground on that reality which Hegel, in the name of the interests of the spirit, had urged men to cast aside, suddenly felt that there lay hidden in the great master's philosophy a treacherous, fatal lie and a terrible temptation. He recognized in it the *eritis scientes* of the Biblical serpent: an appeal to exchange a fearless belief in a free and living Creator for a submission to inflexible truths that rule over everything without exception, but are indifferent to all. He went from the great scholar, from the noted thinker whose praises were sung by everyone, to the "private thinker," to the Job of the Bible; and he not only went but ran, as if to his only savior. And from Job he proceeded to Abraham; not to Aristotle, the master of those who know, but to the man named in the Scriptures as the father of faith. For the sake of Abraham he forsook even Socrates himself. Socrates was also "knowing;" in the phrase γνῶθι σεαυτόν ("know thyself") the pagan god had revealed to him the truth of the unity of the divine and the human natures five centuries before the Bible reached Europe. Socrates knew that for God, as for man, not everything is possible; that the possible and the impossible are determined, not by God, but by eternal laws to which God and man are equally subject. For this reason God has no power over history, i.e., over reality. "To make something which once was into something which never was is impossible in the world of the senses; this can only be done inwardly, in spirit;" so Hegel says; another truth that was certainly not revealed to him in Scripture, where it is repeated so often and so insistently that for God nothing is impossible, and where man is even promised power over all that there is in the world: "If ye have faith as a grain of mustard seed, nothing shall be impossible unto you." But the philosophy of the spirit does not hear these words and does not want to hear them. They are disturbing to it; a miracle, we will remember, is a violation of the spirit. But then the source of everything "miraculous" is faith, and moreover a faith so bold that it seeks no justification from reason, it seeks no justification from any quarter; a faith that instead summons everything in the world to its own tribunal. Faith is above and beyond knowledge. When Abraham went to the Promised Land, explains the Apostle, he went not knowing himself where he was going. He had no need of knowledge, he lived by what he had been promised; the place where he arrived would be the Promised Land, simply because he had arrived there. For the philosophy of the spirit no such faith exists. For the philosophy of the spirit faith is only imperfect knowledge, knowledge taken on trust, which will be proven true only when and if it wins the recognition of reason. No one has the right to quarrel with reason and rational truths, nor the power to contend with them. Rational truths are eternal truths; they must be accepted and assimilated unreservedly. Hegel's "all that is real is rational" is therefore a free translation of Spinoza's *non ridere, non lugere, neque detestari, sed intelligere* ("do not laugh, do not weep, do not curse, but understand"). The created and the Creator alike bow before eternal truths. Speculative philosophy will not give up this position for anything and it defends it with all its strength. Gnosis (knowledge, understanding) is more precious to it than eternal salvation; what is more, in gnosis it finds eternal salvation. This is why Spinoza declared so steadfastly: do not weep, do not curse, but understand. And here, as in Hegel's "rational reality," Kierkegaard perceived, here he discovered, the meaning of that mysterious, elusive link between knowledge and the Fall set forth in the story of Genesis. Now, Holy Scripture did not repudiate or prohibit knowledge in the strict sense of the word. On the contrary, it is said in Scripture that man was summoned to give names to all things. But man did not want to do this, did not want to be content with giving names to the things that the Creator had made. Kant expressed this very well in the first edition of the *Critique of Pure Reason.* "Experience," he said, "shows us what exists, but it does not tell us that whatever exists must necessarily exist thus (as it exists, and not otherwise). Therefore, experience does not give us a true generality, and reason, which eagerly strives for this sort of knowledge, will sooner became irritated than be satisfied with experience." Reason eagerly strives to hand man over to the power of necessity, and not only is not satisfied with the free act of creation described in Scripture, but is irritated, disturbed, and frightened by it. It prefers to hand itself over to the power of necessity, with its eternal, universal, inflexible principles, rather than trust in its Creator. So it was for our forefather, seduced or bewitched by the words of the tempter; so it continues to be for us and for the greatest representatives of human thought. Aristotle twenty centuries ago, Spinoza, Kant, and Hegel in modern times, had an irresistible desire to hand themselves and mankind over to the power of necessity. And they did not even suspect that this is the greatest of Falls; in gnosis they saw not the ruin but the salvation of the soul.

Kierkegaard also studied the ancients and was in his youth a passionate admirer of Hegel. And only when he by the will of fate felt himself wholly in the power of that necessity for which his reason so eagerly strove did he understand the depth and the disturbing significance of the Biblical story of the Fall of Man. We have exchanged faith, which specifies the relationship of the created to the Creator and is in itself a token of unlimited freedom and infinite possibilities, for knowledge, for a slavish dependency on eternal principles which are dead and deadening. Can one imagine a more terrible, more fatal Fall? And then Kierkegaard perceived that the beginning of philosophy is not wonder, as the Greeks taught, but despair: *de profundis ad te, Domine, clamavi*. He realized that there was something to be found in the "private thinker" Job that had not occurred to the renowned philosopher, the noted professor. In contrast to Spinoza and those who before and after Spinoza sought "understanding" (*intelligere*) in philosophy and put human reason in a position to judge the Creator Himself, Job teaches us by his own example that in order to grasp the truth, one should not refuse or forbid oneself "*lugere et detestari*," but should proceed from them. Knowledge, i.e., a readiness to accept as the truth what appears to be self-evident, that is, what we see with the eyes that were "opened" for us after the Fall (Spinoza calls them *oculi mentis;* Hegel uses the phrase "spiritual vision"), inevitably leads man to ruin. "The just shall live by faith," says the Prophet, and the Apostle repeats his words. "What is not of faith is sin"—only these words can defend us against the temptation of "ye shall be knowing," which seduced the first man and holds us all in its power. Job restores to the weeping and cursing, "*lugere et detestari*," rejected by speculative philosophy their primordial right: the right to come forward as judges when inquiries are begun into the whereabouts of truth and falsehood. "Human cowardice cannot bear what madness and death have to tell us;" men avert their eyes from the horrors of life and are

17

satisfied with the "consolations" prepared for them by the philosophy of the spirit. "But Job," continues Kierkegaard, "demonstrated the breadth of his concept of the world by the firmness with which he opposed the subterfuges and insidious attacks of ethics" (i.e., of the philosophy of the spirit; Job's friends told him the same thing that Hegel later on declared in his "philosophy of the spirit"). Furthermore, "The greatness of Job is that his suffering can neither be allayed nor suppressed by lies and empty promises" (of that same philosophy of the spirit). And finally, "Job was blessed; everything he had possessed before was returned to him. This is called repetition. When does repetition begin? Human language has no way of expressing this: *when every conceivable probability, every reliable indication says that it is impossible.*" And he notes in his journal, "Only horror which has turned to despair can develop a man's higher powers." For Kierkegaard and for his philosophy, which to contrast it with theoretical or speculative philosophy he calls existential philosophy, that is, a philosophy which gives man not "understanding" but life ("the just shall live by faith"), Job's wails seem more than mere wails (i.e., meaningless, useless, tiresome cries). For him these cries reveal a new dimension of truth; he perceives an effective force in them, a force that, like the trumpets at Jericho, must make the walls of the fortress crumble. This is the basic motif of existential philosophy. Kierkegaard knows as well as anyone else that speculative philosophy considers existential philosophy great nonsense. But this does not stop him; on the contrary it inspires him. He sees in the "objectivity" of speculative philosophy its basic defect. "Men," he writes, "have become too objective to achieve eternal bliss: eternal bliss consists of a passionate, infinite concern." And this infinite concern is the beginning of faith. "If I renounce everything (as demanded by speculative philosophy, which 'frees' the human spirit through the dialectic of the finite) —this is still not faith," writes Kierkegaard concerning Abraham's sacrifice, "it is only submission. I make this movement by my own powers. And if I do not, it is simply through cowardice and weakness. But in believing I do not renounce anything. On the contrary, I gain everything through faith: if one has faith as a grain of mustard seed, he can move mountains. A purely human courage is needed to renounce the finite for the eternal. But a paradoxical and humble courage is needed to become master of all that is finite by virtue of the Absurd. This is the courage of faith. Faith did not take Isaac from Abraham; Abraham won him through faith." I could cite any number of quotations from Kierkegaard which express the same idea.* "The knight of faith," he says, "is the truly happy man, master of all that is finite." Kierkegaard is perfectly aware that statements of this sort are a challenge to everything suggested to us by the natural human way of thinking. Therefore he looks for protection not to reason, with its universal and necessary pronouncements so eagerly desired by Kant, but to the Absurd, i.e., to faith, which reason qualifies as Absurd. He knows from his own experience that "to believe against reason is martyrdom." But only such a faith, a faith that seeks no justification

---

* [Shestov read Kierkegaard in the German translations of Ketels, Gottsched, and Schrempf (*Gesammelte Werke*, Jena, 1923), Haecker (*Die Tagebücher*, Innsbruck, 1923), and Schrempf (*Erbauliche Reden*, Jena, 1924). All his quotations from Kierkegaard are given as they occur in his text, rather than as they appear in the standard English versions of Kierkegaard's work. Tr.]

from reason and finds none in it, is, according to Kierkegaard, the faith of Holy Scripture. Faith alone gives man the hope of vanquishing that necessity which entered the world and gained control of it through reason. When Hegel transforms the truth of Scripture, revealed truth, into metaphysical truth; when, instead of saying that God took the form of man, or that man was created in the image and likeness of God, he declares that "the fundamental idea of the absolute religion is the unity of the divine and the human natures," he kills faith. Hegel's words have the same import at Spinoza's words: *Deus ex solis suae naturae legibus et a nemine coactus agit*—God acts only by the laws of His own nature and is coerced by no one. And the content of the absolute religion is reduced to another of Spinoza's statements: *res nullo alio modo vel ordine a Deo produci potuerunt quam productae sunt*—things could not have been created by God in any other manner or in any other order than that in which they were created. Speculative philosophy cannot exist without the idea of necessity; necessity is essential to it, just as air is to a human being and water to a fish. This is why the truths of experience irritate reason so. They keep repeating the divine *fiat* and do not provide real knowledge, that is, coercive, compulsory knowledge. But for Kierkegaard coercive knowledge is an abomination of desolation, the source of original sin; it was by saying *eritis scientes* that the tempter brought about the Fall of the first man. Accordingly, Kierkegaard says that "the opposite of sin is not virtue but freedom" and also "the opposite of sin is faith." Faith and faith alone liberates man from sin; faith and faith alone can tear man away from the power of the necessary truths that have controlled his consciousness since the time when he tasted the fruit of the forbidden tree. And faith alone gives man the courage and the strength to look death and madness in the eye and not bow helplessly before them. "Picture a man," writes Kierkegaard, "who by straining his frightened imagination has thought up some unprecedented horror, something completely unbearable. And then suddenly he finds this horror before him; it becomes a reality for him. To the human mind it seems that his destruction is certain. But for God all things are possible. This constitutes *the struggle of faith: a mad struggle for possibility.* For only possibility reveals the way to salvation. In the last analysis one thing remains: *for God all things are possible.* And only then is the way to faith made open. Man believes only when he cannot find any other possibility. God signifies that everything is possible, and that everything is possible signifies God. And only that man whose being has been so shaken that he becomes spirit and grasps that everything is possible, only he has drawn near to God." This is what Kierkegaard writes in his books, and he continually repeats the same theme in his Journal.

III

And here he comes so close to Dostoyevsky that one may say, without fear of being reproached for overstatement, that Dostoyevsky is Kierkegaard's double. Not only their ideas, but also their methods of inquiry into the truth are absolutely identical, and are equally unlike those which form the content of speculative philosophy. Kierkegaard went from Hegel to the private thinker Job. Dostoyevsky did the same. All the episodic digressions in his great novels—"Hippolyte's Confession" in *The Idiot;* the reflections of Ivan and Mitya in *The Brothers Karamazov,* and of Kirillov in *The Possessed;* his *Notes from Underground;* and the short stories he published during the last years of his life in *The Diary of a Writer* ("The Dream of a Ridiculous Man," "The Gentlewoman")—all of them are variations of the theme of the Book of Job, as are the works of Kierkegaard. "Why has dismal sloth destroyed what is most precious?" he writes in "The Gentlewoman." "I will rid myself of it. Sloth! Oh, nature! Men are alone on earth—that is the trouble." Dostoyevsky, like Kierkegaard, "withdrew from the general," or, as he himself expresses it, "from the allness." And he suddenly felt that it was impossible and unnecessary for him to return to the allness; that the allness—i.e., what everyone, in every time and place, considers to be the truth—is a fraud, is a terrible illusion; that all the horrors of existence have come into the world from the allness toward which our reason summons us. In "The Dream of a Ridiculous Man," Dostoyevsky reveals with unbearable clarity the meaning of the words "ye shall be knowing," with which the Biblical serpent tempted our forefather and continues to tempt all of us to this day. Our reason, as Kant says, eagerly strives for generality and necessity; Dostoyevsky, inspired by the Scriptures, exerts all his strength in order to break away from the power of knowledge. Like Kierkegaard, he desperately struggles against speculative truth and the human dialectic that reduces "revelation" to knowledge. When Hegel speaks of "love"—and Hegel has just as much to say about love as about the unity of the divine and the human natures—Dostoyevsky sees it as a betrayal: a betrayal of the divine word. "I maintain," he writes in *The Diary of a Writer* (that is, in the last years of his life) "that awareness of our complete inability to help or to be of any use whatever to suffering mankind, at the same time that we are fully convinced of the suffering of mankind, can turn the love for mankind in your heart into hatred for it." This is the same idea that Belinsky had: an account is demanded of every sacrifice to chance and history—i.e., an account of those whom speculative philosophy considers, in principle, worthy of no attention, since they are created and finite beings, and whom no one in the world is able to help, as speculative philosophy well knows. The following passage from Dostoyevsky's *Notes from Underground* expresses the concept of the futility of speculative philosophy with even greater force and intensity, in his characteristic bold manner. Men, he writes, "yield at once to impossibility. Impossibility means a stone wall! What stone wall? Why, the laws of nature, of course, mathematics, the conclusions of the natural sciences. For instance, once they have proved that you are descended from the ape, it does no good to frown; accept it as it is, for twice two is mathematics. Just try to dispute that! For goodness' sake, they will shout at you, you can't dispute it—twice two is four. Nature does not ask your permission; she is not concerned with your wishes or with whether her laws please you or not. You are obliged to accept her as she is, and therefore you must accept all her consequences as well. A wall, then, is a wall, etc., etc." You see that Dostoyevsky is no less aware than Kant and Hegel of the meaning and significance of those general and necessary judgments, that obligatory, coercive truth to which man's reason summons him. But, in contrast to Kant and Hegel, not only is he not reassured

23

by this "twice two is four" and these "stone walls"; on the contrary, the self-evident revelations of his reason arouse the greatest alarm in him, as they do in Kierkegaard. What handed man over to the power of Necessity? How did it happen that the fate of living human beings came to depend on "stone walls" and "twice two is four," which have nothing at all to do with human beings, which, in general, have nothing at all to do with anyone or anything? The *Critique of Pure Reason* does not raise this question. The *Critique of Pure Reason* would not have paid any attention to this question, if it had been asked. Dostoyevsky himself writes, immediately after the words quoted above: "Lord God, what are the laws of nature and arithmetic to me, if for some reason I do not like these laws and this twice two is four? Obviously, I shall not break this wall down with my head if I really do not have the strength to breach it, *but I will not concede to it simply because it is a stone wall and I lack the strength. As if such a wall were in fact a reassurance and in fact contained any promise of peace. Oh, absurdity of absurdities*" [italics mine]. Where speculative philosophy sees "truth,"—that truth which our reason tries so eagerly to obtain and to which we all pay homage—Dostoyevsky sees the "absurdity of absurdities." He renounces the guidance of reason and not only does not agree to accept its truths, but assails our truths with all the power at his command. Whence came they, he asks, who gave them such limitless power over man? And how did it happen that men accepted them, accepted everything that they brought into the world; and not just accepted, but worshipped, them? One need only raise this question—I repeat that the Critique of Pure Reason did not raise it, did not dare to raise it—in order for it to become clear that there is no answer to it and can be none. More correctly, there is only one answer to it: the power of the "stone walls," the power of "twice two is four," or (to express it in philosophical language) the power of eternal, self-evident truths over man, although it seems to lie at the very basis of existence and therefore to be insuperable, is nevertheless an illusory power. And this brings us back to the Biblical story of Original Sin and the Fall of the first man. "Stone walls" and "twice two is four" are only a concrete expression of what is contained in the words of the tempter: ye shall be knowing. Knowledge has not brought man to freedom, as we are accustomed to think and as speculative philosophy proclaims; knowledge has enslaved us, has put us wholly at the mercy of eternal truths. Dostoyevsky understood this; Kierkegaard, too, found it out. "Sin," wrote Kierkegaard, "is the swoon of freedom. Psychologically speaking, the Fall always occurs in a swoon." "In the state of innocence," he continues, "there is peace and tranquility, but at the same time there is something more: not dissension, not a struggle—for there is no reason to struggle. But what is it then? Nothingness. What effect has Nothingness? It arouses fear." And again: "If we ask what is the object of fear, the only answer will be: Nothingness. Nothingness and fear are attendant on one another, but as soon as the reality of the freedom of the spirit is revealed, fear vanishes. What, upon closer scrutiny, is Nothingness as the pagans feared it? It is called fate. Fate is the Nothingness of fear." Rarely has any writer succeeded in expressing so graphically the meaning of the Biblical story of the Fall. The Nothingness that the tempter pointed out to our forefather prompted his fear before the unlimited will of the Creator; and he rushed to knowledge, to the eternal, uncreated truths, in order to protect himself from God. And so it has continued to the present day: we fear God, we see our salvation in knowledge, in gnosis. Could there be a more profound, more terrible Fall? It is amazing to see how much Dostoyevsky's thoughts about "stone walls" and "twice two is four" resemble what Kierkegaard has just told us. Confronted with eternal truths, men offer no resistance, but accept everything that they bring. When Belinsky "cried out," demanding an account of all those sacrificed to chance and history, the answer given him was that his words had no meaning, that one could not raise such objections to speculative philosophy and Hegel. When Kierkegaard contrasted Job, as a thinker, with Hegel, his words went unheard. And when Dostoyevsky wrote about the "stone wall," no one guessed that there lay the real critique of pure reason: all eyes were fixed on speculative philosophy. We are all convinced that a defect is concealed in Being itself, a defect which even the Creator cannot overcome. The "it is good" which concluded each day of creation is evidence, to our way of thinking, that even the Creator Himself had not penetrated deeply enough into the nature of being. Hegel would have advised Him to taste of the fruit of the forbidden tree, so that He might ascend to the proper level of "knowledge" and understand that His nature, like that of man, is limited by eternal laws and powerless to change anything at all in the universe.

And so Kierkegaard's existential philosophy resolves, as does Dostoyevsky's philosophy, to oppose revealed truth to speculative truth. Sin lies not in being, not in what came from the hands of the Creator; the sin, the defect, the lack are in our "knowledge." The first man was afraid of the limitless will of the Creator; he saw in it the "arbitrariness" that terrifies us so, and began to seek protection from God in knowledge which, as the tempter had suggested to him, made him equal to God, i.e., made him and God equally dependent on eternal uncreated truths by revealing the unity of the divine and the human natures. And this "knowledge" flattened and crushed his consciousness, hammering it down to a plane of limited possibilities by which his earthly and eternal fates are now determined. This is how Scripture represents the "Fall" of man. And only faith, which Kierkegaard, in accordance with Scripture, understands as a mad struggle for possibility (i.e., as we would say, for impossibility, for it is the vanquishing of self-evident truths)—only faith can lift from us the excessive burden of original sin and enable us to straighten up, to "rise" again. Thus, faith is not reliance on what has been told us, what we have heard, what we have been taught. Faith is a new dimension of thought, unknown and foreign to speculative philosophy, which opens the way to the Creator of all earthly things, to the source of all possibilities, to the One for Whom there are no boundaries between the possible and the impossible. Not only is this enormously difficult to put into practice; it is difficult even to conceive of it. Jakob Böhme has said that when God took His hand from him, he himself did not understand what he had written. I think that Dostoyevsky and Kierkegaard could have repeated these words by Böhme. Not without reason did Kierkegaard say: "to believe in spite of reason is martyrdom." Not without reason

Kierkegaard

are the works of Dostoyevsky so full of a superhuman intensity. This is why not enough attention is paid to Dostoyevsky and Kierkegaard, why so few hear what they have to say. Their voices have been and continue to be voices crying in the wilderness.

I

Job and Hegel

Instead of turning for help to the world renowned philosopher or to the professor publicus ordinarius, my friend seeks refuge with a private thinker who knew all that is best in the world, yet afterward withdrew from life: with Job who tosses off fluent observations and hints as he sits in the ashes and scrapes the sores on his body with potsherds. Truth is here expressed more convincingly than in the Greek Symposium.

KIERKEGAARD

Kierkegaard bypassed Russia. Not once did I so much as hear his name in philosophical or literary circles. I am ashamed to admit it, but it would be a sin to conceal the fact that just a few years ago I knew nothing about Kierkegaard. Even in France he is all but unknown; it is only quite recently that a start has been made at translating him. His influence in Germany and the northern countries, however, has been immense. And that fact is of great importance; he has taken hold in the thinking, not only of the more distinguished German theologians, but also the philosophers, and even the professors of philosophy; it is enough to name Karl Barth and his school, on the one hand, and Jaspers and Heidegger on the other. The publisher of *Philosoph. Hefte* went so far as to say that a thorough statement of the philosophy of Heidegger would give us Kierkegaard. And there is every reason to think that the ideas of Kierkegaard are fated to play a great role in the spiritual development of mankind. It is true that that role is of a special kind. He will hardly be accepted among the classics of philosophy and perhaps he will not receive superficial recognition from everyone. But his thought will find a place, unseen, in the hearts of men. So it has already happened; the voice of one crying in the wilderness is not simply a magnificent metaphor. In the general economy of spiritual being, the voices of those crying in the wilderness are just as necessary as the voices which resound in inhabited places, in the public squares and in the temples. And it may be that in some sense they are even more necessary.

Kierkegaard called his philosophy existential—a word which in itself tells us little. And although Kierkegaard uses it often, he was not the one who gave us what might be called the definition of existential philosophy.

"With respect to an understanding of the existential, a desire to avoid definitions shows discretion," * writes Kierkegaard. Kierkegaard does generally avoid detailed definitions; this is connected with his belief that the best means to a common relationship with others is "indirect

* V, 146.

communication." He adopted this method from Socrates, who felt that he had been singled out, not to convey ready-made truths to men, but to help them arrive at truths for themselves. Only the truth which a man has worked out himself can be of use to him. In keeping with this idea, Kierkegaard's philosophy is so constructed that it cannot be assimilated as we usually assimilate any series of ideas. What is called for here is not assimilation, but something different. Well before his death, Kierkegaard was dismayed and infuriated by the idea that after he died *Privatdozenten* would present his philosophy as a complete system of ideas, arranged in sections, chapters, and paragraphs, and that amateurs of interesting philosophical structures would find it mentally enjoyable to follow the development of his thought. For Kierkegaard, philosophy is by no means a purely intellectual activity of the mind. The origin of philosophy is not wonder, as Plato and Aristotle taught, but despair. Human thought undergoes a complete transformation in despair and terror, discovering new powers which lead it to those sources of truth considered unimportant by other persons. Such a man continues to think, but not at all in the way that men think who marvel at what the universe reveals to them, and attempt to understand the nature of that which exists.

In this respect, Kierkegaard's short book *Repetition* is particularly significant. It belongs to the group of his works written and published immediately after, and having to do with, his break with his fiancée, Regina Olsen. In a very short space of time Kierkegaard wrote first his great book *Either/Or*, then *Fear and Trembling* (which came out in one volume together with *Repetition*), and finally *The Concept of Dread*. All these books are on the same

31

theme, which he varies in a thousand ways. I have already indicated the theme: that philosophy originates not in wonder, as the Greeks supposed, but in despair. In *Repetition* he expresses it this way: "Instead of turning for help to the world-renowned philosopher or to the *professor publicus ordinarius* [i.e., Hegel], my friend [Kierkegaard always speaks in the third person when he has to express an idea which is most sacred to him] seeks refuge with a private thinker who knew all that is best in the world, yet afterward withdrew from life: with Job . . . who tosses off fluent observations and hints as he sits in the ashes and scrapes the sores on his body with potsherds. Truth is here expressed more convincingly than in the Greek Symposium." *

The private thinker Job is contrasted with the world-renowned Hegel, and even with the Greek Symposium—i.e., with Plato himself. Does such a contrast have any meaning and has Kierkegaard himself the power to realize it? That is, to accept as the truth, not what was revealed to him by the philosophical thought of the enlightened Hellene, but what was related by a man half-mad from horror and an ignorant man at that—the hero of a narrative from an ancient book? Why is Job's truth "more convincing" than the truth of Hegel or of Plato? Is it really more convincing?

It was not so easy for Kierkegaard to break with the world-famous philosopher. He himself attests to this: "There is no one he dares to trust, no one to whom he can confide his shame and unhappiness at not understanding the great man." † And again: "Dialectical courage is not

* III, 172.
† VI, 111, cf. *ibid.*, 192, 193.

so easily come by: it is only through a crisis that you resolve to oppose the marvelous teacher who knows everything best and has neglected only your problem! Ordinary
people," Kierkegaard continues, "will perhaps not guess
what I am talking about here. For them, Hegelian philosophy is simply a theoretical structure, a very interesting
and diverting one. But there are 'young men' who gave
their hearts to Hegel; finding themselves at the difficult
moment when a man turns to philosophy seeking 'the one
thing that is needful,' such young men will sooner lose
faith in themselves than admit that their teacher was not
looking for the truth, but was pursuing entirely different
problems. If such persons are destined to return to their
senses, they will pay Hegel back with scornful laughter;
and there will be great justice in that."

It may be that they will take even more drastic action.
To leave Hegel for Job! If Hegel could have admitted
even momentarily that such a thing is possible; that the
truth is not in him, but in the ignorant Job; that the
method of inquiry into the truth lies not in a search for
"the self-movement of the concept," (discovered by
Hegel) but in wails of despair which from his point of
view are wild and meaningless, then he would have had
to confess that his whole life's work and he himself
amounted to nothing. And perhaps it is not only Hegel
who would feel that way, perhaps it is not just a question
of Hegel. To seek the truth from Job means to cast doubts
on the basic principles of philosophic thinking. It is possible to give preference to Leibniz or Spinoza or the ancients, and to contrast them with Hegel. But to exchange
Hegel for Job is like forcing time to reverse its course, like
turning back to the age, many thousands of years ago,

when men did not even suspect what our knowledge and our sciences would bring us. Yet Kierkegaard is not satisfied even with Job. He rushes still further into the depths of time—to Abraham. And he contrasts Abraham not with Hegel, but with the man whom the Delphic oracle, and after the oracle all humanity, recognized as the wisest of men—Socrates.

It is true that Kierkegaard does not dare to ridicule Socrates. He respects Socrates, even venerates him. But he takes his need and his difficulties to Abraham, not to Socrates. Socrates was the greatest of men—the greatest, that is, of those who lived on earth before the Bible was revealed to mankind. * One may admire Socrates, but it is not from him that a perplexed soul will find the answers to its questions. In summing up what he had received as a legacy from his teacher, Plato wrote that the greatest calamity that can befall a man is for him to become a μισόλογος, i.e., a despiser of reason. And here I must say immediately: Kierkegaard went from Hegel to Job and from Socrates to Abraham solely because Hegel and Socrates demanded that he love reason, and he hated reason more than anything else in the world.

Plato and Socrates threatened the despiser of reason with every sort of misfortune. But did they have the power to protect the lover of reason from harm? And there is a more disturbing question: must you love reason because if you do not you will be punished? Or must you love it disinterestedly, not looking ahead to see whether it will bring with it joy or sorrow, love it just because it is reason? In my opinion, Plato was far from disinterested, for

---

* *Journal,* II, 343. "Outside of Christianity, Socrates is unique," wrote Kierkegaard in his journal for 1854, a few months before his death.

otherwise he would not have made threats of misfortune. He would simply have said, as a commandment: you must love reason with all your heart and with all your mind, no matter whether this makes you happy or unhappy. Reason demands love for itself and presents no justifications in apology, for it is itself the source, and furthermore the only source, of all justifications. But Plato did not go "as far as that"; even Socrates, to my mind, did not go so far. In *Phaedo*, which declares that the greatest calamity is to become a despiser of reason, we also find it said that when Socrates decided that the νοῦς of Anaxagoras, which had been so alluring to him in his youth, did not guarantee him the "best," he turned away from his teacher. The "best" must come before everything else and the world must dance to its tune. But if such is the case, before we can love reason we must try to find out exactly whether it does guarantee man the best; and consequently we cannot know beforehand whether we ought to love or hate reason. If it gives us the best, we shall love it: if it does not give us the best, we shall not love it. In the event that it brings us something different, or something very bad, we shall hate it and turn away from it, and we shall love its age-old enemy—the Paradox, the Absurd. However, neither Plato nor Socrates posed the question so pointedly. Although the νοῦς* of Anaxagoras did not satisfy Socrates and Plato, they did not stop glorifying reason; they only ceased to be enthusiastic about Anaxagoras. No force could have torn them away from reason.

But there were in fact times when reason yielded them truths that bore little resemblance to the "best," truths that on the contrary, concealed within themselves much

* Mind.

35

that was bad, very bad. Take for instance Plato's admission (*Tim.* 48A) that "creation is mixed, being made up of necessity and mind": or the same statement in a different form: "We may distinguish two sorts of causes, the one divine and the other necessary" (*ibid.*, 68E). And again, if we recall that reason, with its characteristic confidence in its own infallibility, was continually suggesting to Plato that "not even the gods war against necessity" (*Prot.* 345D), then there seems to be really no justification for counting on the blessings at the disposal of reason. Reason has partial control over the world, and it also gives a certain measure of support to the gods: but reason and the gods it glorifies are equally powerless against necessity. Moreover, they are always powerless; reason is well aware of this, allows no one to doubt its knowledge, and therefore rejects, definitely and irrevocably, every attempt to struggle against necessity, as if to do so were madness.

But then necessity, against which both men and gods are equally powerless, may bring with it countless misfortunes. Reason knows this, of course, and indeed has intimated as much to man—but here it suddenly relieves itself of any responsibility and prefers not to talk about it. And yet it continues to demand that men love it, although it is evident that beloved reason may turn out to be just as ill-fated as despised reason, and perhaps even more so; consequently, Plato's famous statement appears in the last analysis to be very weak and even almost entirely without basis when confronted with the facts of experience. Reason, like Diotima's Eros, is not a god but a demon, born of πόρος ("abundance") and πενία ("want"). Socrates and Plato did not pursue this subject further. On the contrary, they tried in every way to turn the probe of thought away from an inquiry into the origin of reason. In order to get around necessity, they invented the famous κάθαρσις. What is κάθαρσις? Plato explains; "Catharsis is the separation of the soul from the body . . . the dwelling in her own place alone, as in another life, so also in this, as far as she can—the release of the soul from the chains of the body." This is all that men and gods together with their reason can muster in opposition to necessity, which does not know reason and does not want to know it. No one has power over the body or over the world. That means there is nothing we can do: let the world exist for itself as it pleases or as it thinks best; we shall learn, and teach others, to do without the world and without the body that belongs to this world. And we shall proclaim this as our greatest triumph, as a victory over invincible necessity before which even the gods have been humbled—or, to put it better, which even the gods can overcome only with the help of a trick invented by reason. Epictetus, the platonizing Stoic, whose intellectual conscientiousness is usually assumed to denote naïveté, openly admitted this. According to him, Zeus told Chryssip: "If it were possible, I would put both your body and all external things completely at your disposal. But I will not conceal from you that I give you all these things in trust only. And since I cannot give you all this as your property, I shall give you instead a certain share from us [the gods]—the ability to decide whether to do something or not, whether to want something or not: in short, the ability to make use of your ideas" (*Discourses*, I, 1). It is difficult, of course, for the man of today to suppose that Zeus actually honored Chryssip with a conversation. But there was no great need of Zeus. He himself must have obtained from some mys-

37

terious source the truth proclaimed by him to Chryssip: that it is "impossible" to give man external things as his property. It is more likely that it was not Zeus who taught Chryssip, but Chryssip, Zeus; that Chryssip himself knew what was possible and what impossible; and that he did not have to bother the gods with his questions. If Zeus had entered into conversation with Chryssip and had attempted to set his own opinions on the possible and the impossible against those of Chryssip, Chryssip would not have listened to him. And if he had listened, he would have refused to believe Zeus: can the gods be superior to the truth? Are not all thinking beings made equal by the truth? Men and devils and gods and angels—all have equal rights, or, more correctly, all are equally without rights before truth, which is wholly subject to reason. When Socrates and Plato realized that the world is ruled not just by the gods, but by necessity also, and that no one has power over necessity, they found the truth for both mortals and the immortals. Zeus is very mighty; no one dares dispute that. But he was not gifted with omnipotence, and as a being no less rational than Chryssip, or even than Chryssip's teacher, Socrates, he must bow before the truth and become a μισόλογος. The only thing that Zeus can do is present man with the ability to conform with the terms of existence. In other words, if all external things, including his own body, can be given to man only in trust, and if there is no possibility of changing the situation (even though it would not be bad, not in the least, if everything could be arranged differently) then let it be so. Man still has a "divine" gift—the freedom to want a thing or not to want it. He is entirely capable of not wishing to own his body and external things as property: he is capable of wishing to possess them only in trust. And then everything will suddenly take a turn for the best and reason will actually boast that for the man who loves and heeds it, life in the world is good, and that there is no greater misfortune than to become a μισόλογος. This is the κάθαρσις of Plato and Aristotle, which the Stoics expressed in their famous theory that "things" have no intrinsic worth, and that autonomous ethics has its starting point in our freedom to consider a thing valuable or worthless as we wish. Ethics makes its own laws. It has the power to declare whatever it pleases (whatever pleases it, of course) worthwhile, important, significant, and also to declare whatever it pleases worthless, unimportant, good for nothing. And no one, not even the gods, can contend with autonomous ethics. Everyone is obliged to yield to it; everyone is obliged to bow before it. The "you must" of ethics came into being at the moment when Necessity said to men and gods alike: "You cannot." The ethical was born of the same parents that produced necessity: πόρος and πενία ("abundance" and "want.") Everything in the world is the product of πόρος and πενία, even the gods. And so, strictly speaking, there are no gods and never were; there are only demons. This is what reason teaches us, this is what is revealed to us by the rational view, by intellectual vision, by speculation. And could reason indeed disclose anything else, if it was itself born of πόρος and πενία?

II

The Thorn in the Flesh

*As for me, a thorn was set in my flesh
early in life. If it were not for that, I
would from the beginning have lived an
ordinary life.*

KIERKEGAARD

Kierkegaard exchanged Hegel and the Greek Symposium for the fiery speeches of Job. Here one must make a very important reservation however; Kierkegaard had a perfect hatred for Hegel and indeed had learned to despise him (although only after a long and difficult inner struggle), but he could never decisively reject the Greek Symposium and the man who was the soul of the Symposium, Socrates—even during that period of incredible strain on all his mental powers when he was writing *Fear and Trembling, Repetition, The Concept of Dread*. He did not even scoff at Spinoza and, in my opinion, treated him with the greatest respect, bordering on veneration (perhaps influenced in this by Schleiermacher). It is as though he felt it necessary to keep Spinoza as well as Socrates in reserve, in case Abraham and Job and the book in which he read of Abraham and Job failed to justify the expectations placed on them. And could it indeed have been otherwise? Can contemporary man reject Socrates and expect to find the truth in Abraham and Job? Usually one would not pose such a question. We prefer to ask: how may the truths of Socrates and the Greek Symposium be "reconciled" with the truths of Abraham and Job? Long before the Bible began to penetrate to the peoples of Europe, this question was posed in just such a way by Philo of Alexandria. He resolved the question by saying that the Bible not only did not contradict the Greek philosophers, but that everything taught by the Greeks was drawn from Holy Scripture. Plato and Aristotle were only disciples of Abraham, Job, the Psalmists and the Prophets (the Apostles did not yet exist).

Philo was not in himself a great philosopher, nor was he in general a very outstanding man. He was an educated, cultured, pious Jew much devoted to the faith of his fathers. But when it needs to, history can make use of mediocre and even insignificant persons to carry out its most grandiose plans. Philo's idea on the relationship between the Bible and the wisdom of the Greeks was fated to play a great historical role. After Philo no one even attempted to understand the Bible as it really was; everyone strove to see in it a special sort of expression of Greek wisdom. In Hegel's *Philosophy of Religion* we read: "In philosophy, religion draws its justification from thinking consciousness. Thought is the absolute judge before which [religion] must justify and explain itself." Two thousand years before Hegel, Philo was of the same mind. He did not "reconcile" Holy Scripture with Greek thought: he made the former justify itself before the latter. And of course he could do this only by first "interpreting" the Bible in the way necessary to achieve the sought-for justification and explanation. Describing the nature of thought in his *Logic*, Hegel said: "When I think, I renounce all my subjective peculiarities, immerse myself in the thing itself, and I think badly if I add anything whatsoever of myself." When Philo interpreted the Bible under the influence of the Greek philosophers, he tried to force the authors of the biblical narratives, and even the One in Whose name they were told, to renounce all their subjective peculiarities. In this regard Philo stood at exactly the same cultural level as Hegel. Philo was brought up on the Greek philosophers and had firmly adopted for himself the thought that not only the heathen gods but also the God of Holy Scripture were subject to the truth that would be revealed to one's thinking self only if that self would renounce its own nature and immerse itself in the thing. After Socrates one could not think otherwise, one must not think otherwise. The mission that history entrusted to Philo consisted of pointing out to people that the Bible did not contradict, and had no right to contradict, our natural way of thinking.

Kierkegaard does not mention Philo, either in his books or in his journals. But we must suppose that if he had happened to mention Philo, he would have called him the forerunner of Judas. For this was the first betrayal, no less shocking than Judas; all the elements were there in full, even to the kiss. Philo praised Holy Scripture to the skies, but in praising it he delivered it into the hands of Greek philosophy, that is, natural thinking, speculation, intellectual vision. Kierkegaard is silent on the subject of Philo.

He directs his thunder against Hegel for precisely the reason that Hegel was a modern-day herald of "objective thinking," which rejects what is revealed by the "subjective" individuality of a living creature, and sees the truth and seeks it in "things." But all the same he respects and spares Socrates—it is, if I may say so once more, as though he were unconsciously insuring himself against the chance that Abraham and Job might not see him through. Even in those moments when he is turning with his terrible *either/or* to complacent laymen and married pastors (or perhaps especially in those moments), he tucks Socrates safely away in some crevice of his soul that even he cannot see. He invokes the Paradox, the Absurd, but all the same he does not let go of Socrates.

And perhaps this will not seem so "improper" if we remember the need with which he turned to Abraham and Job. He says over and over again in his journals that he will never give a concrete description of what happened to him and he even solemnly forbids anyone to try to find out about it. But in his works he cannot help telling about it, in his works he tells of nothing else. It is true that he speaks not on his own behalf, but through various imaginary personages; nevertheless he tells us about it. At the end of *Repetition* * he declares that an event which would have been considered trifling had it happened to someone else became for him a thing of world-shaking significance. In *Stages on Life's Way* he writes: "My suffering is tedious; I know that myself." And a page later he repeats: "Not only did he suffer indescribable torment, but his suffering was tedious. If it had not been so tedious, perhaps someone would have felt sympathetic toward him." And

* III, 207.

again: "He suffered so terribly because of trifles." * Why this tedious suffering? He gives a specific answer: "He felt incapable of that of which everyone is capable—being married." † And again, in the same book, he confesses: "The nine months I spent in my mother's womb were enough to make me an old man." ‡ Such admissions are scattered through all his books and journals; one could cite them endlessly. I shall add just one passage from his journal for 1845, in which, notwithstanding the vow he made, he states in "concrete" words what happened to him.

I am, in the real sense of the word, an unhappy man; I have, from my earliest years, been nailed down to a suffering which is driving me mad, a suffering which is bound up with some sort of abnormality in the relationship of my soul to my body. . . . I spoke of this with my doctor and asked him whether he supposed that the abnormality might be cured, so that I could realize the general. He was doubtful of this. Then I asked him again, whether he did not think that a man's mind could of its own will make some adjustment or set things right there. He had his doubts of this, too. He did not even advise me to try to exert all my strength of will—which, he knew, could destroy everything together. From that moment my choice was made. I accepted this unhappy abnormality (which would probably have led the majority of people capable of understanding such horrible torment to commit suicide) as a thorn set in my flesh, as my limitation, my cross, as the enormous price for which the Heavenly Father has sold me my strength of mind, a strength which has no equal among my contemporaries.

* IV, 315, 314, 269.
† *Ibid.*, 398.
‡ *Ibid.*, 237.

And once again: "As for me, a thorn was set in my flesh early in life. Had it not been for that, I would from the beginning have led an ordinary life." * Kierkegaard gave the title "The Thorn in the Flesh" to one of his most remarkable discourses, remarkable for its profundity and for its stunning power of expression, and the meaning of this can only be understood in the light of the confessions made in those selections from his journals cited here. So also it is only after these confessions that one can understand Kierkegaard's statement that sin is "the swoon of freedom," and that the opposite of sin is not virtue, but faith. The swoon of freedom is described thus in *Repetition:* "I cannot embrace the girl as one embraces a person who actually exists; I can only reach out toward her clumsily, approach her as one approaches a shadow." † Not only Regina Olsen, but the whole world turned for Kierkegaard into a shadow, a phantom. As he more than once repeats in his books and journals, he could not make that "movement of faith" which would have restored reality to the world and Regina Olsen. Can others make it? Kierkegaard does not ask. A large part of the story *Repetition* and that part of *Stages on Life's Way* entitled "Guilty—Not Guilty" seem to strike an entirely different note. The story of unrealized love is not so "simply" or so "tediously" set forth in them. And Kierkegaard is right, of course; if he had only described what really happened to him, who would have "felt sympathetic toward him," who would have been interested in him? That is why the confessions that I have assembled here, although there are not a few

---

* *Journal,* I, 276, 277, and 405.
† III, 184.

of them and they are scattered through the narrative, all seem to amount in their general theme to the same thing: the hero must foresake his betrothed because she is to him not "the beloved of a man, but the muse of a poet." This, of course, is not so tedious and not so ridiculous. But Kierkegaard would rather have his betrothed and everyone else consider him a profligate and a scoundrel than find out his secret. And yet he has an irrepressible need to leave in his writings a trace of his actual experiences. "I am waiting for the storm and repetition. Oh, if only the storm would come! What is the storm to bring me? It must make me capable of being a husband." *

This is why he turned to Job and Abraham, why he turned to Holy Scripture. He despised Hegel, as he despised all speculative philosophy, because in philosophical system no room was allowed for his question. When he said that he concealed from everyone the shame and unhappiness occasioned by his inability to understand the great man Hegel, he did not in the least mean that he could not cope with the abstract complexity of the Hegelian philosophical structure. Kierkegaard had no fear of these difficulties; from his youth he had accustomed himself to read the works of philosophers, had studied Plato and Aristotle in the original, and easily analyzed subtle and complicated arguments. Coming from him, "unable to understand" meant something quite different; almost as if he said, "I understood all too well," understood too well that Hegelian philosophy, in principle, would reduce his question to naught. It can "explain" Kierkegaard's case as it "explained" the case of Socrates, the Thirty Years War, or any other historical event great or small; and then it de-

* III, 194.

mands that a person be satisfied with these explanations and put an end to the questioning. It was this demand which Kierkegaard did not understand in Hegel (that is, in speculative philosophy). He did not understand it, because he supposed that he should in fact submit to this demand, and that in Kierkegaard's place Hegel himself would have been completely satisfied by what speculative philosophy could offer him; but that he, Kierkegaard, was so insignificant and mean-spirited that he was incapable of mounting to those heights where Hegel's thought soared. This is why he spoke about his lack of understanding of Hegel as if it were a shameful and unhappy thing. He might have recalled Plato's μισόλογος ("despiser of reason") and said to himself that he embodied what the divine philosopher had warned against: he who is not satisfied with the world of rational explanations is a μισόλογος and a μισόλογος is doomed to the greatest misfortune. But Kierkegaard hardly ever recalls the Platonic legacy, as if he were trying to forget that the first person who revealed to men the significance and the value of speculation was not Hegel but Plato. He even leaves Aristotle in peace. Both Plato and Aristotle are still too closely bound up with Socrates, and Socrates must be retained. It is likely that Kierkegaard asked himself more than once how the wisest of men would have acted in his place; for Socrates could not have looked to Job or Abraham for help. Yes, and even if he could have, he probably would not have. Epictetus unhesitatingly declared that even the woes of Oedipus and Priam could not have put Socrates at a loss. He would not have taken to complaining, weeping, or cursing; he would have said what he said in prison to Crito: "Oh, good Crito, if it pleases the gods, let it be so." Hegel's speculation amounted to the same thing. All his "explanations" had the same meaning as Epictetus' reflections on Socrates and Oedipus: reality is rational. And one cannot and must not argue with reason. Presumably—and a further explanation will support this theory—Kierkegaard would not have attacked Hegel with such indignation and scorn if the reality which Hegel happened to embody in his life had been the same as that which fell to Socrates' lot. If Hegel had lived in poverty, had suffered every sort of persecution, and at the end had been poisoned for being faithful to his ideas, then Kierkegaard would have considered Hegel's philosophy not empty twaddle at which the gods of Olympus would laugh, but a serious piece of work. He would have called it existential and would have recognized Hegel himself as a "witness for the truth." However, Hegel declared that reality is rational (that reality is as it should be and that there is no need for it to be anything else) solely because he had succeeded in safely avoiding those submerged rocks against which others had been dashed. What is such a philosophy worth? Not long before his death, Kierkegaard made an attack upon Bishop Mynster. Like Hegel, Mynster was sincerely able to think that the reality that had been prepared for him by fate, or created by him for himself, was rational. For many years he was head of the Danish Christian Church, which did not interfere with his being a wealthy man, married, respected and honored by all. His Christianity had no quarrel with his reason. Christianity was for him both "comprehensible" and "desirable"; for Hegel's "reality is rational" meant also that reality can be comprehended and, being comprehensible, can be accepted as the best of all that is possible and even impossible. Mynster died a very old man, con-

scious that he had lived his life as a devoutly believing
Christian should. And over his grave his pupils and
friends, who were also believing Christians and enlightened men, solemnly proclaimed in the words of his son-in-
law Martensen, a professor of philosophy (and a firmly
convinced Hegelian), that the deceased had been a "witness for the truth." Kierkegaard did not attack Mynster
while he was alive. Mynster had been confessor to his father whose memory Kierkegaard venerated, he had carried Kierkegaard himself in his arms, and he was
considered in their family an example of every virtue.
Kierkegaard was raised on Mynster's sermons; he heard
them constantly and read them repeatedly. But all the
while an aversion to Mynster's complacent Christianity
was growing in his heart; and when Mynster died as
peacefully as he had lived, and not only did not repent and
confess before his death his guilt before God but somehow
managed to cast a spell over all those who had known him,
leaving behind the memory of a man who "bore witness
for the truth," it was too much for Kierkegaard. With all
the impulsiveness that distinguishes his writings he declared in the harshest way over the bishop's open grave his
protest against Martensen's words. Kierkegaard himself
had not long to live, and he knew it. And yet, almost dead
as he was, he made a furious attack upon an adversary
who was quite dead. Could he have acted in any other
way?

In *Repetition*, from which we have already quoted a
number of passages, the hero of the story speaks of the
fate that has overtaken him: "What force is this that
wishes to take from me my honor and my pride, and in
such a meaningless way? Can it be that I am beyond the

protection of the laws?" * And in *Stages on Life's Way,* as if to clarify the meaning of this question, Kierkegaard writes:

"What is honor," asks Falstaff? "Can it set to a leg? No. Or an arm? No. Ergo, honor is an expression, a word, a mere scutcheon . . ." This "ergo" is false. It is true that honor, if you possess it, can give none of these things, but if you lose it, it can do the opposite; it can cut off an arm, cut off a leg, send you into an exile worse than Siberia. And if it can do this, it is then no longer just an expression. Go out onto a battlefield and look at the dead; go to a hospital and look at the wounded; neither among the dead nor among the wounded will you find a man so maimed as the one upon whom honor has revenged itself.†

There can be no doubt that Kierkegaard "bore witness for the truth," although of course not in the same sense as Mynster who also, in Martensen's words, bore witness for the truth. To put it another way: Kierkegaard tells the truth about himself. He was deprived of the protection of the laws and covered with dishonor as if he were a leper. It was no accident that he included his horrifying "Memoirs of a Leper" in *Stages on Life's Way.* Can there be a common language between him and Martensen and Mynster? Is it not obvious that some primordial and terrible *either/or,* merciless and relentless, was drawing near him? It is either Hegel, Mynster, Martensen, complacent Christianity, and the "laws" that protect their reality, or else new "laws" (or perhaps not even laws, but something that does not resemble laws at all) that will do away with the old laws, cast down the false witnesses for truth, and

* III, 184.
† IV, 320.

raise Kierkegaard to his rightful place, Kierkegaard who has been trampled underfoot. It is true that "honor" has not the power to restore to a man the arm or leg that has been torn off, but on the other hand it has the ability not only to tear off arms and legs, but to set the hearts of men afire. From whom did Kierkegaard learn this truth? Outside of Christianity, he told us, there was no man equal to Socrates. Then does not Socrates remain, in Christianity as before, the sole source of truth?

III

The Suspension of the Ethical

> *Abraham oversteps the boundaries of the ethical. . . . Either the ethical is not supreme, or Abraham is lost.*
>
> KIERKEGAARD

"From my early youth," says Kierkegaard, "I have lived a perpetual contradiction: to others I appear uncommonly gifted, but in the depths of my soul I know that I am fit for nothing." * Who was right, those others who considered Kierkegaard to be uncommonly gifted, or the man himself who knew that he was fit for nothing? Can one even pose such a question in regard to Kierkegaard? He himself says: "It is only in a religious way that I can understand myself, alone before God. But between me and others there stands the wall of misunderstanding. I have no common language with them." † Just so; how are we to reconcile Kierkegaard's inquiries with that which "ev-

* IV, 218.
† IV, 318.

erybody" is seeking? "Everybody" considers him a very gifted man; he knows that he is fit for nothing. Everybody supposes that he suffers because of trifles, but for him, his suffering is a universally historic event. His certainty that "everybody" will never consent to admit that his "sufferings" are worthy of any attention whatever makes it impossible for him to share his secret with others; this forces his anguish to an extreme pitch and it becomes unendurable. Where are we to find a court of law to judge between Kierkegaard and "everybody," between Kierkegaard and the "general"? Is there indeed such a court? At first glance it seems that there is not even a question here: it is wholly evident that the individual must first of all be prepared to give in to the general, however difficult this may be for him, and he must be ready to find the meaning of his existence in this act of conforming. Moreover, and this is the most important thing, what specific gravity do such words as suffering, torment, horror, possess with regard to truth, whether they be uttered by Kierkegaard, or Job, or Abraham? Job says: "Oh, that my grief were throughly weighed, and my calamity laid in the balances together! For now it would be heavier than the sands of the sea." Even Kierkegaard decided not to repeat these words of Job's. What would Socrates have said, had he been able to hear such a thing? Can a "thinking" man talk this way? Nevertheless, Kierkegaard left the distinguished philosopher Hegel for Job, the "private thinker," solely because Job dared to talk like that. Job, as he expresses himself in Kierkegaard's words, also "withdrew from the general," also had no common language with others. The horrors that befell Job drove him to madness, and "human cowardice cannot bear what death and madness have to say about life." * Kierkegaard continually repeats that most people do not even suspect what terrible things life conceals within itself. But is Kierkegaard "right," is Job right? Isn't it an indisputable and self-evident truth that madness and death are "simply" the end of everything, just as it is indisputably and self-evidently true that the calamities and griefs of Job, and even of all humanity, will not on any scales outweigh the sands of the sea? And does not "everyone," that is, he who does not know and does not want to know the horrors of life, thus find himself more favorably situated to grasp the truth than a person who has experienced these things?

We now come to Kierkegaard's basic question: on whose side is the truth; on the side of "everybody" and "everybody's cowardice," or on the side of those who have dared to look madness and death in the eye? It was for this and this alone that Kierkegaard forsook Hegel and turned to Job, and at that moment determined the characteristics that distinguish existential philosophy from speculative philosophy. To abandon Hegel meant to renounce Reason and rush toward the Absurd without a backward glance. However, as we shall presently see, the path to the Absurd proved to be barricaded by "ethics"; it was necessary to suspend not only reason, but also the ethical. In his journals Kierkegaard says that he who wishes to understand existential philosophy must understand the meaning concealed in the words "suspension of the ethical." As long as the "ethical" stands in the way, it is impossible to break through to the Absurd. The truth is (and this must be said now) that if we do not turn from the path of the "ethical,"

* III, 185.

we cannot penetrate to the Absurd; but this still does not mean that the "ethical" is the only obstacle existential philosophy must overcome. The greatest difficulty lies ahead. We already know that the ethical originated at the same time and had the same parents as the rational, and that necessity is obligation's own sister. When Zeus, compelled by necessity to limit man's rights over his world and his body, decided to give him something "better, from the gods themselves," by way of compensation for what he had lost, the "ethical" was that something better. The gods were able to save themselves and human beings from necessity by one stratagem alone: obligation. Having suspended the ethical and having refused the gift of the pagan gods, man finds himself faced with necessity. And here there is no longer a choice; one must enter into a final desperate battle with necessity, a battle from which even the gods would shrink, and the outcome of which no one can predict. Or to be more accurate: as much as we would like to predict it, it must be said that we cannot be of two minds about this. Even the gods do not contend with necessity; the greatest sages have retreated before necessity. Not just Plato and Aristotle, but Socrates himself admitted that no one can fight against it and, inasmuch as a struggle for the unattainable is unthinkable, it follows that there ought not to be any struggle. If at this point there is anyone who does not see where the meeting ground between the rational and the ethical lies, then perhaps he will see it now: as soon as reason looks at necessity and announces "Impossible," the ethical is right alongside to say "You must." The words that the friends of Job addressed to that tormented old man, lying in filth, show them to be no less educated than the Greek philosophers. Their lengthy

55

speeches, put more concisely, all come down to what Socrates was in the habit of saying, or, if we may believe
Epictetus, what Zeus said to Chryssip: if it is impossible
to prevail, then men and gods alike must accept their fate.
And on the other hand, if a brief version of Job's answer to
his friends is wanted, it could be stated this way: nowhere
in the world is there a force strong enough to make him
"accept" what happened to him as proper and unquestionable. In other words, not just necessity's "right" but also
its "power" is being questioned. To be exact, does necessity really have the power to arrange the fates of men and
of the world? Is this a "self-evident truth" or a dreadful
nightmare? How did it happen, how could it happen, that
human beings accepted this power and humbled themselves before it? Furthermore, how could the "ethical,"
which men associate with all that is most important, most
essential, most valuable in life, come forward with its "you
must" to champion that meaningless, disgusting, dull, stupid, blind thing, Necessity? Can a man live in peace as
long as he is dominated by necessity? Is it possible for him
not to give in to despair if he has convinced himself that
necessity, not satisfied with the methods of outward coercion at its disposal, has managed to win over to its side his
own "conscience," and forced it to sing the praises of its
evil deeds?

It was this that drove Kierkegaard away from Hegel
and speculative philosophy to Job, the "private thinker."
Job demonstrated the "breadth of his concept of the world
by the firmness with which he opposes all the subterfuges
and attacks of 'ethics,' " * writes Kierkegaard. Let Job's
friends "berate" him as much as they please, he goes on to

* III, 192.

say, let not only those friends, but all of the wisest men of all times and nations, berate him in order to convince him of the justness of the "ethical," which demands that he cheerfully submit to the fate which has befallen him. For Job, the ethical's "you must" is an empty phrase, and the "metaphysical consolations" that his friends tossed at him by the handful simply nonsense. And not because his friends were not sufficiently wise and educated. On the contrary, they had mastered all human wisdom and would have been ornaments to any Hellenic symposium. By quoting their words, Philo was able to prove without difficulty that the great Greeks drew their wisdom from the Bible—not, it is true, from the Prophets and Psalmists, but from the opinion expressed by Job's friends: ethics (obligation) is the shield of necessity; a person has no right to wish for the impossible. Precisely: if reason, which is all-seeing, can determine exactly where the possible ends and the impossible begins, then ethics, which shields reason and is supported by it, is safe and sound in the *saecula saeculorum,* and the wisdom of Job's friends becomes holy, just like the wisdom of the Greeks. If?! But here the question arises: what sort of thing is this necessity? And how does it hold on to its power? Why is it that both men and gods behave as though bewitched by it, and dare not or cannot renounce their obedience to it? Once more I repeat the question I posed earlier: how did it happen that ethics, invented by the wisest of men, acted in support of this power and gave it its blessing? Before the court of ethics, it is not Job who is right but his friends; an intelligent person cannot think it probable that the laws of the universe will be remade for his benefit, cannot demand this! But that is just the way Job behaves; he does not want to "think anything probable," he does not want to think . . . he demands, and has but one answer to everything put forward by his friends: "Miserable comforters are ye all." Kierkegaard echoes Job, sacrifices Hegel for his sake, suspends ethics, renounces reason and all the great conquests that humanity, thanks to reason, has made in the course of its age-old history. To everything suggested to him so far by his teachers he replies as though in oblivion, not with words but with sounds that our ears can scarcely distinguish; and he does not even give an answer, but cries with all his might: "What power is this, that has taken from me my honor and my pride, and in such a meaningless way?" He cries out as if his cries had some force, as if he expects that those cries, like the trumpets at Jericho, will make the walls begin to topple.

Where, then, is the "absurdity"—in the power that took from Job (more precisely, from Kierkegaard) his honor and his pride, or in Kierkegaard's fantasy of walls toppling because of his cries? It is true that something unheard of, almost unbelievable, had happened to him, something neither he nor others could comprehend: he, a man like any other, found himself beyond the protection of the laws. Suddenly, without any apparent reason, he was exiled for life from the realm of reality; everything he touched was transformed into a shadow, just as everything the mythical Midas touched turned into gold. For what reason? why? Job's friends, like Kierkegaard's friends, had no particular difficulty finding enough, and more than enough, reasons for this. That both Job and Kierkegaard are insignificant links in the endless chain of the universe's endlessly changing phenomena is in itself a completely satisfactory explanation for a person of "normal" consciousness. Even

Job himself at the beginning, when news of his first misfortunes began to arrive, said with dignified serenity, in full compliance with the demands of the ethical, as befits a wise man: the Lord gave and the Lord hath taken away (just as Socrates would have spoken, so Epictetus assures us, if he had been in Priam's or Oedipus' situation). But the more misfortunes rained down upon him, the more impatient he became and the more suspect grew his "knowledge" of the inescapable and the irrevocable, and his moral philosophy, which had inspired his readiness to accept cheerfully the fate which had befallen him. "The greatness of Job," says Kierkegaard, "manifests itself not when he says: the Lord gave and the Lord hath taken away, blessed be the name of the Lord—this is how he spoke in the beginning, and afterward he did not say it again; the significance of Job is in the fact that he carried his fight to the boundaries where faith begins." * And once more: "The greatness of Job is that his suffering can neither be allayed nor suppressed by lies and empty promises." † All this is so. But it is still not the main point. The main point, both for Job himself and for Kierkegaard, is to be found elsewhere—least of all in the greatness of Job. Is Job really in need of compliments and distinctions? Is he really waiting for any scrap at all of approval from any source whatsoever? Does not even Kierkegaard have to be reminded about this, Kierkegaard, who turned to Job for the very reason that Job had "suspended the ethical"? The question here is not whether Job was or was not a great man or a worthy man; all such questions were abandoned long ago. The question is whether it is possible to go

* III, 191.
† *Ibid.*, 189.

against the eternal laws of nature, armed with shouts, laments, and curses; or, as we would put it, with bare hands. Job perhaps did not know, but Kierkegaard knew, that in modern philosophy this question is settled once and for all: *non ridere, non lugere, neque detestari, sed intelligere.** This is Spinoza's thesis, with which there can be no quarrel. And if the existential philosophy of Job, the "private thinker," wishes to turn this thesis around and expects to get the truth not from understanding but from its own wails and curses, then it is hardly fitting to transfer these questions to the level of a subjective evaluation of Job's personality. Nevertheless, it is not by chance that Kierkegaard twice speaks of the greatness of Job. Apropos of this, he has no difficulty explaining why Job shows himself to be great not when he speaks the words: "The Lord gave and the Lord hath taken away," but when he says so passionately that his grief is heavier than the sands of the sea. Who decides in these cases where greatness lies and where insignificance? But what if the opposite is true: if Job is great as long as he accepts his misfortunes with inward serenity, but he becomes pitiful, contemptible, and ridiculous when he loses his serenity and peace of mind. Who is to resolve this question? Up to that time Job had been completely subject to the jurisdiction of ethics. We even have a ready-made formula for this, minted long ago by the Greeks. Cicero and Seneca put it in these words: *fata volentem ducunt, nolentem trahunt.* A man whom fate drags along as if he were a drunkard being taken to the police station cannot be called great: the great man is he who goes of his own will when fate has ordained that he should go. Oedipus cried out, wept, and cursed, but Socra-

* "Do not laugh, do not weep, do not curse, but understand."

tes, as Epictetus has explained to us, would have been just as imperturbably serene in Oedipus' place as he was when he accepted the cup of poison from his jailer. There can be no question that were Socrates and Job to come together before the court of ethics, Job would lose the case. Kierkegaard is aware of this. He knows that the only way for Job to get what he wants is to impugn the competence of ethics in his case. He writes: "Job was blessed; everything that he had possessed before was returned to him twofold. This is called repetition . . . And so it is repetition. When does it begin? Human language has no way of expressing that. When did it begin for Job? When every conceivable probability, every reliable indication, told him it was impossible." And here, drawing a parallel between his own experience and Job's, he goes on to say: "I am waiting for the storm and the repetition. What is the repetition to bring me? It must make me capable of being a husband." *

Is there any hint in all this of that which we call greatness? Is ethics at all interested in the fact that Job recovered his cattle, his gold, and even his children (and twofold at that)? Is ethics interested in whether Kierkegaard regains his ability to be a husband? The "blessings of this world," as the spirit defines them, are of no concern: Kierkegaard himself tells us this at the end of *Repetition*. And he goes on to explain that everything finite becomes insignificant for a person with a proper understanding of his relationship with God. But then, this was known long ago to the wise men of pagan times, who invented self-regulated (autonomous) ethics. And if it is true that everything worldly is a matter of indifference to the spirit, and the essence of the "religious" is that it teaches one to scorn

* III, 193, 194.

what is finite, then why bother, why turn away from Socrates? Why take up arms against Hegel? Hegel, too, taught that everything finite is in the process of development, has no independent meaning, and takes on significance only in that endless process. There was, moreover, no need to bother about repetition or to announce solemnly that "repetition is fated to play an important role in the new philosophy," and that "the new philosophy will teach that all life is a repetition." * What if Job regains his cattle, and Kierkegaard his ability to be a husband—these cannot seriously matter to anyone and it is unnecessary to turn such trifles into universally historic events. Job would have wept, would have cried out, and would have fallen silent. Kierkegaard, too, finally ceased his weeping and cursing; for not only are life's blessings (which they were both denied) transitory things: Kierkegaard and Job themselves were no less transitory than their cries, tears, and curses. Eternity swallows up everything, as the sea swallows the rivers emptying into it and becomes no fuller thereby. And in the long run even the praise and censure of the ethical come to nothing in the limitless expanse of eternity. Yes, as we have seen, neither Job nor Kierkegaard had need of them. They sought repetition, which human reasoning, knowing full well what is possible and what is impossible, absolutely refused them. On the other hand, it never refuses to praise anyone, on the condition, of course, that the person humble himself, admit that what is real is rational, and with the pure joy characteristic of a spiritual nature accept the fate, however burdensome, that falls to his lot. Kierkegaard knows this and now and then is even tempted by it. It is all very well if Job

* *Ibid.*, 119.

can overcome necessity and attain repetition! But what if he should fall in the unequal struggle? It is all very well if Holy Scripture does contain truth of which the ancient philosophers knew nothing! But what if Philo was right and one should accept from the Bible only that which does not contradict the wisdom of Socrates, Plato, and Aristotle? And what if even the despised Hegel was right in summoning religion before the court of reason?

These misgivings never entirely left Kierkegaard. That is why he spoke only of the "suspension of the ethical," although he was aware that more was called for, that for him the moment of that most inexorable *either/or* was approaching. He himself at times speaks of this with great power and intensity. "Abraham," we read in *Fear and Trembling*, "by his own action oversteps the boundaries of the ethical. His τέλος ("goal") lay further on, beyond the ethical; fixing his gaze upon this τέλος, he suspends the ethical." And once more: "We find ourselves faced with a paradox. Either the individual, as such, stands in absolute relationship to the Absolute, in which case the ethical is not supreme; or Abraham is lost." * Still, the ethical is suspended only to make possible a return to its protective shadow if need be (i.e., in the case of Job's victory over necessity), even though that would require Kierkegaard to subscribe to the sentence passed on Abraham. This instinctive caution in a thinker who was otherwise always impulsive is profoundly significant. The fight he has taken up is too daring; even the boldest of men cannot avoid being frightened by it. Everything has been taken from Kierkegaard. He has "withdrawn from the general," he is "deprived of the protection of the laws." And then for him to

* III, 56 and 107.

refuse the protection of ethics, which has the power to pronounce us *laudabiles vel vituperabiles!* This is why (and I shall speak of this further on in greater detail) Kierkegaard persistently introduces an ethical element into his understanding of "religious thought" and attaches more and more significance to this element in each succeeding book. We will recall that he was speaking of the "greatness of Job" as early as *Repetition,* and it is there that he calls religious persons "aristocratic natures." * In *The Sickness Unto Death* he even often uses his opinions on ethics to support his opinions on religion, as if he had forgotten what he said about the relationship between the religious and the ethical, that if the ethical is supreme, then Abraham is lost. "What determining factor did Socrates (i.e., the pagan world in its best aspect) fail to consider in his definition of sin? Human will, human stubbornness. Greek intellectualism was too genial, too naïve, too esthetic, too ironical, too clever, too sinful, to understand that anyone can consciously refrain from doing a good thing, or consciously (i.e., knowing what is right) do something wrong. The Greeks proposed an intellectual categorical imperative." † At first glance, this seems true: Socrates taught that no one who knows what good is will do evil. But this has nothing in common with what Kierkegaard says about the pagan world. One need only recall Alcibiades' speech in Plato's *Symposium* in order to be won over to the opposite side. Or Ovid's *video meliora, proboque, deteriora sequor,* quoted by almost all philosophers (among them Leibniz and Spinoza), along with the corresponding words of the Apostle Paul. Just as though he had never read *The Symposium* or heard of that line by

* III, 204.
† VIII, 87, 90.

Ovid (he must have read it, if not in Ovid's own writings, then in Spinoza's work, where it is quoted several times), Kierkegaard goes on to say: "Where is the confusion? It is in the fact that the dialectical transition from understanding to action is lacking. The role of Christianity begins here, at this transition; now it becomes clear that sin lies in will, and we arrive at the concept of stubbornness." There can hardly be any doubt that these words open up the possibility of a *restitutio in integrum* of the "ethical" that Socrates brought to mankind and which, at the decisive moment, Abraham had to "suspend." But we already know what protected the ethical and from what it drew its power and strength. Moreover, Kierkegaard is here speaking not on his own behalf, not on behalf of philosophy, but in the name of Christianity. He sees sin in human stubbornness, in the obstinacy of the will, which does not consent to obey decrees emanating from a higher power. In that respect, however, Job was the sinner par excellence; his sin was in not wanting to adhere to the traditional "the Lord gave and the Lord hath taken away," daring instead to show resentment of the ordeals which had descended upon him. Job's friends spoke the truth: Job is a rebel, an insurrectionist, opposing his own will to the eternal laws of the universe in a blasphemous and wicked manner. It is not from Hegel to Job that one must flee, but from Job to Hegel; not from the general to the particular, but from the particular to the general. As for Socrates, not only is he outside Christianity, but he has no equal within Christianity itself. Abraham became a transgressor when he resolved to pass beyond the realm of the ethical. The Absurd, in which Kierkegaard sought protection, protects nothing; behind ethics and its "you must," Necessity, with its heavy, stone-like tread, is closing in on helpless man.

IV

The Great Offense

The greatest provocation to offense comes when man admits that what lies outside the realm of possibility for human reason is possible for God.

KIERKEGAARD

I have had to dwell somewhat on Kierkegaard's "inconsistencies," but by no means have I done this to demonstrate a lack of self-control in his thinking. The constant substitution of the "religious" for reason (of the Absurd for the ethical) we observe in his work does not in the least resemble what is called in logic μετάβασις εἰς ἄλλο γένος. When he wishes Kierkegaard can employ the strictest consistency in his thinking. But there is a reason for his repeating so often and so fervently that Christ's words, "Blessed is he, whosoever shall not be offended in me," are basic to Christianity.* "The greatest provocation to

* "Taking the responsibility upon myself before the Most High, I have dared to say that the words 'blessed is he, whosoever shall not be offended in me' belong with (the essentials) proclaimed by Christ" (VIII, 121).

offense comes when man admits that what lies outside the realm of possibility for human reason is possible for God." * When Kierkegaard's thinking does an about-face, it is not because he is insufficiently consistent, but because he is overcome by the offense he speaks of in the lines just quoted. How is one to admit that what is evidently impossible to our human minds is possible for God? Descartes admitted this "theoretically," but he constructed his entire philosophy on *cogito ergo sum* (borrowed from St. Augustine, and St. Augustine could not have done without it!)—which meant that the truths of reason are equally compulsory for us and for the Supreme Being. In our time Husserl, whose thinking derives from Descartes, also states that what is true is true not only for us but for every thinking being, for the devil, for an angel, for God—and with this he seems to be bridging contemporary thought with Hellenic thought. And, throughout the whole history of human thought—even after the Bible had become widespread among the peoples of Europe—we can name scarcely one philosopher who completely overcame this offense. Kierkegaard sought the Absurd with all the impulsiveness characterizing him, and with an infinitely passionate intensity. He notes in his journal: "Only horror that has turned to despair can develop a man's higher powers." † But even by thus straining all his powers he did not always succeed in driving offense from him. He was wholeheartedly with Job, but he could not dispel the fascination of Hegel, could not "think" that for God the possible does not end where human reason believes all possibilities end. He went to Job only to convince himself

* *Ibid.,* 115.
† *Journal,* II, 204.

of his right and his power to transform his little case into a universally historic event. For as far as that goes, even the case of Job is very trivial. Quite a few men have their wealth taken from them, lose their children, fall ill with a serious and incurable disease. Kierkegaard says of himself that his suffering is "tedious." But Job's case is no more remarkable or more diverting! Kierkegaard knows this, and is *frightened* by it. It is here that we must seek the reason he spares the ethical and "suspends" it only temporarily to be able, if necessary, to rescue it from Hegel. For, and this no one can know in advance, Hegel might manage to prove, by relying on self-evidency, that neither the misfortunes of Job nor the misfortunes of Kierkegaard have any significance in the general economy of being. Hegel "explained" the fate of Socrates; why not assume that the fate of Job or Kierkegaard can also be explained, and once explained stricken from the records. Earthly misfortunes, however terrible or grand they may be, do not give man a deciding voice at the council of the great and eternal forces of nature. If Kierkegaard wishes to speak and wishes to be heard, he must win over the ethical to his side and put on its vestments. And if he does the opposite and appears naked before people, without any ceremonial robes—just as man looked when he came from the hand of the Creator, and just as each of us will appear sooner or later before the Creator (so Kierkegaard is convinced)—no one will stop to listen to him, or if any one does, then it will likely be to laugh at him. Fear of the power of necessity and the judgment of men never left Kierkegaard. He knew that his voice was the voice of one crying in the wilderness and that he was condemned to absolute loneliness and hopeless abandonment by circumstances which he could not alter. He constantly and incessantly speaks of this, both in his journals and his books. If he turned from Hegel, it was primarily because he no longer expected anything for himself from the universally recognized philosopher, and placed his hopes with Job, whom men had forsaken. But misgivings that the final truth and consequently the decisive power are to be found, if not on the side of Hegel, then on the side of Socrates, were his inseparable companions during his life. It might be expressed thus: he did not suspend the "ethical"; at a difficult moment, the "ethical" suspended itself from him. His soul was attracted to the "private thinker" Job; he hated Hegelian speculative philosophy ("Hegel is not a thinker but a professor," he wrote in his journal), but to the end he could not rid his soul of a fear of the eternal truths discovered by the Hellenes. And this fear, hidden in his soul, repressed yet irrepressible, vanquished yet invincible, accompanied him in his approach to the ultimate mysteries of existence—the mysteries of knowledge, faith, sin, redemption. Not for nothing did he give the name *The Concept of Dread* to one of the most remarkable of his works. He had discovered in himself and others a fear that was unaccountable, unjustifiable, and unreasonable, and moreover, as we shall presently see, a fear of Nothingness. And to anticipate what will be explained later, it must here be said that in his struggle with his fear of Nothingness, he remained as before in the power of Nothingness. I must add that the fear of Nothingness, in the sense given it by Kierkegaard, is not a personal, subjective trait of his. Owing to the special conditions of his existence, he merely exposed this fear and the Nothingness that gives rise to it with a precision distinguished by its clarity and its great vividness. Or perhaps we might put it this way: that which exists only potentially, and therefore invisibly, in the souls of other men became for him an actuality, an everyday reality. This is why he maintained that the beginning of philosophy is not wonder but despair. As long as a man wonders, he has not yet touched on the mysteries of being. Only despair brings him to the brink, to the limits of the existing. And if philosophy, as we have always been told, seeks the beginnings, sources, and roots of everything, then whether it wishes to or not it must pass through despair.

But—and here lies Kierkegaard's final question—has despair the power to dispel the fear of Nothingness? We have just now seen that Kierkegaard could not renounce the support of the ethical, even after he had forsaken Hegel and gone to Job. We shall see this problem recurring further on, and in an even more, much more, clear-cut and obvious form. And still his truly titanic struggle with fear and Nothingness produces a shattering impression, unmasking for us those aspects of being of whose existence people have not the least notion. When he cried out, like Job, "What force is this that has taken my pride and my honor from me?" the ethical suspended itself from him. The ethical is unable to answer this question. It experiences the very same fear of Nothingness that paralyzed Kierkegaard's will. It is continually obliged to look directly at necessity, that terrible Medusa's head which turns to stone all those who gaze upon it. But Kierkegaard still managed from time to time to find the courage and the strength to tear himself away from the enchanted circle into which he had stumbled, and to search in life for another principle, a principle that knows no fear, not even fear of Nothingness. This is what led him to existential philosophy. It is pertinent to say here that even in those moments when like the prodigal son he returns to the ethical, he does in such a way that there is some doubt whether he is not more of a danger to the ethical when he returns to it than when he leaves it; more of a danger when he testifies for it than when he testifies against it. In this connection it is most helpful, in reading Kierkegaard's edifying discourses and the chapters corresponding to them in his later works (*The Sickness Unto Death, Training in Christianity,* and *The Moment*) to recall Nietzsche's *Toward a Genealogy of Morals;* Kierkegaard is no less zealous than Nietzsche in his glorification of cruelty, and his discourse on love for one's neighbor is as pitiless as Nietzsche's discourse on love for the far-off; the Nietzschean superman is only a different, less usual word than the "Christian" "you must" with which Kierkegaard assails the married pastors and the comfortably settled laity. When replying to the question asked by Shakespeare's Falstaff: can honor (for honor comes from the ethical) give a man back his arm or leg?, Kierkegaard answers with obvious triumph and joy, no, it cannot, but on the other hand when its demands are not fulfilled it can maim a man as the most vicious torturer cannot. Should not Kierkegaard ask himself what moved him to welcome a force which is able to smash, to burn, to reduce to ashes—but unable not only to build, but also to rebuild? Particularly if we recall that he, like Nietzsche, showed so little cruelty in his life, attacking Job's friends so fiercely because they did not want to acknowledge his laments and curses as lawful? Is not such a celebration of the "ethical," in Kierkegaard's work as well as Nietzsche's, simply an ex-

pression of profound, irreconcilable, ineradicable hatred
for it? It is as if Kierkegaard wished to say: men think
the ethical to be a superior vital principle, but look what
it promises you: do you accept this? Do not think to rid
yourself of it by giving it a pittance in alms. It demands
from you what you consider most precious in the world.
It comes to Job as he lies in filth and says to him: I cannot
give you back your flock, your riches, your children, or
your health. But if you agree to renounce all this and admit that my praise is worth more than all the good things
in the world, I will sustain you, I will take you to my
bosom. If you do not agree, if you insist as before that all
that was taken from you be returned, then I will censure
you, will turn you from my bosom, and add to the horrors
that fell to you from my brother Necessity new horrors,
much more terrible than those you already know. Nor
will I do this in my own name, but in the name of Him
who called to Himself the laboring and the heavy-laden,
promising them rest. For even He cannot, as even I
cannot, give you "repetition," and the rest that He promised shall be many times worse than the misfortunes you
have suffered.* It cannot be disputed that the "ethical"
has thus led astray those who have trustingly placed all
their hopes in it. But neither can it be disputed that the
"ethical" has never used this sort of language and has not
revealed in this manner the meaning of the bliss promised

* This will be discussed in greater detail further on; here I shall cite
one short passage from Kierkegaard so that the reader may more easily
see the direction in which his thought tended: "Oh, the singular effect
of love; oh, the unfathomable misfortune of love: God cannot—true, He
does not want to, and cannot want to—but if He did want to, He could
not arrange matters so that His loving assistance would not lead to the
opposite result, to the greatest unhappiness. He can make men more
unhappy by His love than they could ever be without it" (VIII, 119,
120).

to men. Plato and the Stoics did not talk like this. Aristotle in his *Ethics* sets as a condition of bliss a definite minimum of life's blessings. Even the Pelagians did not dare to defend the ethical thus when St. Augustine made a relatively weak attempt to dispute its right to apportion the higher blessings to men (*quo nos laudabiles vel vituperabiles sumus*), and this was precisely because they acted not out of fear, but out of conscience. And is it in fact a defense or the most monstrous, violent accusation masquerading as a defense? The ethical sets as the condition of its benevolence man's readiness to submit without a murmur to whatever necessity brings him; does not such a clear representation of the nature of the ethical have the effect of fixing it to the pillory and bringing everlasting dishonor upon it? Kierkegaard, as I have already indicated, repeated insistently that existential truths call for indirect communication. Indeed, as we will remember, he took pains to conceal, and did not want to give a concrete name to, that actual experience of his fated to be transformed by his will (or perhaps by the will of another) into a universally historic event. And in my opinion he had every reason for doing so. Perhaps it was because, like the princess in Andersen's fairy tale, he hid his pea under eighty feather beds that it grew to such gigantic proportions, not only in his own eyes, but also in the eyes of remote posterity; had he shown it openly to everyone, no one would have stopped to look at it. Moreover, when he took it out from under the innumerable covers, it seemed even to him (we have heard often enough about this) to be insignificant, dull, pitiful, and ridiculous. But concealed from men's eyes it took on universally historic significance, both for him and for others. He even forgot his unconquerable fear and found the strength and the courage to look into the empty eyes of the Nothingness that had overwhelmed him. It was not easy for him to convince himself that it is Job with his wails, and not Hegel and speculative philosophy, that leads to the truth. It was not easy for him to renounce the protection of ethics, even for a while. And these were only the first steps. The most difficult lay ahead. He had to accept the Fall of man—not as it is commonly represented, but as it is described in Holy Scripture; he had to accept the Absurd, to tear faith from the clutches of reason, and to look to faith, the Absurd, and Holy Scripture for the deliverance refused to man by rational thinking; and to accomplish all this in the face of Necessity and Ethics, and that invincible fear of them we have already heard about. This is natural, if in the future we are expected to be witnesses for the indirect manner of communication and those strange, innumerable, not always coordinated movements, sometimes almost convulsive and spasmodic, called for by the struggle he has undertaken. For Kierkegaard, reason and ethics became, to use Luther's words, *bellua qua non occisa homo non potest vivere* ("the monster man must kill so that he may live"). Existential philosophy has its point of origin here; man must not "understand," but live; and he opposes, he dares to oppose his *ridere, lugere,* and *detestari* to the understanding achieved through speculative philosophy. Holy Scripture gives him its blessing in this enterprise: *justus ex fide vivit* ("the just shall live by faith"), the Prophet tells us, and the Apostle after him. And what is more, "if ye have faith as a grain of mustard seed, nothing shall be impossible unto you"— οὐδὲν ἀδυνατήσει ὑμῖν.

V

The Movement of Faith

I cannot accomplish the movement of faith; I cannot close my eyes and fling myself without a glance into the abyss of the Absurd.

KIERKEGAARD

The way leads from Job to the father of faith, Abraham, and his terrible sacrifice. The whole of the book *Fear and Trembling*, which takes its title from the Bible,* is devoted to Abraham. Kierkegaard had difficulty enough with Job, great difficulty; we remember what an effort it cost him to decide to oppose the sedate and sober thinking of Hegel with the tears and curses of Job. But more, much more, was demanded from Abraham than from Job. Job's misfortunes descended upon him from an external, outside force—Abraham himself raised a knife to the one who was dearest to him in all the world. Men avoided Job, and even the "ethical," sensing its complete lack of power, imperceptibly suspended itself from him. Men were obliged

* Psalms 2:11 and Philippians 2:12.

not to avoid Abraham, but to take up arms against him; ethics not only suspended itself from him, but pronounced a curse on him. In the judgment of ethics, Abraham is the greatest of transgressors, the most despicable of men: he is a filicide. Ethics cannot help man, but, as we know, it commands sufficient means to torment anyone who does not please it. Abraham is at the same time the most unhappy and the most culpable of men; he loses his beloved son, the hope and support of his old age, and in addition he, like Kierkegaard, loses his honor and his pride.

What sort of person is this mysterious Abraham, and what sort of enigmatic book is it, in which the case of Abraham is not deservedly branded as a disgrace, but is glorified and exalted as an example and lesson for posterity? I will remind you again of the words of Kierkegaard, which I have quoted once before: "Abraham by his own action oversteps the boundaries of the ethical. His τέλος (goal) lay further on, beyond the ethical. Fixing his gaze upon this τέλος, he 'suspends the ethical'." We will also recall that the ethical acted as a shield for Necessity, which has the power to turn to stone anyone who looks at it. How did Abraham dare to suspend the ethical? "When I think about Abraham," writes Kierkegaard, "it is as if I were utterly destroyed. At every moment I see what an unheard-of paradox is presented by the content of Abraham's life; at every moment something thrusts me back and, as hard as it tries, my thought is unable to penetrate into the paradox. I do not move forward by so much as a hairsbreadth. I exert my entire being in order to achieve my aim, but I immediately feel that I am totally paralyzed." And he explains this further: "I can think deeply about the hero, but my thought cannot fathom Abraham.

As soon as I attempt to rise to his heights, I immediately fall, because what is revealed to me turns out to be a paradox. But I do not on that account belittle the importance of faith; on the contrary. To me, faith is the highest gift to man, and I consider it dishonest for philosophy to substitute something else for faith, and make light of it. Philosophy cannot and is not obliged to give man faith, but it ought to know its own limitations, it ought not to take anything away from man, and least of all has it the right to deprive man, with its glib talk, of what he possesses as if it were a trifle, as if it were nothing." * Here, of course, we must pause and ask in turn: by what right does Kierkegaard assert that faith lies beyond the realm of philosophy? And can one shake off so "easily" philosophy's claims "to be the absolute judge" before which, as Hegel has told us and as almost all philosophers think, "the content of religion must justify and explain itself"? But Kierkegaard, as we have already been able to understand in some degree from what he has told us about Abraham, is himself aware of the difficulties that confront him. He writes: "I looked into the eyes of the horror and I was not afraid, I did not tremble. But I know that even if I courageously offer resistance to the horror, my courage is not the courage of faith; compared with the latter, it is nothing. I cannot accomplish the movement of faith; I cannot close my eyes and fling myself without a glance into the abyss of the Absurd." He repeats this innumerable times: "No, I cannot make this movement. As soon as I try to do so, everything begins to whirl about me." And he even expresses it this way: "To make the final movement, the paradoxical movement of faith is simply impos-

* III, 28 and 29.

sible for me. And I run to take shelter in the bitterness of resignation." *

Whence came all these "I cannots" and "impossible's"? Who or what paralyzes Kierkegaard's will, prevents him from making what he calls the movement of faith, and imperiously drives him into the sorrowful vale of resignation and inaction? Philosophy (that is, rational thinking) does not, as he tells us, have the right to take man's faith away with its glib talk. But can there be a question of right here? Necessity also had no *right* to limit the power of the father of the gods, but both the divine Plato and the austere Epictetus were nevertheless obliged to admit that it was *bona, optima fide* for Zeus the all-powerful to submit to Necessity and resign himself to it, even though against his will; he wanted to give men both their own bodies and the entire world as their absolute property, but he had to be satisfied with letting them hold them "in trust," and limit himself to the sensible advice to find happiness in little. What? had neither Plato nor Epictetus nor Zeus himself enough courage to do battle with Necessity? Did they, too, flee from the field of battle to hide in "the sorrowful vale of resignation," as Kierkegaard put it? If we were to address this question to the Greek philosophers or gods, they would indignantly reject Kierkegaard's explanation. They had enough courage, much more than enough; it was not a question of courage. But every reasonable person well knows that Necessity is what it is, that it cannot be overcome, and that the sorrow of resignation is the only consolation in life, which the immortals share with mortals, giving of their own ability to adapt themselves to the conditions of existence. Kierkegaard

* *Ibid.,* 46.

continually challenges Socrates, the teacher of Plato and Epictetus. But did Socrates lack courage? And could Kierkegaard admit even for a moment that Socrates would have been on the side of Job or Abraham? Socrates, who always laughed at the courage that overestimates its strength and rushes headlong into danger! There is no doubt that Socrates would have directed all the venom and acerbity of his irony and sarcasm against Job's ravings, and even more so against Abraham, who throws himself with eyes closed into the abyss of the Absurd. Philosophy has no right to take a man's faith away, no right to laugh at faith! Where did Kierkegaard get this precept? Should it not be the other way round? is it not the basic task of philosophy, after making fun of faith, to return men to the sole source of truth—to reason? Especially such a faith as that celebrated by Kierkegaard and Abraham? The case of Job is bad enough; a person must be senile and completely ignorant besides, to call upon creation for an answer to his personal misfortunes, however great they may be. And he must be extremely naïve—like the unknown author of the Book of Job—in order to be seriously convinced that God could return Job's stolen cattle and riches, and even his slain children. All this is plainly an invention, a tale for the nursery, and if Kierkegaard, relying on the story he read in the Old Testament, declares that the starting point of philosophy from now on will be, not recollection, as Socrates and Plato taught, but repetition, then this is evidence only that he thinks badly, that he cannot, as Hegel quite rightfully demanded, renounce his subjective desires and immerse himself in the thing itself. Or else it means that, scorning the advice of Leibniz, he did not take with him in his quest for truth the law of contradiction and the law of sufficient basis, which are as indispensable to the thinker as compass and chart are to the sailor; and so he took the first fallacy he saw for the truth.

But Kierkegaard, I repeat, was very well aware of all this; if he had thought that he could get rid of philosophy so easily and simply, he would not have written his two-volume *Philosophical Fragments,* devoted exclusively to the struggle with theoretical philosophy. The unadorned assertion that faith is sustained by the Absurd would not strike anyone as convincing; if faith places its every hope in the Absurd, then anything at all will pass for the truth, just as long as it smacks of absurdity. The same thing can be said about the suspension of the ethical. It is enough merely to consider the kind of need which requires that the ethical be suspended. Thus, Socrates would have said —and here Socratic irony could not be more appropriate— that Job suspends it in order to get back his cattle, and Kierkegaard, in order to regain the ability to be a married man. One must suppose that even Abraham, the father of faith, was not far removed from Job and the hero of *Repetition*. . . It is true that Abraham's decision was about a matter that to our minds is shocking: he raised a knife to his only son, his hope, the comfort of his old age. This, of course, required a great effort. But not without reason has Kierkegaard told us that Abraham suspended the ethical—that Abraham "believed." In what did he believe? "Even at the moment when the knife was already glittering in his hand, Abraham believed that God would not demand Isaac from him. . . . Let us go further. Let us assume that he really did sacrifice Isaac—Abraham *believed.* He did not believe that he would find happiness somewhere in another world. No, he would still be happy *here, in this world* [underlined in the original]. God would give him another Isaac; God would return his sacrificed son to life. Abraham believed by virtue of the Absurd; he had long ago finished with human reckoning." * And in order to dispel any doubts about how he regards Abraham's faith and the meaning of his action, Kierkegaard links his own case with the Biblical story. Of course, he does not do this directly or straightforwardly. We already know that men do not speak openly of such matters; this is even more true of Kierkegaard, and that is why he devised his "theory" of indirect communication. It is true, by the way, that when the occasion arises he tells us this: "Every man decides for himself and by himself what his own Isaac is" †—but the meaning and the "concrete" significance of these words can be guessed only after one has heard the story Kierkegaard "invented" about the poor youth who fell in love with the king's daughter. It is perfectly evident to everyone that the youth is never going to get the princess. Ordinary common sense, as well as the lofty wisdom of mankind (in the last analysis there is no essential difference between common sense and wisdom), advises him to put aside his dream of the impossible and to aim for the possible; the widow of a wealthy brewer is the most suitable match for him. But the youth forgets both common sense and the divine Plato, and suddenly, just like Abraham, throws himself headlong into the embrace of the Absurd. Reason refused to give him the daughter of the king, whom it had intended, not for him, but for a king's son; and the youth turns away

* III, 32.
† *Ibid.*, 68.

from reason and looks to the Absurd for his happiness. He knows that in "the ordinariness of everyday life" there reigns a most profound assurance that the king's daughter will never be his. "For reason is right: in our vale of sorrow, where it is lord and master, this has been and will remain an impossibility." * He also knows that the wisdom which the gods have given men recommends in such cases, as the only way out from the situation which has been created, a calm resignation to the inevitable. And he even passes through this resignation—passes through it in the sense that he perceives reality with all the clarity of which the human mind is capable. Perhaps, explains Kierkegaard, another man would consider it more tempting to do away with his desire to win the king's daughter, to blunt, so to speak, the sharp edge of his sorrow. Such a man Kierkegaard calls the knight of resignation, and even finds words of sympathy for him. But just the same "it is a wonderful thing to win the king's daughter"; "the knight of resignation is a liar if he denies this" † and his love is not true love. Kierkegaard contrasts the knight of resignation with the knight of faith: "Through faith, says this knight to himself, through faith, by virtue of the Absurd, you will win the daughter of the king." And he repeats this once more: "All the same, how wonderful it is to win the daughter of the king. The knight of faith is the only happy one: he is master over the finite, while the knight of resignation is merely an outsider and a stranger there." ‡ But here he admits: "And yet I am incapable of this bold [movement]. When I try to perform it, my head whirls

* III, 43.
† *Ibid.,* 46.
‡ *Ibid.,* 46.

and I rush to take shelter in the sorrow of resignation. I am able to keep afloat, but I am too heavy for this mystical soaring." And in his journals we read, more than once: "If only I had had faith, Regina would still be mine."

Why is a man who strives so passionately, so frantically for faith unable to attain it? Why can he not follow the example of Abraham and the poor youth who fell in love with the king's daughter? Why has he become so heavy and incapable of soaring? Why has resignation befallen him, why has he been denied this final act of daring?

We will recall that Kierkegaard, in comparing paganism with Christianity, said that paganism did not understand that sin is bound up with the stubbornness and obstinacy of the human will. We will also recall that, upon investigation, this contrast turns out to be false; paganism always understood vice as originating in evil will. But the obstacle between Kierkegaard and faith was not evil will. On the contrary, his entire will, of the sort to be found only in man—a will both good and evil—sought faith with an infinitely passionate intensity, but it did not arrive at faith and went no further than resignation. To realize the ideal of resignation is within the power of the man, but he does not find in his soul the capacity for the final act of daring. "Resignation brings me awareness of my eternity; this is a purely philosophical movement and I am convinced that if it is demanded of me, I will make it, will find within me the strength to force myself to submit to the strict discipline of the spirit. . . . I make this movement by my own powers." * And Kierkegaard is not exaggerating; he knew what is meant by the discipline of the spirit—he did not pass through the school of Socrates in vain. If it were

* III, 44.

simply a matter of self-renunciation or, to put it better, of a feat of self-renunciation, Kierkegaard would emerge the victor from the struggle. But he is not much attracted by "awareness of one's eternity"—that which Spinoza expressed in the words *sentimus experimurque nos aeternos esse,* and which was such an inspiration to Schleiermacher—this is the *consolatio philosophiae* and of theoretical philosophy; one would not turn to Job or to Abraham with such "consolations." Kierkegaard goes on to explain: "I can renounce everything by my own efforts. But I cannot gain by my own powers anything that belongs to the finite world. . . . By my own powers I can give up the king's daughter without a murmur and bear the sorrow in my heart cheerfully, with a feeling of peace and seren-ity. But am I to find the king's daughter again? Through faith, the wondrous knight tells us, through faith you can attain her, by virtue of the Absurd." * Kierkegaard's aim is now made clear. Socrates was a knight of resignation and all the wisdom he bequeathed to mankind was the wisdom of resignation. (Spinoza, with his *sub specie aeternitatis,* echoes Socrates.) Socrates "knew" that a man can give up a king's daughter by his own powers, but win her he cannot. He also "knew" that even the powers of the gods are limited, that they have no authority in the finite world, and that their realm includes only the "eternal," which they are willing to share with mortals. This is why Socrates thought that all those who are not satisfied with what the gods can do for them and who do not agree to find happiness, peace, and serenity in a renunciation of

* Cf. *Ibid.,* 45: "A purely human courage is needed to renounce the transitory for the sake of the eternal; but a paradoxical and humble courage is needed to become master over all that is finite, by virtue of the Absurd. Abraham did not lose Isaac through faith; he gained him."

the finite are obstinate and inveterate sinners who deserve all the misfortunes reserved for those who are μισόλογοι. Since knowledge comes from reason, to reject knowledge means to reject reason—and *quam aram parabit sibi qui majestatem rationis laedit*—at what altar will the man worship who has insulted the majesty of reason, as Spinoza, the *Socrates redivivus*, said, two thousand years after Socrates?

And yet Job rejected all the *consolationes philosophiae*, all the "deceitful consolations" of human wisdom—and the God of the Bible not only did not see evil will in this, but condemned his "comforters," who had suggested that he exchange his "finite" blessings for the contemplation of eternity. For his part, Abraham did not repudiate the "finite" Isaac even at the moment when the knife glittered in his hand—and he became the father of faith for countless generations to come; Kierkegaard cannot find words and images too strong to celebrate his daring.

VI

Faith and Sin

> *The opposite of sin is not virtue, but faith: all that is not of faith is sin (Romans 14:23). This belongs to the most explicit of Christianity's definitions.*
>
> KIERKEGAARD

Two things have, I hope, become fairly clear to us by now. On the one hand, Kierkegaard resolves to suspend the "ethical," which is the expression of "resignation," and to a certain degree he is successful; not only Job and Abraham, but also the poor youth who fell in love with the king's daughter, renounce the "deceitful consolations" suggested to them by reason and by Socrates, and have no fear of the judgment of the "ethical." They do not care whether ethics recognizes them as *laudabiles* or *vituperabiles* (worthy of praise or blame); they are aiming at something entirely different: Job demands the restoration of the past; Abraham, the restoration of his Isaac; the poor youth, the restoration of the king's daughter. Let ethics threaten them with all its thunders and anathemas;

let Socrates be as ironical as he pleases, let him point out that "a contradiction is concealed in the infinitely passionate striving for the finite"—none of this will disturb Job or Abraham or Kierkegaard. They will answer indignation with anger and scoff at Socrates himself, if need be. But ethics is not alone; behind its gibes and its indignation stands Necessity. Necessity cannot be seen; it says nothing, it does not jeer or reproach. It is impossible even to say where it can be found; it is as though it were nowhere at all. It only strikes, silently, indifferently, at the man who is unprotected, who obviously does not even suspect the existence in the world of the indignation, the anger, the horror, of Job, Abraham, and Kierkegaard, and does not in any way take them into account.

With what are we to oppose Necessity? How to cope with it? Reason not only does not dare to contend with it, it is entirely on its side. Indeed, reason led even the divine Plato to Necessity; it won ethics over to the side of Necessity, and ethics began to sing Necessity's praises, to justify it, and to demand of gods and men a loving resignation to the inevitable. Man must not only accept, but even give his blessing to everything prepared for him by Necessity, and he must see this as the supreme task assigned to him in life. We must not strive for finite happiness—must not aim for the flocks and lands of Job, or the return of a son, or the winning of the king's daughter—for everything finite passes; such is the fundamental law of existence. We do not know why, when, or by whom this law was established, but it is primordial and immutable. All that is finite, precisely because it is finite, has a beginning, and all that has a beginning also has and must have an end. Such, I repeat, is the unalterable law of existence, and although we know not when, where, and why it arose, our reason knows for a certainty that it will never go away. By its side, also revealed by intellectual vision, stand Eternity and her sister Infinity. Perhaps human daring already has the power to cope with ethics—but is there a power capable of vanquishing Eternity? Eternity devours everything and never returns what she has seized. She does not recognize "repetition" and takes from man with equal indifference all that is most precious to him—his honor, his pride, his Isaac, his Regina Olsen. The greatest daring has been obliged to humble itself, and has been humbled, before Eternity; worse yet, daring is unmasked before Eternity, revealed for what it really is—insurrection, mutiny, which is, moreover, doomed from the start to fail. Greek thought, almost from its very beginnings, discovered γένεσις and φθορά (birth and destruction) in all that exists, inextricably bound up with the very nature of existence. Could Job, Abraham, and Kierkegaard change any of this? Could the gods themselves make any change whatever in it?

Kierkegaard is no less aware of this than Hegel.* And precisely because he is aware of it, he opposes Greek reason with his Biblical Absurd, philosophical speculation with the thinking of Job and Abraham. This is the most difficult point in his "existential" philosophy, but at the same time the most important, the most essential, and the most remarkable. Here, to a greater extent than in all the rest of Kierkegaard's ideas, one must be prepared to put

---

* III, 43: "He understands that [he is seeking] the impossible; but it is at precisely this moment that he believes in the Absurd. For if he, without having grasped impossibility with all the passion in his soul and all the strength in his heart, imagines that he possesses faith, then he is deceiving himself and his testimony is groundless."

into practice his fundamental precept, or, if you please, his methodological principle, his *either/or:* it is either the thinking of Abraham, Job, the Prophets, and the Apostles; or the thinking of Socrates. It is either theoretical philosophy, which takes wonder as its starting point and seeks "understanding"; or existential philosophy, which proceeds from despair (I repeat once more: from the biblical *de profundis ad te, Domine, clamavi*) and leads to the revelation of Holy Scripture. Here, and only here, is the meaning of Kierkegaard's pairs of opposites: Job–Hegel, Abraham–Socrates, reason–the Absurd. And it would be a mistake to think that the Absurd signifies in itself the end of thinking. It was not by chance that Kierkegaard said that he had gone from Hegel to the private thinker Job. For Kierkegaard, Hegel, who as he expresses it, "deified reality," * is not "a thinker, but a professor." Thinking not only is retained in the "Absurd," but achieves an unprecedented intensity, achieves, as it were, a new dimension, totally unknown to Hegel and speculative philosophy; this is the distinguishing characteristic of existential philosophy. According to Hegel, a man thinks badly if he does not surrender wholly to the power of a thing external to him, and if he adds anything of himself; man is obliged to accept existence as it is given to him, for all that is given, or, as he prefers to say, all that is real, is rational. In saying this, Hegel shows no originality; a thousand-year-old philosophical culture lies behind him. Spinoza's formulation of the same thought—*non ridere, non lugere, neque detestari, sed intelligere*—is far more brilliant, more meaningful, more profound; it still retains the traces (completely obliterated in the Hegelian

* IX, 73.

formula) of a struggle with a truth that thrusts itself upon us from somewhere without. But Kierkegaard learned something different from Job; man thinks badly if he accepts what is "given" to him as final, irrevocable, forever unchangeable—however horrible and repellent he may find it. Of course, he understands perfectly well that to oppose Job to Hegel, or Abraham to Socrates is the greatest offense, and the height of folly for the ordinary consciousness. But this is precisely his problem: to tear himself free from the power of the commonplace; not for nothing has he told us that the starting point of philosophy is not wonder, but despair, which reveals a new source of truth to man. Moreover, he does not forget for a moment that theoretical philosophy, which is supported by the given and the real, is a terrible and implacable enemy; that even the greatest thinkers in the world have retreated and bowed low before the given, and not of their own will, be it good or evil; and that these great thinkers have compelled the gods to bow and retreat before it also. And yet he dares to go all but barehanded against an adversary armed from head to toe. He proceeds against the argumentation, the proofs, the evidence of theoretical philosophy with the wails and curses of Job, with the "groundless" faith of Abraham. He does not even offer any "proof" —what can one prove when all is over, all is lost? But on the other hand, will "proofs" still be able to prove anything to a man for whom all is lost, all is over? Will there not be an end to proofs, in that case? There is the abyss, in the depths of despair, thought itself will revive; this is the meaning of those puzzling words of the Psalmist: *de profundis ad te, Domine, clamavi.* That which we call "understanding" is like an enormous stone, fallen from

God knows where, which has crushed and flattened our consciousness, beaten it down to the two-dimensional plane of an illusory half-existence, and weakened our powers of thought. We can only "accept"—we are not yet able to challenge, we are convinced that "challenging" only spoils and corrupts human thought; Job, Abraham, and the Psalmist, in our opinion, think badly. But for existential philosophy, the greatest defect in our thinking is its loss of the ability to "challenge," because it has thus forfeited the one dimension that alone is able to guide it to the truth.

This is the source of the sarcasm which Kierkegaard directs at theoretical philosophy. "It seems strange to me," he writes, "that people are always saying: speculation—as if it were a person, or as if speculation were human. Speculation does everything; it questions everything, etc. The man who speculates, on the other hand, has become too objective to speak of himself; therefore he does not say that it is he who questions something, but that speculation does this and he is speaking in the name of speculation." * The very qualities which theoretical philosophy considers to be to its particular credit—its objectivity, its lack of passion—are seen by Kierkegaard as its greatest deficiency, its basic shortcoming. "Men," he says in another passage, "have become too objective to attain eternal happiness: for eternal happiness consists precisely of a passionate and infinite personal concern. And they renounce this in order to become objective: objectivity robs their souls of passion and 'infinite personal concern.'" † The unlimited power of "objectivity" seems to Kierkegaard

---

* VI, 141 and 142.
† *Ibid.,* 121.

unnaturally strange, mysterious, and enigmatic. And here is something to ponder, even though not one of the innumerable extollers of objectivity has ever pondered it, has ever posed the question of whence and when this power came to objectivity, and why the "infinitely passionate concern" of living man and living gods should have yielded to objectivity, which is indifferent to all and certainly has no concern for anything. At times one might even think that the philosophers who glorify objectivity and place all of creation in its clutches are, seemingly without knowing it, using the Kierkegaardian method of indirect communication; it is as if they were asking themselves: how much longer are the people to be scourged? The people are long-suffering, however; the people will endure everything, even objectivity. Then, too, objectivity has fascinated and will always fascinate the thinker because it offers him the possibility of announcing its truths with assurance—as universal and necessary truths. In the *Critique of Pure Reason* Kant openly asserts (I almost said: lets slip): "Experience tells us what exists, but it does not tell us that this must necessarily be the way it is or otherwise. Therefore experience does not give us a true generality, and reason, which eagerly strives for just this kind of knowledge, will sooner become exasperated with experience than be satisfied with it." But if it is a matter of "eager striving," of passion—then has not a substitution been made here? To express it in the words of Kierkegaard: has not the man who speculates—he who was hiding behind the impartiality of speculation—regained his voice at this point? And are we then not right to suspect that this so-called objectivity of theoretical thinking is only an outward show, a superficial appearance, perhaps even a conscious deception; should we not, following the example of Kierkegaard, oppose reason's eager striving for general and necessary judgments, with man's subjective concern for eternal happiness? This question does not exist for speculative philosophy; it does not see the question and does not wish to see it. It says, not openly, but with inward certainty, that man can laugh, weep, rail, curse, but this will make no impression on Necessity, which will continue as before to crush, smother, burn, and reduce to ashes everything "finite" (above all, man) that it finds in its path. As we shall more than once again find opportunity to prove, this is the *ultima ratio* of theoretical philosophy, which is upheld only by Necessity and Necessity's companion, Obligation. Our reason, as if bewitched by some magic spell, is making straight for the place where man's destruction awaits him. What is this? Is there not concealed here that *concupiscentia invincibilis* which led our forefather to the Fall?

This question is the principal theme of Kierkegaard's *The Concept of Dread,* in which he sets forth the most basic and irreconcilable difference (which he had mentioned in part before) between biblical revelation and Hellenic truth. Although Kierkegaard, as we will recall, assured us that Socrates, in his definition of sin, left out the concepts of stubbornness, of obstinacy, of evil will, conveyed to us by the Bible—in actuality, as we shall presently see, he not only felt and thought, but even said, something entirely different. "The opposite of sin," he writes, "is *not virtue, but faith.* That is why it is said in Romans 14:23: all that is not of faith is sin. And this belongs to the most explicit of Christianity's definitions: that the opposite of sin is not virtue, but faith." * He repeats this many times throughout all his works, just as he repeats countless times that, in order to attain faith, one must renounce reason. In his last writings he even formulated in this way: "Faith is against reason—faith dwells beyond death." † But what sort of faith is spoken of in Holy Scripture? Kierkegaard's answer is: "Faith means precisely this: to lose reason in order to find God." ‡ Kierkegaard had written earlier, with regard to Abraham and his sacrifice: "What an incredible paradox is faith! The paradox can transform murder into something that is holy and pleasing to God. The paradox returns Abraham's Isaac to him. Thinking cannot master the paradox, for faith begins at the exact point where thinking ends." Why is it necessary to renounce reason? Why does faith begin where rational thinking ends? Kierkegaard does not avoid this question and does not conceal from himself the difficulties and the pitfalls connected with the question thus posed. He had already written, in *Philosophical Fragments*: "To believe against reason is martyrdom. The man who speculates is free from this martyrdom." § And that is just the point: to renounce rational thinking, to deprive oneself of the support and protection of the ethical—is this not the ultimate horror for man? But Kierkegaard has anticipated us: existential philosophy begins in despair. Even the questions he sets before us are dictated to him by despair. This is how he himself describes it: "Picture a man who by straining his frightened imagination has

* VIII, 77.
† XI, 88.
‡ VIII, 35.
§ VI, 285.

thought up some unprecedented horror, something completely unbearable. And then suddenly he actually finds this horror before him. To the human mind it seems that his destruction is certain. He wrestles with the despair in his heart over whether to give himself up to that despair in order to find (if I may use the expression) peace of mind thereby. And so, by human standards, salvation is a complete impossibility for him. But for God all things are possible. Faith consists of this: a mad struggle for possibility. For only possibility opens the way to salvation. If someone falls in a faint, people run to fetch water and restoratives. When a person falls into despair, we cry: possibilities, possibilities, only possibility will save him. Possibility appears, and the one who was in despair revives, begins to breathe again. Without possibility, just as without air, man suffocates. At times it seems that his inventive imagination is itself the creator of possibility. But in the last analysis one thing remains: for God all things are possible. And only then is the way to faith laid open." * Kierkegaard is inexhaustible on this subject. He repeats in every conceivable way: for God all things are possible. He declares unhesitatingly: "God signifies that all is possible; or, that all is possible signifies God. Only the man whose being has been so profoundly shaken that he becomes spirit, and understands that all things are possible, only he has come near to God." † And here he adds: "The absence of possibility means either that everything has become necessary or that everything has become commonplace. The commonplace, the trivial do not know what possibility is. The commonplace tolerates only probability, in which hardly

* VIII, 35.
† Ibid., 37.

more than a trace of possibility is preserved; but that all this (that is, the improbable and the impossible) is possible does not occur to it and it has no notion of God. The commonplace man (be he a tavern keeper or a minister of state) is devoid of imagination and lives in the sphere of limited, banal experience: as generally happens, what is generally possible, what has always been. . . . The commonplace imagines that it has caught possibility in the trap of probability or shut it up in a madhouse; exhibits it in the cage of probability and thinks that it possesses God knows what power." Kierkegaard has no mutual language with the commonplace—we must suppose that the commonplace, in turn, has no mutual language with Kierkegaard. Moreover, one certainly ought not to include brewers and the philosophy of brewers under the heading of the commonplace and the philosophy of the commonplace (notwithstanding the fact that Kierkegaard himself often identifies the commonplace with triviality and is tempted thus to simplify the matter.) The commonplace exists everywhere that man still relies on his own powers, his own reason (Aristotle and Kant, owing to their undoubted genius, do not, in this sense, cross over into the realm of the commonplace), and comes to an end only where despair has its beginning, where reason demonstrates with full clarity that man is faced with impossibility, that all is finished forever, that any further struggle is senseless— in other words, the commonplace ends where and when man feels his total powerlessness. Kierkegaard had to drink more deeply than anyone else from the bitter cup given to man by the knowledge of his powerlessness. When he says that some terrible force took from him his honor and his pride, he has in mind his own powerlessness,

powerlessness that made him feel that the woman he loved became a shadow when he touched her, powerlessness that made him feel that for him all reality was becoming a shadow. How did this happen? What sort of force is it, where can it be found,—this force which can so ravage a man's soul? In his journal he writes: "If only I had had faith, I would not have left Regina." * This is no longer indirect communication of the sort Kierkegaard put in the mouths of the heroes of his stories, this is a man's direct testimony about himself. Kierkegaard "felt" the absence of faith as powerlessness, and powerlessness as the absence of faith. And through this terrible experience he discovered that most people do not even suspect that the absence of faith is an expression of the powerlessness of man, or that the powerlessness of man expresses in itself the absence of faith. This makes clear to us his words: the opposite of sin is not virtue, but faith. Virtue, as we have already been told by Kierkegaard, is maintained by man's own powers; the knight of resignation achieves by himself all that he needs, and, having achieved it, finds serenity and peace of mind. But is man thus freed from sin? All that is not of faith, as Kierkegaard reminds us in the enigmatic words of the Apostle, is sin. Are the peace and serenity of the knight of resignation therefore a sin? Was Socrates, who quietly accepted the cup of poison from the hands of his jailer, to the astonishment of his disciples and all succeeding generations, a sinner because of that? Kierkegaard nowhere says this directly; even when the subject of the most famous of the world's wise men arises, he places Socrates in a special category. But this does not alter the case. The "best of men" was satisfied with the

* *Journal,* I, 195; cf. *ibid.,* 167.

position of a knight of resignation, accepted his helplessness before necessity as inevitable and therefore right, and for several hours before his death bolstered the "peace and serenity" in the hearts of his disciples with his edifying words. Is it possible to "surpass" Socrates? Many hundreds of years after him, Epictetus, faithful to the spirit of his incomparable master, wrote that the beginning of philosophy is a sense of powerlessness before Necessity. For him, this sense is also the end of philosophy, or, to be more precise, philosophical thought is altogether limited by man's sense of his absolute powerlessness before Necessity.

Here, for Kierkegaard, the meaning of the Biblical story of the Fall is made plain. Socratic virtue does not save man from sin. The virtuous man is a knight of resignation, who has experienced all the ignominy and horror associated with his powerlessness before necessity, and has stopped at that. He can move no further: something has whispered to him that there is nowhere to go, and therefore no need to go on.

Why did he stop? Whence came this "nowhere" and "no need"? Whence came this resignation, this cult of resignation? We know: "nowhere" was revealed to the pagan world by reason, and "not obliged" comes from the ethical. Zeus himself proclaimed them to Chryssip—we must suppose that Socrates and Plato found out about them from the same source. As long as man is guided by reason and bows before the ethical, "nowhere" and "not obliged" are insuperable. Without taking this into account, man decides, instead of seeking "the one thing that is needful," to put himself at the disposal of the "general and necessary" judgments for which reason, followed by its servant Ethics, so "eagerly strives." And, indeed, how can one suspect reason and ethics of anything bad, for they are our support, everywhere and in everything. They protect us from loss of honor and loss of pride! Can man think even for a moment that they, by their solicitude, are affording shelter to that "horror" which lies in wait for us at every step— that they are concealing from man's powerlessness not only his, but also their own powerlessness before Necessity? Even Zeus, compelled to admit the limitation of his powers, is transformed into a knight of resignation and does not feel that his powerlessness means his honor and his pride have been taken from him, that he is no longer God the all-sustaining, but the same sort of weak and helpless being as Chryssip, Socrates, and Plato, or any other mortal. Zeus, of course, was not lacking in virtue—at least, not the Zeus invoked by Chryssip, Plato, and Socrates; however, this is not the Zeus of popular mythology and of Homer, whom Plato had to re-educate in his *Republic*— but even he could not accomplish everything "by his own powers." Falstaff's sly question (can you restore a man's arm or leg?) might well have been addressed to him. Kierkegaard, who attacked Falstaff so angrily, himself turns to reason and ethics with the fat knight's questions: can you restore Job's children, Abraham's Isaac, can you give back the king's daughter to the poor youth, and Regina Olsen to me? If you cannot, then you are not gods; however much wise men may assure us of the contrary, you are but idols, creations, if not of human hands, then of human imagination. God means that everything is possible, that nothing is impossible. And this is why reason, which asserts that the power of God is limited and that God cannot cross over the boundaries set for Him by the very nature of things, not only does not inspire love for itself, but inspires the most profound, unyielding, implacable hatred. This is why even "ethics," which is always supported and glorified by reason, must be suspended. And here a question arises which appears completely senseless to speculative philosophy: where did reason obtain the gift of knowing what is possible and what impossible? And has it indeed such a gift? And furthermore, is it just *that one sort* of knowledge, or knowledge in general? It is not empirical knowledge, which arises from experience; such knowledge not only does not satisfy reason, but irritates and offends it. Kant himself told us this, and Spinoza said that to offend reason is the most grievous of crimes, *laesio majestatis*. Reason eagerly strives for universal and necessary truths which are uncreated and dependent upon no one! Is not reason itself in the power of some hostile force that has so bewitched it that the fortuitous and the transitory seem to it necessary and eternal? And ethics, which suggests to man that resignation is the highest virtue—is it not in the same position as reason? It, too, has been bewitched by mysterious spells; man's destruction awaits him where ethics promises him happiness and salvation. One must escape from reason, escape from ethics, without trying to find out beforehand what the end of the journey will be. This is the paradox, this is the Absurd, which was concealed from Socrates, but revealed in Holy Scripture: when it was necessary for Abraham to go to the Promised Land, writes the Apostle Paul, he went, not knowing himself where he was going.

VII

Fear and Nothingness

In the estate of innocence, there is peace and serenity, but in addition to that there is something else. . . But what is it? Nothingness. What effect has Nothingness? It arouses fear.

KIERKEGAARD

The opposite of sin is not virtue, but faith. Faith is faith in God, for whom all things are possible, for whom nothing is impossible. Human reason, however, is not willing to assume that all is possible; for it, this means thinking that there is unlimited arbitrariness at the foundation of the universe. It does not in any way alter the case for us to say, as did Kierkegaard, that for God all things are possible—for this implies an admission that God does not take into account either our reason or our ethics. Can one entrust his fate to God without having first been convinced that God is a rational and ethical being? What if God is insane, what if God is evil and cruel? *Abraham, who went, not knowing himself where he was going, is an ignoramus and a fool; Abraham, who raised a knife to his own son, is a transgressor and an evildoer.* To us, this is self-evident; there is no disputing it. Even St. Augustine himself wrote: "Before I can believe, I must ask myself: *cui est credendum.*" God created everything; but reason and ethics are not created—they are timeless and primordial.

Here, for the second time, Kierkegaard has come up against the idea of sin as it was imagined by the pagan consciousness and as it is represented in Holy Scripture. He has assured us that the idea of sin in Socrates' definition left out the moment of "evil will." But we are certain that this is historically false. The fact is that the pagans linked sin inseparably with evil will and even, I might add, attempted to impose their own notion of sin upon Christianity in its infancy. The famous Pelagian controversy arose over this very point. For Pelagius, to use Kierkegaard's words, the opposite of sin was virtue—which is why he insisted so vehemently that man has the ability to save himself by his own powers, and why he showed such indignation toward those who relied not on their own merits, but on the grace of God. It is true that Pelagius was condemned, but even St. Augustine, who had been the first to offer a proper objection to Pelagius, could never (and did not want to!) relinquish the concept of sin as an expression of evil will; and in the history of theological thought we observe constant attempts (clandestine, of course) to return, on one pretext or another, to Pelagianism. Men have always been inclined to rely upon their own powers and to trust their own reason more than God. Kierkegaard, who, of course, disavowed the Pelagian doctrine and was generally far removed from it, nevertheless could not rid his heart of the conviction that sin originates in evil will and stubbornness, and that virtue is fated to play a certain, and indeed not the least, part in the matter of our salvation. He not only could not, but did not want to—and, as we have just seen, he was more unwilling than unable to do so. At the same time, though, he felt that the radical difference between the pagan and the biblical concepts of sin was by no means to be found here.

In his book *The Concept of Dread*—one of his most profound works and the one that brings us nearest to him—he closely considers the greatest enigma set before man by Holy Scripture, the story of the Fall of the first man. He makes a tremendous effort to link the Biblical narrative dealing with original sin and the Biblical concept of faith with his personal experience; and to free himself of those ready-made ideas which he had absorbed during his study of the works of the pagan and Christian philosophers. "The thought of finding a logical explanation of how sin came to the world," he writes, "is a piece of nonsense which could occur only to men who are preoccupied to a ridiculous degree with perpetually explaining everything, no matter what." And again, a page later: "Each man must understand for himself how sin came into the world—for if he wishes someone else to teach him this, it means that there is some hidden misunderstanding here. . . . And if any sort of science makes an appearance at this point with its explanations—it will only confuse everything. *It is truly said, that a scholar should forget about himself: but this is exactly why sin is not a scientific problem*" (italics mine).*

But, if this is so, what then can Kierkegaard tell us about sin? And what is the source of what he tells us? The Bible?

* V, 44.

But the Bible is open to everyone, even without him. Moreover, as we are about to see, he refuses to accept part of what the Bible says about the Fall of the first man. He does have some sources of information: not without reason has he told us that each man must know for himself how sin came to the world. Let us listen to him: "Innocence is ignorance. In innocence, man is limited, not spiritually, but mentally, in direct union with the natural state. Man's mind is still sleeping. This idea fully agrees with the Bible, which does not recognize that man in the state of innocence has any knowledge of the difference between good and evil." * The contrary is completely indisputable: this idea does not agree in any way with the Bible, but is very similar to what theoretical philosophy sees in the biblical narrative. It is true that, according to the Bible, the innocent man (that is, man before the Fall) has neither knowledge in general nor knowledge of the difference between good and evil. But in the Bible there is not even a hint that the mind of man, as he came forth from the Creator's hand, was lulled to sleep, and still less that knowledge and the ability to distinguish good from evil signify in themselves the awakening of man's mind. Exactly the opposite; the entire meaning of the enigmatic story of the Fall of man lies in just this: that knowledge and the ability to distinguish good from evil, that is, what the fruit of the forbidden tree brought man, did not awaken his mind, but put it to sleep. It is true that when the serpent tempted Eve, he promised her that, having tasted of this fruit, men would awaken and be as gods. But then, the serpent, according to the Scripture, was the originator of every sort of lie, and only men of Hellenic education—in ancient

* *Ibid.*, 36.

times the Gnostics, and afterward, nearly all philosophers
—thought otherwise, considering it unlikely that the
knowledge and the ability to distinguish between good
and evil would not awaken a sleeping mind, but would
put to sleep a wide-awake one. Hegel, whom Kierkegaard
despised, persistently and confidently repeated that in the
story of the Fall of man the deceiver was not the serpent,
but God: the serpent revealed the truth to the first human
beings. It would seem least of all appropriate for Kierkegaard, who sang the praises of the Absurd so ardently, to
connect the awakening of the mind with knowledge; and
since he had surmised that the knight of faith was obliged
to suspend the ethical, it would be even less fitting for him
to see any spiritual advantage in the ability to distinguish
good from evil. But not for nothing did he lament that he
was not able to make the final movement of faith. Even at
the moment of greatest inward strain, when his entire soul
is rushing in a frenzy toward the Absurd, he turns to
"knowledge," demands an examination of the Absurd, and
asks the question (asks it of reason, of course, whom else
could he ask?): *cui est credendum*. And that is why he,
who recklessly surrendered his soul to Holy Scripture,
does not find it at all difficult to say that the role of the
serpent in the Biblical narrative is incomprehensible to
him. In other words, he almost (and maybe not almost)
repeats what Hegel had said: it was not the serpent that
deceived man, but God!

And yet, even though Kierkegaard reserved the right
and the possibility of verifying with his own reason what
the Bible revealed to him, he still felt with all his heart
its profound truth, perhaps even confirming it indirectly
by this very interpretation, as he had confirmed it by his

admissions that he could not make the movement of faith and that, if he had had faith, he would not have left Regina. Immediately after the words quoted above, he goes on to say: "In that state (i.e., in the state of innocence) there is peace and serenity, but in addition to that there is something else: not confusion, not a struggle—for there is no reason to struggle. But what is it? Nothingness. What effect has Nothingness? It arouses fear. The great mystery of innocence lies in this: that it is, at the same time, fear." *

Original sin, the Fall of the first man, as the result of fear of Nothingness, is the basic concept of the book by Kierkegaard mentioned above. We must suppose that this is the most precious, most necessary, most sacred, most deeply felt idea in his extraordinary spiritual experience. And yet, in the words which I have just cited, he expresses this idea inadequately. He says: "The great mystery of innocence lies in this: that it is, at the same time, fear." If he had heard someone else say that, he would probably have felt uneasy and called to mind all the things he had said about theoretical philosophy and the objective truth acquired by theoretical philosophy. "Innocence is, at the same time, fear." Who gives us the right thus to expose the great mystery of innocence? This is not to be found in the Bible, just as one cannot find there even the slightest hint of the idea that man in the state of innocence is limited, not spiritually, but mentally. Kierkegaard could have learned all this, I repeat, either from the Gnostics, who took over both the gnoseological ideas of the Greek philosophers and their axiology, and, accordingly, drew a contrast between the spiritual condition of man and the men-

* *Ibid.,* 36.

tal, the latter being considered superior; or he could have learned it from thinkers contemporary to him who had yielded to Gnostic influences. At any rate, we are hardly likely to "know" anything about the state of innocence, even in a general way. Kierkegaard's approach to the Fall includes his own personal experience, but in his experience of the sinful man, there could not be any data that would enable him to draw conclusions about the innocent man, i.e., the man who has not sinned. And least of all had he the right to express the opinion that "innocence is, at the same time, fear." The most that he had the right to say is that "There was innocence; then suddenly, for an unknown reason, from an unknown place, came fear." But Kierkegaard is afraid of any sort of "credo." Is not this fear of "suddenly" the fear we already know, the fear of Nothingness, which destroyed our forefather, but was not itself destroyed, and a thousand generations later continues to be passed down to us, the remote descendants of Adam? . . .

Kierkegaard insists that the fear felt by the first man must be distinguished from terror, apprehension, and other such states of mind that are always aroused by certain definite causes; this fear is, as he puts it, "the reality of freedom, as the possibility of possibilities." In other words, Adam's fear was not motivated by anything—and yet it seemed insurmountable. Perhaps it would have been better if, instead of defining fear as "the reality of freedom" (we shall see in a moment that, according to Kierkegaard, the most terrible "result" of the Fall was man's loss of his freedom), and as "the possibility of possibilities," Kierkegaard had expressed himself more concretely, that is, had said that the freedom of the innocent man knows no bounds. This would correspond with what he, in complete agreement with the Bible, told us earlier: for God all things are possible; and with what he has further to tell us about fear. It is just as incorrect to find fear in the state of innocence as it is to find the sleep of the mind there. Both the sleep of the mind and fear—according to the Bible—came after the Fall. Therefore the serpent is evidently introduced into the Biblical narrative to serve as an external, but active, principle. The serpent inspired the first man's fear; although a false fear—fear of Nothingness—it was overwhelming and insuperable. And this fear has lulled the human mind to sleep, paralyzed the human will. Kierkegaard takes exception to the serpent, declaring that he cannot associate him with any sort of definite idea. I am not about to dispute the notion that the role of the serpent is "incomprehensible" to our reason. But then, even Kierkegaard himself continually assures us that the persistent desire to "grasp," to "understand" the meaning of the Fall, no matter what, only bears witness to our reluctance to experience the entire depth and significance of the problem that lies therein. In this case, "understanding" not only does not help, it is a hindrance. We have entered the region where the "Absurd" rules with its "suddenly," which ceaselessly flares up and dies down again; every "suddenly," every unexpectedness is the implacable foe of "understanding," and so, too, is the Biblical *fiat*—for ordinary human thinking it is a *deus ex machina* which theoretical philosophy quite rightly sees as the beginning of its destruction.

It is my opinion—and I hope that the following explanation will bear this out—that Kierkegaard behaves contrary to his nature whenever he tries to amend the Bible (alas, he does this more than once), and that therefore we will come far closer to him if we say this: the state of innocence did not include fear, because it had no knowledge of limited possibilities. The innocent man lived in the presence of God, and God signifies that all is possible. The serpent, in the temptation of man, had at his disposal only Nothingness. This Nothingness, although it is only Nothingness, or, more probably, all the more because it is Nothingness, has lulled the human mind to sleep, and the man whose mind is asleep has become the prey or the victim of fear, even though there is no reason or basis for fear. But then, Nothingness is only Nothingness. How did it happen to turn into Something? And once having become Something, how did it acquire such limitless power over man, and even over all existence?

The concept of Nothingness was already well known to the ancients. According to Aristotle (*Met.* 985 B 6), Democritus and Leucippus affirmed the existence of Nothingness: οὐδὲν μᾶλλον τὸ ὂν τοῦ μὴ ὄντος εἶναι, they said. The same thought is put forward by Plutarch in far more expressive words: μὴ μᾶλλον τὸ δὲν ἢ τὸ μηδὲν εἶναι ("Being has no more existence than nonbeing"). It is true that Leucippus and Democritus identify Nothingness with emptiness, and Something with matter. But whether in this aspect or another—at the same time as, and in contrast to, Parmenides, whose point of departure was the position that only being exists, that nonbeing not only does not exist, but cannot even be conceived of—Greek philosophy assumed the existence of Nothingness and even held that the existence of Nothingness was a prerequisite of thinking. It is obvious that this idea was not entirely foreign to the Eleatics, and that when Parmenides insisted that

Nothingness has no existence, he had to overcome and reject, after an inward struggle, the suspicion that perhaps Nothingness manages nevertheless in some way to exist; "natural" thinking is obliged, in the quarrel between the Eleatics and the Atomists, to incline to the side of the latter. Nothingness is not perfect; that is, Nothingness is devoid of existence. It stands in opposition to Something, and opposes it as an equal. This is how we must understand Plato's words about the two causes—the divine and the necessary. He was merely clarifying the idea of the Atomists; for him, Nothingness had become Necessity. The conviction that Necessity is separate from divine power over what exists was, for the Hellenists, one of the most insuperable of self-evidencies and even, perhaps, the fundamental postulate of Hellenic thinking. And so it has remained down to our own day. In modern philosophy it has been expressed in the Hegelian dialectic, where it is called "the self-movement of the concept"; in the opinion of Schelling, who states that there is "something else" in God besides Himself—His nature; and in the thesis that Spinoza, the spiritual father of Hegel and Schelling, formulated in his famous theorem: *Deus ex solis suae naturae legibus et a nemine coactus agit* (God acts only by virtue of the laws of His own nature and is coerced by no one).

The "natural" human way of thinking, which strives for what is self-evident, i.e., which obtains the kind of knowledge that finds that what is not only is, but necessarily is (only this sort of thinking, as Kant explained to us, gives us genuine knowledge)—this natural thinking must cherish as its most precious treasure the idea of Necessity. However much reason may sing the praises of freedom, it still wants to, and has to, fit it into the mold of Necessity.

This Necessity is indeed that Nothingness which we must say exists, for although it is nowhere and there is nowhere to search for it, it still in some mysterious fashion bursts forth into human life, which it makes ugly and monstrous, in the guise of fate, luck, destiny, *Fatum,* from which there is no hiding place and no salvation.

Kierkegaard has much to say about the role of fate in the consciousness of the ancient Hellene, about the horror the ancients felt for Destiny. All this, of course, is true, just as it is true that, for Biblical revelation, fate does not exist. Revelation is revelation precisely because, in spite of all that is self-evident, it tells us that for God all things are possible and that there is no power equal to the omnipotence of God. When Jesus was asked which was the first commandment of all, he replied: "The first of all the commandments is, Hear, O Israel; The Lord our God is one Lord" (Mark 12:29). How, then, could Kierkegaard assume that innocence (i.e., the state of man as he stood in the direct presence of God) presupposes fear of Nothingness and, therefore, contains within itself the source of, or the potential for, those horrors of which human life is full and which he himself depicts with such incomparable, stunning power both in his journals and in his other works? The reason I insist so upon this question is that, for Kierkegaard himself, either the question or its answer conceals the *articulus stantis et cadentis* of existential philosophy. Neither Job, nor Abraham, nor any one of the Prophets and Apostles would ever have admitted the idea that innocence—which, as Kierkegaard says, quite rightly and in full agreement with the Biblical text, is ignorance—is inseparable from fear. Such an admission could only arise in the soul of a man who has lost his innocence and found "knowledge." We have just been speaking of how Socrates and Plato saw by intellectual vision that the power of Necessity is equal to divine power; how Leucippus and Democritus with similar confidence added the predicate of Being to their Nothingness; and how even Parmenides himself could only fight against the idea of Nothingness' right to existence, and yet was barely able to uproot it from his soul. As long as we put our trust in reason and the knowledge which reason brings, the rights of Nothingness and the rights of Necessity will be guaranteed by self-evidencies which we have not the power to overcome, and which we dare not even try to overcome. Kierkegaard went to Job, went to Abraham, invoked the Absurd and craved Faith, only because he hoped in this way to blow up the impregnable fortress behind whose walls speculative thought was hiding all-destroying Nothingness. And at the very moment when the Paradox and the Absurd were presented with the chance to realize their sovereign rights and enter upon a great and final struggle with the self-evident, they fell exhausted, robbed of their strength by some mysterious and enigmatic power.

VIII

Genius and Fate

> *The genius reveals fate everywhere, all
> the more profoundly as he is more pro-
> found . . . The existence of such genius
> is, in spite of its brilliance, its beauty,
> and its great historical significance, a sin.
> It takes courage to understand this.*
>
> KIERKEGAARD

The fear of Nothingness is thus made plain to us, not as
a condition inherent in Innocence and Ignorance, but as a
condition inherent in sin and knowledge. There was no
need to amend Holy Scripture. It is true that in the case
at hand the entire responsibility for this cannot be
ascribed to Kierkegaard. The story of the Fall has always
been a veritable *crux interpretuum,* and even the faithful
have thought it their right, indeed their obligation, to add
their own corrections to it. The unknown author of the
famous *Theologia deutsch,* whom Luther enthusiastically
praised as one of the most remarkable mystics of the Middle Ages, flatly states that sin did not come into the world

from the fruit of the tree of knowledge of good and evil. Adam, he declares, could have eaten even ten apples—and no harm would have come of it. Adam's only sin was his insubordination, his disobedience to God. Kierkegaard always disassociated himself from mystics and obviously did not trust them. He reproaches them for their impetuosity and even for their obtrusiveness. What he says about them might be more succinctly expressed in the words of Holy Scripture: they already have their reward. The more gifted, the more fiery, the more daring a mystic is, the more one feels, both in his writings and in his life, that he has already received his full reward and there is nothing more to be expected from any quarter. This is no doubt why modern life, weary of positivism and disillusioned by it, but possessed of neither the strength nor the desire to go beyond the boundaries it has established, has made such a fierce attack upon the work of the mystics. The religion of mystics, even though it is a lofty one, or more probably precisely because it is lofty, is nevertheless a religion within the limits of reason. The mystic becomes united with God, the mystic himself becomes God; in mysticism God has just as much need of man as man has of God. Even Hegel, *bona fide* and with every right to do so, adopted the famous line by Angelus Silesius, and for this he did not have to go to Job or Abraham, or call upon Faith or the Absurd. Mysticism exists in peace and concord with human reason and human perception, and the reward which it promises men does not presuppose, but excludes, any supernatural intervention; everything proceeds naturally, everything is achieved by one's own powers. In my opinion, this too repels Kierkegaard from mysticism; if we say "by one's own powers," it means that there is no repetition, it means that Job does not regain his riches and his children, that Abraham loses his Isaac forever, it means that the youth who fell in love with the king's daughter will have to be content with the brewer's widow, it means that Kierkegaard is never again to see Regina Olsen. The God of the Bible, Who listens to the wails and curses of Job, Who turns Abraham's hand from his son, Who bothers about the youth hopelessly in love, the God Who, in Kierkegaard's words, numbers the hairs on a man's head, is for the mystics not the real God. As cultivated persons (Hegel, again, or Renan) have said, it is impossible to worship this God in truth. Such a God can exist only in the crude and naïve notions of ignorant people—shepherds, carpenters, and fishermen—almost barbarians or half-barbarian. Even the works of the mystics, to the degree that they still retain traces of these outdated and ridiculous notions, must here and there be subordinated and adapted to the level of our concept of the world. But Kierkegaard avoids enlightened mysticism. He is irresistibly drawn to the God of Abraham, the God of Isaac, the God of Jacob—and away from the God of the philosophers, who imagine that they are worshipping in spirit and in truth. But he has told us that it was not given him to make the movement of faith, and this is true. In his journal, in regard to Luther, we read: "It is well enough known that certain states of mind seek refuge in what is opposite to them. A man bolsters himself with forceful words and the more he vacillates, the more forceful they become. This is not deceit, but devout endeavor. Man does not want to give expression to the uncertainty of his fear, does not even want to call it by its real name, and violently wrings from himself assertions to the contrary, in the hope that this will help." * We are not about to touch upon the matter of how far these observations are correct with respect to Luther, but they are completely applicable to Kierkegaard. He approached the mystery of the Fall without having rid himself of the "uncertainty of fear" (is it indeed possible to get rid of fear; has anyone ever succeeded in driving it away?), and then he found it necessary to misinterpret, i.e., to amend and alter the Biblical story and even to invest the state of innocence with what he had found in his own experience, the experience of a sinful, fallen man. He achieved a "logical explanation" which he had so stubbornly resisted.

And, in fact, if fear is already inherent in innocence, then sin becomes inescapable and unthinking; it is therefore explicable and "not irritating" to reason, as Kant said, but satisfactory to it. Even if the result is not the "self-movement of the concept," as Hegel wished, then it is, in any case, "self-movement," and even for Hegel it is not the second, but the first part of the formula that is essential. It is important that there be self-movement, that a thing move by itself, but the thing that moves is of secondary importance; the end has come for hateful unexpectedness, for "suddenly," for *fiat,* and for the free will behind them, even though it be God's. Man's sin is not that he tasted the fruit of the tree of knowledge of good and evil, not that he began to distinguish good from evil. Adam could have eaten even twenty apples; he would have lost nothing by this, but would have gained by it. It is also not true that the serpent tempted the first man—there is surely no need to bring the serpent into the story of the Fall. Our reason knows all this definitely and positively, and there is no re-

* *Journal,* I, 229.

sort to a higher authority than the knowledge of reason, nor can there be. . . . The Absurd once more retreats before self-evidencies which it has not the power to overcome.

But the fear of Nothingness has remained, and Kierkegaard cannot and does not want to forget about it. However, in order to retain at least the semblance of consistency, he performs a μετάβασις εἰς ἄλλο γένος which is almost completely imperceptible to the inexperienced eye. He began with pointless and causeless fear; next he substitutes for the word "fear" the quite similar word "terror," and then, as if it were perfectly natural, he proceeds to the real horror of life, from which his mind can never free itself. But in fact, fear of Nothingness, by which sin is maintained, has nothing in common with the terror experienced by children as they listen to tales of perilous adventure and the like. Kierkegaard himself observed correctly that inherent in terror there is a moment of "sweetness" which always accompanies our fancies of the mysterious, the extraordinary, and the marvelous. The origin of fear of Nothingness is altogether different from the origin of terror; it is also impossible to demonstrate any direct link between fear of Nothingness and the horrors of which human life is full. That is precisely why this fear is pointless and causeless, and, in its pointlessness and causelessness, so incomprehensible to us. To approach it with the "laws" of inconsistency and of sufficient basis, with which Leibniz armed himself when he set out to seek the truth, means to do everything to ensure the impossibility of examining it. Only the serpent of the Bible (or, as a concession to our habits of thinking, only the intervention of some force external to man) can introduce us, in some degree at least, to that incandescent atmosphere in which the Fall took place, and at the same time reveal to us—so far as it can be or should be revealed to man—what the Fall actually is. And here Kierkegaard's experience, breaking through every prohibition, every veto imposed upon our minds by reason and morality, can render a priceless service. "Fear," he says, "may be compared with giddiness. A person who must look down into an abyss opening before him will feel that his head is spinning . . . . And fear is the giddiness of freedom. It occurs when the mind, wishing to realize a synthesis, peers into its own possibility, but simultaneously grasps at the finite in order to retain it. This giddiness causes freedom to fall to the ground. Psychology can tell us nothing more. But in that moment everything is changed and when freedom gets up again, it sees that it is guilty. Between these two instants there is a leap that no science has ever explained or could explain. Fear is the swoon of freedom, like a woman's swoon. Psychologically speaking, the Fall always takes place in a swoon." * These words, together with what Luther told us about human freedom in his *De servo arbitrio,* should be classed among the most profound and wonderfully penetrating achievements of the human mind. "Fear is the giddiness of freedom" and "the Fall always takes place in a swoon"—says Kierkegaard to us. And at the same time, this fear is fear of Nothingness. "The Nothingness of fear thus seems to be a complex of premonitions which the individual considers more and more closely all the time, even though they have practically no meaning as far as the fear is concerned (that is, they offer it no sustenance, so to speak): nevertheless this is not the kind of Nothingness to which the individual

* V, 56.

has no relationship, but a Nothingness which has a vital mutual relationship with the ignorance of innocence." Kierkegaard is absorbed in examining, with intense concentration, the Nothingness revealed to him and the connection between Nothingness and fear. "If we ask what is the object of fear," he writes in another passage from the same book, "there will be but one answer: Nothingness. Fear and Nothingness are always found in company with one another. But as soon as the reality of freedom and the mind comes into its own, fear disappears. What exactly is Nothingness as the pagans feared it? It is fate . . . Fate is the union of Necessity and Chance. This has been expressed in the representation of destiny as blind; one who walks along blindly is moving forward just as much by necessity as by chance. A necessity which does not recognize itself as such is chance *eo ipso*, in regard to the next moment. Fate is the Nothingness of fear." * The man of greatest genius—Kierkegaard goes on to explain—has no power to vanquish the idea of fate. On the contrary, "the genius reveals destiny everywhere, all the more profoundly as he is more profound. To a superficial observer this, of course, is nonsense; but in fact, there is greatness here, for man is not born with the idea of Providence . . . . This is an exact statement of the innate strength of the genius—that he reveals destiny—but therein also lies his weakness." † And he concludes his observations with these provocative words: "The existence of such genius, in spite of its brilliance, its beauty, and its great historical significance, is a sin. It takes courage to understand this, and he who has not learned the art of satisfying the hunger of a

* *Ibid.*, 93, 94.
† *Ibid.*, 96.

yearning spirit will hardly be able to grasp it. And yet it is so." *

Space does not permit me to cite further passages. Kierkegaard rings every possible change on the ideas set forth in the excerpts just quoted, culminating in his assertions that fear of Nothingness leads to the swoon of freedom; that the man who has lost his freedom is made powerless, and in his powerlessness takes Nothingness to be unconquerable Fate, omnipotent Necessity; that the more firmly he is convinced of this, the more penetrating his mind becomes, and the more mighty his talent. In spite of all his reservations, which have already been mentioned, Kierkegaard, as we shall see, makes a complete return to the Biblical narrative of the Fall of the first man. A genius, the greatest genius, before whom all bow and whom all consider mankind's benefactor, who can expect posterity's immortal praise just because he is a genius, because he, with his sharp-sighted, alert gaze, pierces the farthest depths of all that exists—is "also the greatest sinner, the sinner par excellence." Socrates, at the moment when he discovered "general and necessary truths" in the world, which even today are still the prerequisite of the possibility of objective knowledge, repeated anew the transgression of Adam —he stretched forth his hand to the forbidden tree—and therefore, in spite of all his immense historical significance, in spite of all his fame, he is a fallen man, a sinner. Perhaps, I might add, he may be that sinner over whom, as the eternal Book so exasperatingly says, there would be more rejoicing in heaven than over ten righteous men, but nevertheless he is a sinner. He tasted the fruit of knowledge—and empty Nothingness became for him Necessity

* *Ibid.*, 99.

which, like the head of Medusa, turns to stone all who gaze upon it. And he did not even suspect the significance of what he was doing, just as our forefather did not when he accepted from Eve's hand that fruit which was so alluring to the eye. In the words uttered by the tempter: *eritis sicut dei scientes bonum et malum,* there lies concealed the invincible power of Nothingness which paralyzes man's previously free will.

Kierkegaard observes with some truth that as long as Adam was innocent he could not understand what was meant by God's words forbidding him to taste the fruit of the tree of good and evil, for he did not know what good and evil were. But is it necessary or even possible to "understand" them? We accept them, we know that good is good and evil is evil. But there is another possibility, related in Holy Scripture, which is hidden from us, and will probably always remain hidden from our "understanding." It is not that Adam "did not know" the difference between good and evil: *there was no such difference.* For God, and for Adam so long as he walked in the presence of God, evil did not exist: everything in creation was good. When the serpent promised man that, once having tasted of the tree of knowledge, he would become equal with God and know the difference between good and evil, he deceived him doubly. Man did not become equal with God, and God in general has no knowledge and in particular has no knowledge of good and evil, that knowledge which the fallen man, the man bewitched by the treacherous spells of Nothingness, thinks of, even today, as his highest attribute. Socrates, the wisest of men, an incomparable genius, was the greatest of sinners—he was not the free Socrates he thought himself to be, but an enchained, enchanted

Kierkegaard

Socrates, Σωκράτης δεσμώτης. Fear of the Nothingness shown him by the tempter had paralyzed his will. Moreover, he did not even suspect that his will was paralyzed. He was certain that his will was free and that the reason directing that will was of the best; he believed that the promise: *eritis sicut dei scientes bonum et malum* had been realized in him and in every man, that he had become like God, and become like God because he "knew." Here we find the meaning of the words of the Apostle Paul quoted by Kierkegaard himself: all that is not of faith is sin. The knowledge for which our reason so eagerly strives is a most grievous, mortal sin. This is why Kierkegaard made such haste for the Absurd and warned against the claims of the ethical. Reason, with its eager striving (I shall repeat once more—*concupiscentia invincibilis*) for necessary truths, and goodness with its categorical demands, are what the fruit of the forbidden tree has brought to man. Man has been weakened by that fruit, and has lost the ability to perceive any misfortune in his weakness, has lost the desire to struggle against it. He has become a knight of resignation; he sees merit and virtue in this resignation, and identifies knowledge with truth. He has lost his freedom—but this does not dismay him; rather, he thinks it not unusual that there is no freedom and can be none, and that the world is upheld by coercion, expressed in the "laws" of existence, which he has identified with truth, and in the "laws" of obligation, which together make up his morality. He sees it as his duty to recognize the laws of existence and to carry out in his own life the laws of morality: *facienti quod in se est deus non denegat gratiam* (God will not refuse His blessing to the man who does what is within his power). However strange it may seem, one observes in the thinking of Kierkegaard, in spite of all his impulsiveness, a constant tendency toward the concept of sin adopted by theoretical philosophy. This is why he said that Adam in his innocence did not yet know the difference between good and evil. But if such is the case, we must again ask: what then is the relevance of Job with his wails, Abraham with his terrible sacrifice, and the Apostle Paul with his assertion that all that is not of faith is sin? And what has become of the paradox, what of the Absurd? For the Absurd is the Absurd for the very reason that it wishes to free itself from every sort of "law," that it cannot reconcile itself with "laws," but is in opposition to them. Kierkegaard himself tells us: "Faith begins where thinking comes to an end." * Or, again, he says this: "Faith is a paradox by virtue of which the individual stands out above the general . . . or that the individual, as an individual, finds himself in an absolute relationship to the absolute." † And none of these ideas were uttered by him casually—faith is, for Kierkegaard, the *conditio sine qua non* of existential philosophy. But, if this is so, can we look for "laws" when we enter the realm where faith contends with sin? And is sin the breaking of laws? In other words, is sin guilt? It must be said once more that Kierkegaard displays a continual readiness to substitute the concept of guilt for the concept of sin. And, in fact, if we wish to understand how the pagan idea of sin differs from the Biblical idea of it, we must first of all say to ourselves that, while the pagans considered that the concept of guilt had completely put an end to and superseded the concept of sin, Holy Scripture saw these ideas, not even as opposed to one

* III, 50.
† *Ibid.*, 53.

another, but simply as having nothing to do with each other. There is a famous Russian proverb: he who is not sinful in the eyes of God is not guilty in the eyes of the Tsar. In contrast to what Kierkegaard has written, the fact is, as we have seen, that for the pagans sin always presupposed evil will, and therefore κάθαρσις, i.e., purification, constitutes, according to Plato, the essence of philosophy. "No one who has not studied philosophy and who is not entirely pure at the time of his departure is allowed to enter the company of the gods" (*Phaedo*, 82), says Socrates, expressing a thought which was most sacred to him. On the other hand, we read in the *Republic* (613, a): "God never abandons the man who tries to be just, who practices virtue, . . ." In keeping with this, the fifty-third chapter of the Book of Isaiah, which speaks of the one who has taken upon himself all our sins, a chapter which Christianity sees as a prophecy of the coming and the mission of Christ, could only seem highly deceitful to the pagans, a decisive challenge both to the pagan conscience and to pagan reason. To transfer one's sins to another is both impossible and extremely reprehensible. Equally challenging and deceitful to the pagans were those other words of Isaiah included by the Apostle Paul in his epistle (Romans 10:20) as an example of amazing audacity: Ἡσαΐας δὲ ἀποτολμᾷ καὶ λέγει ("I am sought of them that asked not for me; I am found of them that sought me not"). Human reason plainly and distinctly sees and admits as a self-evident truth that there is no possibility of transferring sin from oneself to another; and conscience, which always follows upon reason, declares definitely and categorically that it is immoral to pass on one's own sin (one's own guilt) to another. And here, more than anywhere else, it is appropriate to recall Kierkegaard's

Absurd, or better yet, the original words of Tertullian which reached Kierkegaard in the abbreviated formulation *credo quia absurdum.* In Tertullian's *De carne Christi* we read: *crucifixus est Dei filius: non pudet quia pudendum est; et mortuus est Dei filius: prorsus credibile quia ineptum est; et sepultus resurrexit, certum quia impossibile.*

Tertullian had learned from the Prophets and the Apostles that all the *pudenda* of our morality and all the *impossibilia* of our reason were suggested by a hostile power which has enchained man's will, and in this mysterious power he perceived, as Luther was later to do, the *bellua qua non occisa homo non potest vivere.* For God nothing is impossible, and nothing is shameful. Shame, which Alcibiades said Socrates had given him, was passed down to Socrates himself by the sinner Adam. Innocence knew no shame, according to the Scriptures, and shame was unnecessary for innocence.

All this is paradox, all this is Absurd; but then, the prophecy of the fifty-third chapter of Isaiah can enter our consciousness only under cover of the Absurd and the Paradox. It is impossible to "understand" that a sinless one has taken sin upon himself. It is even less comprehensible that sin can thus be destroyed, uprooted from existence: for this means causing something which once had existence to become nonexistent. It is natural that the most profound and devout of men have tried with all their might to win reason and morality over to the side of the truth of revelation. We read in the writings of Bonaventura: *non est pejoris conditionis veritas fidei nostrae quam aliae veritates; sed in aliis veritatibus ita est, ut omnis (veritas) qua potest per rationem impugnari, potest et debet per rationem defendi; ergo, pari ratione, et veritas fidei nostrae.* ("The truth of our faith is in no worse position than other truths; all other truths can be proved by the same means which can be used to attack them, that is, by the arguments of reason; consequently, the truth of our faith is in exactly the same situation.") Bonaventura, like all other medieval philosophers, was firmly convinced that if the truth of faith cannot be defended by the same rational proofs which can serve to dispute it, this means that it is in a worse position than other truths. From what source did he draw this conviction and what sustains it? There will be more said about this later on. Meanwhile I shall say only that the power and the possibility of absolving sin cannot be defended with the same arguments by which they can be disputed. It would not have been difficult to convince Bonaventura himself of this, using Matthew 9:5-7, and similar passages from the other synoptic Gospels. When Jesus understood the thoughts of the scribes who upbraided him among themselves for saying to a sick man: your sins will be forgiven; he did not start to dispute with them and defend himself with the same methods by which they had attacked him, but chose an entirely different way: he healed the sick man with his words. "For whether is easier, to say Thy sins be forgiven thee; or to say, Arise and walk? But that ye may know that the Son of man hath power on earth to forgive sins, (then saith he to the sick of the palsy), Arise, take up thy bed, and go unto thine house. And he arose, and departed to his house." The power to take away sin from man, to destroy sin, lies not in him who looks to reason and morality for help and protection, but in him by whose words a sick man regains his strength, that is, in him for whom nothing is impossible.

IX

Knowledge as the Fall

If I might express my wish, it would be that not one of my readers displays his depth of thought by proposing the question: what would have happened if Adam had not sinned?

KIERKEGAARD

In order to forgive sin, it is necessary to have power, just as one must have power in order to return strength to the sick. Natural reason says that it is as impossible to do one as the other, impossible not only for man, but also for a higher being: Zeus, may I remind you once again, himself disclosed this secret to Chryssip—or, more probably, both Chryssip and Zeus received the revelation of this ultimate secret of existence from the one eternal and inexhaustible source of all truths. To use the words of Bonaventura, the truth of Chryssip and Zeus is in no worse position than all other truths; if someone should think to attack it by citing reason, then it could just as well be defended by reason. Such is not the case with the truth claimed by Jesus in the

Gospel: all reasonable arguments are against it, and not one is adduced in its favor. It is forced to say of itself, as Kierkegaard said of himself, that it is deprived of the protection of laws. Or, in simple language: neither Jesus of Nazareth, nor generally speaking, anyone else in the world has the power to forgive sin, as no one has the power to return strength to a sick man. Reason *proprio motu,* consulting no one, having inquired of no one, proclaimed this truth—without, I insist and repeat once more, having asked anyone, gods or men, whether or not they wanted it. Indeed, reason itself proclaimed this truth, not because it wanted it, not because it valued it or needed it; it simply proclaimed it in a tone which admits of no objection. Thereupon, this truth began to gain the upper hand in life; and all living beings, secretly sighing (Zeus himself sighed as he confessed his helplessness to Chryssip), have submitted to it.

Why this submission? Where does reason get the power to impose its truths upon existence—truths which it does not need itself and which are detestable and at times completely intolerable to existence? No one asks this question—neither men nor gods, at least not the gods of enlightened pagandom, and not the God of enlightened Christianity, either. For this would be a more grievous insult to reason, to the greatness of reason, than the *laesio majestatis* against which Spinoza, that profound thinker, warned us. The Pelagians defended morality desperately in order to realize their ideal of *homo, emancipatus a Deo.* Theoretical philosophy aspires no less fervently after *ratio, emancipata a Deo;* for it, the only truth is that which has succeeded in freeing itself from God. When Leibniz announced so triumphantly that eternal truths exist in the understanding of God independent of His will—he was only confirming openly what had been the mainstay of medieval philosophy, passed down to it by the Greeks: the human mind has always directed all its efforts toward obtaining for itself *veritates emancipatas a Deo*. Reason dictates the laws which it takes a fancy to dictate, or more probably, which it is obliged, by virtue of its nature, to dictate. For it, too, has no freedom of choice; it, too, could not, even if it wanted to, give back the world to man, not merely to be held in trust, but as an absolute possession. But reason itself does not ask why and wherefore it dictates these laws, and it does not permit others to ask questions about them. So it is, so it has been, so it will always be. The fates of mankind and of the universe have been foreordained *in saecula saeculorum* and nothing that has been foreordained since time began can or should be altered. Existence has been bewitched by some impersonal and indifferent power and it cannot shake off the magic spells. Philosophy, which has always asserted proudly that it seeks the beginnings, the sources, the roots of everything—ριζώματα πάντων—does not even try to find out the nature of this force that has been able to bewitch the world, but "simply" recognizes it and rejoices over its own success in "exposing the invisible." Even *The Critique of Pure Reason* halted at this point, obviously in full agreement with the wise vision of Aristotle who said that an inability to know when to stop asking questions is the mark of ill breeding in a man.

Only in the Bible is there an indication that all is not well with reason and the eternal truths conveyed by reason. God warned man against knowledge: thou shalt surely die. But can it be that this is an *objection* to knowledge? Can one thus disparage knowledge? Bonaventura was not present in Eden, nor was theoretical philosophy there. It seems to me that for the first man the words of God actually did appear to be an objection; he would not have stretched forth his hand to the forbidden tree on his own initiative, of his own will. For the ignorant, "law" meant the words which were later to be declared by the Prophet and repeated by the Apostle: *justus ex fide vivit*. Faith leads to the tree of life, and from the tree of life comes, not knowledge, not theoretical philosophy, but existential philosophy. According to Genesis, the intervention of the serpent was necessary so that the first man might take his fateful step; made weak by some mysterious spell, he gave himself up to the power of the truths of reason, *veritates emancipatae a Deo,* and exchanged the fruit of the tree of life for the fruit of the tree of knowledge.

Kierkegaard does not decide to accept the story of Genesis about the Fall of the first man without reservations and without making corrections. He takes exception to the Biblical serpent, he cannot grant that the ignorance of the first man revealed the truth to him and that knowledge of good and evil implies sin. And yet Kierkegaard is the one who told us that sin is the swoon of freedom; that the opposite of sin is not virtue, but freedom (or—as he also says—the opposite of sin is faith); that freedom is not, as is commonly thought, the possibility of choosing between good and evil, but possibility; and finally, that God signifies that all is possible. How could man, in spite of this, have exchanged freedom for sin, renounced the boundless possibilities set before him by God, and taken instead that limited possibility offered him by reason? Kierkegaard has no answer to this question—but he does ask it, although in a different form. "If I might express my wish, it would be that not one of my readers display his depth of thought by proposing the question: what would have happened if Adam had not sinned? At the very moment that reality takes hold, possibility moves aside as if it were nothing, which tempts all those who do not like to think. And why can this kind of science (perhaps it would be better to say, knowledge!) not conclude that it is holding man back and understand that even it has limitations! But when someone asks you a stupid question, beware of answering it—you will become just as stupid as the questioner. What is ridiculous about this question is not so much the question itself as the fact that it is addressed to science." There can be no argument here; this question should not be addressed to science. For science, reality always puts an end to possibility. But, does it follow from this that, generally speaking, the question ought not to be raised at all? And that Kierkegaard himself did not raise it—if not *explicite,* then *implicite?* When he proposes that we forget about the serpent-tempter, was this not his answer to the question which he now forbids us to ask? And he answered in the name of science, which is naturally forced to admit that there is nothing necessary in the Biblical narrative of the serpent, and that it is, moreover, a purely external, childish fantasy. In rejecting the serpent, Kierkegaard evidently hesitated in the face of some rational truths, which are emancipated from God, and in fact uncreated and eternal. But, at the same time, it is here, right at this point, more than anywhere else, that we ought to recall the enigmatic words: "blessed is he, whosoever shall not be offended in me," of which Kierkegaard himself reminds us so often. Indeed, what an offense the Biblical serpent offers for rational thinking! But then, the entire story told in the Bible about original sin is no less an offense. The Fall of Man, as described in the Scriptures, is completely incompatible with our notions of what is possible and what ought to be, no less incompatible than a serpent who holds a conversation with a man and tempts him. However much we may be convinced of the truthfulness of the Biblical story, every conviction must fall before the logic of common sense. If there is, nevertheless, some "truth" to be found in this story, it is indisputable that it cannot be defended by the same means with which it can be demolished. And so, if the truth of faith, like the truth of knowledge, is maintained only by the possibility of rational defense, then that chapter of Genesis in which the story of the Fall is told ought to be erased from the pages of Holy Scripture. Not that it would be stupid to ask what would have happened if Adam and Eve had not surrendered to the blandishments of the serpent and had not picked the forbidden fruit; it can be confidently asserted that our ancestors would never have given in to temptation, that the serpent would never have tempted them, and, what is even more, that the fruit of the tree of knowledge was not more harmful and dangerous, but instead more useful and necessary, than the fruit of the other trees in Eden. In short, if we rely upon our own insight and perspicacity, then we must assume that sin began with something that is quite dissimilar from what we have been told about Adam and Eve; that it did not even begin with Adam, but, let us say, with Cain, who murdered his brother. Here we see with our own eyes—*oculis mentis*—both the presence of sin and the presence of guilt, and there is no need whatever to resort to such a fantastic *deus ex machina,* considered totally inadmissible by philosophy, as the serpent tempter and betrayer. Consequently, even the idea of sin loses the fantastic character lent it by the Biblical narrative, and fully deserves the honorable title of truth, for it can be defended with considerations of the same sort that can be used to attack it.

Evidently Kierkegaard was thrown off guard: the Biblical story of the Fall offended him. But then, who can guard against offense, who can overcome it? All our "spiritual" being cries out: let the origin of sin be anything but the tree of knowledge of good and evil. No less shocking to us is the idea that the serpent had the power to paralyze or lull to sleep man's will. Therefore, we surely must look for another, more acceptable explanation of sin. But does not every "explanation"—and in particular the attempt to "explain everything," which Kierkegaard himself ridiculed—still bear witness to the "swoon of freedom"? So long as man is free, so long as man's freedom is not paralyzed, so long as man is free to do everything he wants to, everything he needs to, he does not make explanations. The man who explains is the one who does not have the strength to act on his own, who has submitted to a power outside himself. One who is free not only does not seek explanations, but with unerring perceptiveness guesses that the greatest threat to his freedom lies in the very possibility of explanations.

Consequently, we not only can but must ask: what would have happened if Adam had not sinned? And if man is indeed fated to awaken from his swoon and shake off the spell cast over him by the serpent, then perhaps he will find the courage to ask: is the story of Adam's Fall an "eternal truth"? And has not the moment come for him to regain the genuine primordial freedom which he shared with God during his existence in Paradise; the moment when, in spite of all reason's prohibitions, he will "suddenly" realize that the truth about the Fall had a beginning, as do all the truths which experience conveys to us, and that, by the will of the One who creates all truths, it can also have an end? Of course, reason will offer resistance to this; such an assumption means the end of its rule, which, it is convinced, can have and must have no end, since it had no beginning. But Kierkegaard wrote so many inspired pages about the Absurd! Is it possible that the protests and the indignation of reason would alarm him or move him to pity? or that existential philosophy would, at the decisive moment, tremble and give way before its enraged opponent?

I must emphasize here that existential philosophy, as conceived by Kierkegaard, has a double meaning, or, more precisely, it has set two problems for itself, problems which, moreover, seem at first glance to be opposed to each other, and even mutually exclusive. And this is not mere chance, not "involuntary inconsistency." It has a very close, organic connection with his method of "indirect communication," which I have already mentioned more than once and which at times makes Kierkegaard's thoughts, complicated and involved to begin with, totally incomprehensible to the hasty reader.

We meet in Kierkegaard's work almost at every step the expression "religious-ethical," which is familiar to everyone and therefore distasteful to no one, indeed even caressing to the ear. By quoting numerous passages from

his writings, and without making any far fetched interpretations, it is possible to state that the goals which existential philosophy has set for itself are religious-ethical. It is
true that we have heard him say that Abraham, the father
of faith—at a grave and terrible moment of his life, the
moment when his destiny was decided, when the fateful
question "to be or not to be" rose before him, not as a
theoretical, abstract problem, but as that to which his
entire existence was linked—had to "suspend the ethical,"
which was blocking his path to God. "If the ethical is
eternal—Abraham is lost": this Kierkegaard clearly understood. And, indeed, it is true that if the ethical were the
highest court, the last stage of appeal, if it had no beginning and were uncreated, if it were not of God, if it
were *veritas a Deo emancipata*—then there would be no
salvation for Abraham. Kierkegaard himself exposed *that*
sort of ethics (in the philosophy of recent years it is called
autonomous, self-regulated): when Abraham raised the
knife above Isaac, he did believe that Isaac would be returned to him. In the court of religion, this is the strongest
argument in Abraham's favor, but in the court of reason
and ethics, which have their own laws (let me remind you
again that both reason and ethics are autonomous), Abraham's faith compromises him and makes his action worthless. Reason firmly declares that there is no power capable
of returning a murdered Isaac to life, and ethics demands,
no less firmly, that Abraham slay his son without any hope,
without any "expectation" of ever regaining him. It is only
upon the fulfilling of this condition that ethics is willing
to consider his action a sacrifice, and only at the price of
such a sacrifice can its praise and approval be purchased.
Shakespeare's Falstaff asks: can ethics replace a man's

severed arm? It cannot. Therefore ethics is merely a word. But Kierkegaard's Abraham echoes Falstaff. Can the "ethical" return a murdered Isaac? If it cannot, then the ethical must be "suspended." Abraham made his decision to raise the knife to his son only because God, unlike ethics which can do nothing, could and would return his son to him. What difference is there between the "father of faith" and the comical personage of Shakespeare's play? Faith, which possesses such exceptional, incomparable value in the sphere of religious existence ("all that is not of faith is sin"), turns out to be a defect, and a great defect, in the commonplace world of rational thinking. The "ethical," whose function is to shield and protect rational truths—although it is powerless to replace a man's severed hand, and generally powerless to give man anything except its blame and praise—is still required to direct all its blame, all its thunders, all its anathemas, in equal measure against both Abraham and Falstaff.

And once more I must add: Falstaff laughs at the threats of ethics. If ethics cannot give back a man's arm or leg, this means that it has no might, that it is powerless, that it is only an illusion, only a word—and its thunders are an illusion also. For by what right does one who cannot bless assume the power to curse? We have not forgotten how, according to Kierkegaard, the ethical takes its revenge upon those who dare to disobey it. *Sine effusione sanguinis*, of course, as befits its pious nature—but it is worse than the most merciless torturer, the most violent murderer. This, I say, is the mysterious "contradiction" in Kierkegaard's work: in the presence of Abraham, ethics falls silent. And before Job—after prolonged and desperate resistance, it is true—ethics is obliged to withdraw. If

Socrates himself had approached Job, all his irony and dialectic would have come to nothing. Job appeals from ethics to another "principle"—to God, to God, for Whom nothing is impossible, Who can restore a severed arm, Who can raise Abraham's murdered Isaac from the dead, Who can give back the king's daughter to the poor youth, and Regina Olsen to Kierkegaard himself. He overturns the commandment of Spinoza—the commandment of speculative philosophy: *non ridere, non lugere, neque detestari, sed intelligere.* Man will not live by "understanding." "Understanding" is the terrible *bellua, qua non occisa homo non potest vivere.* Out of man's weeping and curses new strength is born, which sooner or later will help him to triumph over the despised enemy. As the Psalmist said: *de profundis ad te, Domine, clamavi.* This is what Kierkegaard calls existential philosophy: "the mad struggle of faith for possibility." Theoretical philosophy subsides into flatness, into two dimensions. Existential thinking is aware of a third dimension which does not exist for theoretical thinking: faith. . . .

But as soon as Kierkegaard turns from Job and Abraham and begins to deal with the commonplace, he is overwhelmed by an unconquerable fear, fear that, with the elimination of the rational and the ethical, the Falstaffs will become the lords of existence. And then he hastens back to the ethical. The ethical cannot return Regina Olsen to him; it is, generally speaking, powerless to give man anything. But it can take away, it can warp and make hideous the lives of those who do not obey it; for it is the ally and companion in arms of necessity, which is protected by the exalted shield of reason. However much Falstaff may vaunt his courage, however much he may bluster, the ethical will overtake him in the end. It will transform itself into infinity, into eternity, bringing with it death and destruction. The most frivolous and heedless of men will be driven to despair when faced with the arsenal of horrors at the disposal of the ethical—and will surrender. And now when Kierkegaard feels that, as he expresses it, "he cannot make the final movement of faith," he turns to the ethical with its menacing "you must," and gives what seems to be an entirely different meaning to existential philosophy. It is no longer a mad struggle for the impossible, but a calculated struggle (at times well, at times poorly calculated) for a possible victory over dissenters. Instead of fighting against the terrible enemy "necessity," he attacks those who, of course, are also terrible, but who are nevertheless armed only with human weapons similar to his own. Fear has carried out its destructive purpose; it has paralyzed Kierkegaard's freedom, or, to use his own words, it has caused him to fall into a swoon. The self-evident truths of reason replace the revelation of Holy Scripture.

X

Cruel Christianity

My severity is not of my own making. If
I knew a milder word, I would gladly
comfort and encourage man. And yet! It
may be that the sufferer needs something
else: suffering that is crueler still. What
fiend dares to say this? My friend, it is
Christianity, the doctrine which is offered to us under the name of gentle
consolation.

KIERKEGAARD

This contradiction in Kierkegaard's existential philosophy contains all that is difficult to understand not only in
the task he set himself, but also in the whole array of
problems that arise when the revelation of Holy Scripture
encounters the truths naturally obtained by our reason.
We strive with our entire being and with all our thoughts
to bridge the abyss separating revelation from truth; together with Hegel and all the philosophers in whose
schools the teachings of Hegel were formed, we are con-

vinced in advance that revelation cannot and must not contradict reason and rational understanding; that, on the contrary, it must place itself under their protection and in their keeping. It is true that both the Prophets and the Apostles tell us over and over again about the madness of faith. It is true that Kierkegaard himself, with fear and trembling, never wearies of repeating his magic formula: in order to achieve faith, one must give up reason. But the thundering words of the Prophets and the Apostles and the fervent incantations of Kierkegaard have no effect, or almost none, and they cannot awaken our freedom from its dreaming swoon. The "fear" that freedom which is unverified and unjustified by reason will lead, and can only lead, to unlimited trouble has become so entrenched in our souls that there is probably no way to get rid of it. We are deaf even to thunder; we reject all incantations.

Whence came this fear? Whence came the conviction that reason has more to offer man than does freedom? Plato taught that to despise reason is the greatest misfortune, but we have not tried to find out where he obtained this truth. What is more, we have had the opportunity of assuring ourselves that reason does not very often direct its entire might against man. It will be said that this is not an "objection" to the legality of reason's claims—and, consequently, man will never succeed in freeing himself in this way from the power and spell of rational truths. Let us even suppose that Plato was mistaken, that reason will, in the last analysis, turn out to be the enemy of man, or even his executioner; still there is no end to its rule, nor is any end in sight. How can one then oppose freedom to reason? Because freedom is freedom, we cannot know in advance what it will bring; it may be something good, but it may be something bad, very bad. Unlimited freedom cannot be permitted even for God: we do not "know" in advance what God may bring us. An inescapable fear continually whispers this disturbing question in our ear: but what if God should bring us something bad? Here, in this fear, is the origin of the custom of linking the religious with the ethical, and speaking of the religious-ethical. It is as if man were insuring himself against the religious with the ethical. The religious is something new, unknown, remote; the ethical, however, is something known, familiar, ordinary. Kierkegaard, and all of us after him, can confidently say of the ethical that even if it is not mighty enough to give a man back his arm or leg, there is no doubt that it has the power to deform and torment the human spirit. The ancients knew this, even before the time of Socrates; the ethical has always had at its disposal the horde of raging Furies, who mercilessly pursue every deviation from its laws. Everyone knows this, and such knowledge does not in the least presuppose faith. And yet Kierkegaard himself is always repeating what the Apostle Paul said: all that is not of faith is sin. The ethical with its Furies is certainly not of faith. This is knowledge, knowledge of what is real, and the "unbelieving" pagans could speak of it just as well as Kierkegaard. It cannot return a man's severed arm—however, it is not the only one that cannot; no one in the world can do this. The "religious" is in this case just as powerless as the "ethical": Zeus himself attested that the gods can give men the world only in trust, but not as their property. It is true that Kierkegaard says, or, rather, cries out in a frenzy: for God nothing is impossible; God signifies that everything is impossible. He can return a severed arm or leg; He can raise Job's slain children from the dead; He can raise Isaac from the dead, and not just the one whom Abraham sacrificed, but every Isaac sacrificed to Necessity; and, what is more, Kierkegaard, as if inspired, as if in a transport of self-oblivion and desperation, assures us that God allows every man to decide for himself what his own Isaac will be and where he is to be found, allows him that unlimited freedom in the presence of which a case like Kierkegaard's, considered by reason to be "insignificant," "pathetic," "tedious," even "comical," becomes, in the words of Kierkegaard himself, a universally historic event, possessing an importance unsurpassed by the campaigns of Alexander of Macedonia and the great migrations of peoples. As Kierkegaard suggests to us: "The man who is not mature enough to understand that immortal fame through countless generations is only an attribute of temporality, and who does not understand that a striving for this sort of immortality is a pitiful thing in comparison with the immortality which awaits every man and which would justifiably inspire universal envy, were it prepared for one man only, will not go very far in the understanding of what the soul is and what immortality is." *

Who gave Kierkegaard the right to make such an assertion? Does the personal immortality of the first person who comes along mean more than the fame through countless generations of Alexander of Macedonia? Did he consult the ethical? Evidently he forgot this or overlooked it; for if he had consulted it, he would have had to cool his ardor. Personal immortality—his own or that of someone else— not only is not comparable with the fame in posterity of Alexander of Macedonia, but does not bear comparison

* V, 100.

with the far more modest fame of Mucius Scaevola or Regulus. Even Herostratus was, in his estimation of the significance of fame in posterity, much closer to the truth than Kierkegaard. Nevertheless, he did not permit himself to judge arbitrarily, as he pleased, but awaited the judgment of history. All values that exist in the world are true values only insofar as they find room for themselves in the categories which have been established, not by the arbitrariness and caprice of man, but by higher laws, standing outside of and above every arbitrariness and caprice. Kierkegaard's claim to immortality has as little basis as his claim to have turned his meeting with Regina Olsen into an event of universally historic significance. And this is no secret to Kierkegaard. In a burst of frankness, speaking as usual, of course, not directly, but in the third person, he confesses that he does not trust the "ethical," that he hides from it, although he knows it is very easily insulted and demands of man that he lay before it, as before a confessor, all his innermost thoughts and desires.* In Kierkegaard's life, the ethical not only is not indissolubly bound up with the religious, but is continually at war with it. In the moment when the ethical, according to the dictates of its nature, turns its gaze upon the rational and pronounces its decisive and final sentence, when all "possibility" ends for the ethical, the "religious" has its beginning. The religious dwells above and beyond the sphere of the "general." It is not protected by any laws, it is not concerned with what our thinking finds to be possible or impossible, or with what ethics declares to be permissible

---

* III, 82. "Ethics cannot help them; it is insulted. For they have a secret they have concealed from ethics. A secret they have accepted as their personal responsibility." And he is speaking here, not of Job, not of Abraham, but of a couple in love.

and obligatory. For a religious man, "personal immortality" is more precious than the greatest fame in posterity; to him, those gifts which he has received from the Creator are worth more than all the praises and distinctions with which the "ethical" lures us. Everything that Kierkegaard tells us, both in his books and in his journals, is evidence that he did not place his hopes in the possibilities revealed by reason (he disdainfully calls them probabilities), and the rewards promised by the ethical (which he calls deceitful consolations.) This is the source of his hatred for reason and his ardent glorification of the Absurd. One can find few writers in the literature of the world who sought the truth as passionately and recklessly as Kierkegaard.

But not for nothing does he so often repeat the words: "Blessed is he, whosoever shall not be offended in me." The offense lies in wait for faith everywhere and at every moment. There is a certain connection between them, incomprehensible to us, but seemingly unbreakable: he who has not experienced offense will not come to experience faith. Only, I must add that the offense begins earlier than even Kierkegaard supposes. In Kierkegaard's opinion, the event which is most incredible, and therefore most offensive, is the incarnation of Christ. How could God lower himself to take human form, and, what is more, the form of the humblest of men? Kierkegaard spares no detail to depict for us the humiliation to which Christ was subjected during his life on earth. Poor, persecuted, despised not only by outsiders, but by those close to him; rejected by his own father, who was suspicious of Mary; * etc., etc.—how could such a one turn out to be God? This is truly a great offense. But the source and the beginning of

* XI, 136.

the offense are nevertheless not to be found in God's decision to take the shape of a lowly person. The offense begins for human reason even earlier, in the very assumption
that there is a God for Whom everything is possible, Who
can take the shape, not only of a lowly person, but also of
a king and lord. And it must be said that the second possibility is far less acceptable to reason than the first, and
that Kierkegaard himself never lost sight of this, least of
all in those moments when he tells, with his characteristic
sombre pathos, of the horrors of Christ's earthly existence.
It is easier for us to assume—keeping within the limits of
our experience and understanding—that, if there are
beings higher than man, which we therefore call gods,
they are nevertheless not so mighty as to be able to break
through all the impossibilities revealed by reason and overcome all the prohibitions established by morality; and are
thus, when faced with unfavorable circumstances, doomed
to every sort of hardship—it is easier to assume this than
to acknowledge the existence of a being for whom "everything is possible." Reason, as we have seen, knows for
certain that even God is the product of $\pi\acute{o}\rho os$ and $\pi\epsilon\nu\acute{\iota}a$, and
that it is therefore more fitting for Him to appear as a
lowly person than as an unlimited lord and master. And
this is a matter which concerns not only the pagan philosophers. Every time we try to give an answer to the question: *cur Deus homo*, we inevitably come up against the
moment of Necessity, which is evidence of the existence
of some primordial principles of existence over which even
God has no power; in order to save man, God is *obliged* to
become man, to suffer, to accept death, and so on. And the
more profoundly thought out the explanation, the more
insistently it emphasizes, on the one hand, the impos-

sibility of God's achieving His aim in any other way, and, on the other hand, His sublimeness, expressed in His readiness to accept the conditions set for Him by Necessity, for the sake of the salvation of mankind. The situation is altogether the same as in human affairs: reason shows God the limits of possibility, ethics praises God for scrupulously fulfilling all the "you must's" stipulated by impossibilities. Here lies the ultimate and greatest offense, of which Kierkegaard was always aware, and against which he always fought desperately, but which to the end he never succeeded in overcoming, which no mortal ever succeeds in overcoming, and which, by all evidence, mortals cannot overcome by their own powers: we are not able to reject the fruit of the tree of good and evil. In other words, our reason and our morality are emancipated from God. God created everything, but morality and reason were before everything, before God; they have always existed. They were not created—they have no beginning.

This is why the endeavors of existential philosophy always have a tendency to run aground on what Socrates, according to Plato, taught: μέγιστον ἀγαθὸν ὄν ἀνθρώπῳ τοῦτο, ἑκάστης ἡμέρας περὶ ἀρετῆς τοὺς λόγους ποιεῖσθαι ("The highest good for man is to converse every day about virtue.") When the religious is combined with the ethical, the former disappears into the latter without a trace; the tree of knowledge drains all the sap from the tree of life. Existential philosophy, seeing as its task the struggle, however mad, "for possibility," becomes edification, which by its very nature results in a readiness to compromise with those limited possibilities at the disposal of the "rational" and the "ethical." Man does not dare, or does not have the strength, to think in the categories in which he lives, and he is compelled to live in these categories in which he thinks. And, what is more, he does not even suspect that this is his greatest Fall, that this is original sin. He is entirely in the power of the *eritis sicut dei* inspired in him by the serpent. Kierkegaard probably had this in mind when he said of himself that he could not make the final movement of faith. And this was the real reason for his unrestrained attacks upon the clergy and the church, upon "the Christianity which has abolished Christ," just as it was the reason for that virtually unprecedented cruelty and severity of which his sermons (or, as he prefers to call them, his "edifying discourses") are full. Kierkegaard's most ardent admirers are not prepared to go along with him in this direction to the very end, and they make all sorts of attempts in the way of "interpretations" to adapt them for ordinary understanding. But this only alienates us from both Kierkegaard and the questions he poses, which persistently call attention to all the implacable *either/or's* concealed in existence. If Kierkegaard could have "relented," he would have done so, and would not have delegated the task to anyone else. In 1851, in the same book in which he announced with such fury that Christianity had abolished Christ, he wrote: "My severity is not of my own making. If I knew a milder word, I would gladly comfort and encourage man. And yet! And yet! It may be that the sufferer needs something else: suffering that is crueler still. Crueler still! What fiend dares to say this? My friend, it is Christianity, the doctrine which is offered to us under the name of gentle consolation." * At this point he returns once more to the sacrifice of Abraham, about which he told us so much in his earlier works: "To

* XI, 67.

147

destroy with your own hands what you so passionately desired; to allow what you already possess to be taken from you—this cuts to the very heart of the natural man. But this is what God demanded of Abraham. Abraham himself was obliged—terrible to relate!—obliged by his own hand—horror and madness!—to sacrifice Isaac—the gift of God for whom he had waited so long and with such yearning, for whom he had thanked God all his life and could not give thanks enough, Isaac, his only child, the child he had been promised! Do you believe that death could sting so? I do not believe it." There is no doubt that life stings more keenly than death—and, on the other hand, there is also no doubt that Kierkegaard's severity was not of his own making. It was not he who demanded the terrible sacrifice from Abraham; he is not the author of those horrors of which human life is full. They existed before him, they will continue after him, and perhaps will grow and increase in number. He is only a spokesman transmitting to us words and phrases which he did not originate. He only sees and hears what until now has gone unheard by others. But he is the one who must guess the "meaning" of his words, the "significance" of what he has seen and heard. And here we are witnesses to an unprecedented inward struggle that tore his already tattered soul to shreds, a struggle that he nevertheless could not refuse, since through it existential philosophy is freed from the intolerable self-evidences established for man by theoretical philosophy. In *Fear and Trembling*, Kierkegaard could still speak of "temptation" in connection with the sacrifice of Abraham. And in his later works he brings up "temptation" at every turn and continually asserts that no science can make clear and explain what is concealed in the Biblical expression "temptation." But he rejected the "serpent"—and is there much left of temptation without the serpent? Or, to put it better—was this not a concession to contemporary enlightenment, which accepts only what it can understand and explain? Kierkegaard, of course, did not admit the thought that his readiness to cleanse the story of the Fall of elements for which our understanding has no room could have such fateful consequences for our thinking, if not directly, then indirectly. But then, the intervention of the serpent with his *eritis sicut dei* ("you will be as gods") is nothing but an appeal to *lumen naturale*, to natural light: the fruit of the tree of knowledge will turn man into God, and by this very act, all that is unnatural, all that is supernatural will cease and become a fantasy, an illusion, Nothingness. There is real artistry in this, the beginning of every possible temptation, all the more threatening and dangerous because it does not in the least resemble temptation. Who could suspect that knowledge, the ability to distinguish good from evil, conceals in itself any danger whatever? It is completely obvious that, on the contrary, all dangers have their source in ignorance and the inability to distinguish good from evil. We will recall how unconcernedly the author of *Theologia deutsch* passed over the Scriptural story of the tree of knowledge. We will recall that Kierkegaard himself saw the sleep of the mind in the ignorance of the innocent man. Man is ready and willing to seek and find the source of sin anywhere but where Holy Scripture tells him it is. What is more, our "natural" thinking assures us that the greatest sin, man's most terrible Fall, his spiritual death, is his reluctance to participate in the knowledge of what good is and what evil is. Kierkegaard, who regards the

Bible as a divinely inspired book, cannot rid his soul of this conviction. He does not doubt that, if the ethical, i.e., the fruit of the tree of knowledge, is supreme, then Abraham, his favorite hero, the father of faith—is lost. He knows that if Abraham's faith is humiliated by knowledge, then all human beings are lost. But the ethical does not loosen its grip on him and holds him firmly in its clutches.

What is this? Kierkegaard himself has told us: sin is the swoon of freedom. Man does not even choose; he has no power to choose. The choice is made for him by Nothingness, which—Kierkegaard, again, has told us of this—turns out to be a Proteus. In the beginning it assumes the form of Necessity. Now it has adopted the guise of the "ethical." And it will not stop at this. Before our eyes it will take the shape of Eternity, Infinity, love. And consequently existential philosophy will retreat further and further before the objective truth of theoretical philosophy, against which Kierkegaard fought so desperately, and which he considers to be mankind's most terrible enemy.

XI

Fear and Original Sin

*Much has been said about the nature of
original sin, but the main category has
been overlooked:* fear. *Its real definition
is to be found here. Fear is an alien, external force which takes possession of
the individual; he cannot tear himself
away from its power.*

KIERKEGAARD

Let me remind you once more—because it is extremely
important for an explanation of the problem that existential philosophy has set itself—of what Kierkegaard tells
us about sin, about fear, and about freedom. "Fear is the
swoon of freedom," he writes in his book *The Concept of
Dread.* And there also he adds: "Psychologically speaking,
the Fall always takes place in a swoon." * In his journal
we read the same thing, almost word for word: "Fear
weakens man, and the first sin takes place in a swoon."

* V, 57.

Kierkegaard

The words just quoted are introduced by Kierkegaard in this manner: "Much has been said about the nature of original sin—and yet the main category has been overlooked: fear. Its real definition is to be found here. *Fear is an alien, external force which takes possession of the individual; he cannot tear himself away from its power* because he is afraid; what we fear, we at the same time desire" * [italics mine].

I think scarcely anyone, including even the most profound religious thinkers, has succeeded in coming close to the problem of the Fall. Nietzsche, perhaps: however, Nietzsche, having renounced Christianity, was obliged to speak, not of the Fall, but simply of the fall of man. But Nietzsche's "decadence" is indistinguishable in nature from Kierkegaard's original sin. For Nietzsche, Socrates—the wisest of men, the greatest of geniuses—was the fallen man par excellence. Fearing the "Absurd" revealed to him in life, he sought reassurance and salvation in the confines of rational thought. We know that, for Kierkegaard, Socrates was the most remarkable phenomenon up to the time of Christianity. But for him, Socrates was also the sinner par excellence, for the very reason that he was an incomparable genius, i.e., a man who "revealed" knowledge and placed all his hopes in the knowledge revealed by him. Knowledge was to him the only source of both truth and good. Knowledge showed him the natural limits and boundaries of the possible; good was the art of finding the greatest blessing in the limits pointed out by knowledge. His inspiration was the Delphic "γνῶθι σεαυτόν," † which led him to the conviction that the greatest blessing for man is to converse every day about virtue.

* *Journal*, 171.
† "Know thyself."

It is astonishing that Nietzsche not only guessed the existence of the decadent, that is, the fallen man, in Socrates, but also—just as though he had undertaken to illustrate the Biblical story with the example of Socrates—was able to understand that the fallen man cannot save himself by his own powers from the catastrophe which awaits him. Everything the decadent does to save himself only hastens his ruin, says Nietzsche. However much he may struggle and try to gain control of himself, his methods of fighting and his attempts to save himself are only an expression of his "Fall"; everything he does, he does as a fallen man, i.e., as a man who has lost his freedom of choice and is doomed in advance, by a power hostile to him, to see his salvation in that which brings his ruin. When Kierkegaard said that the greatest genius is the greatest sinner, he did not, as we know, name Socrates, but doubtless he had him in mind. For him, Socrates embodies the great offense of which Holy Scripture speaks. And indeed, what could be more of an offense than the Delphic commandment: know thyself? Or the wisdom of Socrates: to converse every day about virtue? But then, this is just how the Biblical serpent led the first man astray. And led him so far astray, that even today we persist in seeing the truth where a fatal lie is concealed. All men, even those inclined to mysticism, are attracted to knowledge, but Kierkegaard simply rejects the serpent, for reasons which seem to him and to everyone else to arise from the depths of the soul awakened from its "sleep of ignorance." It is probably here that we must seek the source of the mysterious certainty that the man who has knowledge cannot act badly, and, no doubt, of our certainty that sin could not come from the tree of knowledge. On the contrary, sin came, if we may still use the Biblical images, from the tree of life. All evil that exists on earth came from the tree of life. And yet Kierkegaard, even though he rejected the serpent, always kept aloof, as if instinctively, from the teachings of the mystics, as I have already pointed out. The mystics maintained a semblance of faithfulness to the Biblical revelation, but the principle of "knowledge," proclaimed by Socrates, was realized both in their teaching and in their lives. They sought and found their salvation in themselves, and only in themselves, and their aim was to set themselves free from the world. But, no matter how often Kierkegaard managed to resist Socrates and the mystics, they gained the upper hand once more each time his strength failed him. It was evidently at one of these moments that he resolved to reject the serpent, and it seemed to him then that the narrative of Genesis could only be the better for such correction, that the Fall of man would become clearer and more comprehensible. But the result was quite different. The story of the Fall of the first man is too closely connected with the entire content of the rest of the books of the Old and New Testaments. Further amendment was necessary. And Kierkegaard's existential philosophy began to take on that contradictory character of which I spoke earlier. To reject the serpent not only does not mean to rid oneself of his power, but means just the opposite: to surrender oneself wholly to his power—that is, to give up the struggle with him. Unseen or unrecognized, he is even more completely our master: we do not know who our true enemy is, and we set ourselves against a nonexistent enemy. As Nietzsche said, the fallen man, in saving himself, destroys himself. When he should be listening, he instead begins to teach, to expound, to preach. But can a man who "teaches" "surpass" Socrates? Can one be a "better" teacher than Socrates? In one of his edifying discourses, Kierkegaard asks the question: "What is the difference between the apostle and the genius?" (The discourse was published under that title.) One would think, from what Kierkegaard has already said about genius, that his answer to this question would clarify still further the principal conflict between existential and theoretical philosophy which he has so inspiredly set forth for us. It would seem that here Kierkegaard was presented with a particularly favorable opportunity to express the thoughts dearest to him. But Kierkegaard puts together a work of edification: and everything changes as if a magic wand had been waved. His answer goes like this: the apostle speaks with an authority that the genius does not and cannot possess. Apostles become teachers and exhorters whose only advantage over the genius or the wise man is that they possess authority, and that, on the strength of this, everyone must obey them. In his eyes, even Jesus becomes a teacher who possesses authority and who therefore rightfully demands obedience of men. He possesses the authority, but not the power: in other words—it is not the world and the elements that obey him, but only men. Even the God of Biblical revelation does not signify that everything is possible: and much (perhaps even what is most important) continues to remain impossible for the God of the Bible, as for the god whom Socrates knew, and the god with whom, according to Epictetus, Chryssip conversed. The most that we can expect from God is instruction, edification, a willingness, like that of the pagan god, to share with us the results of His rational understanding. Anything more is merely superstition, even though it may be conveyed to us through the pages of Holy Scripture. And on this point we read in Kierkegaard's writings: "In general, unbelievable confusion arises in the sphere of religion if in the relationship of man to God the "you must," which is the only possible rule here, is abolished." * This is one of the basic themes of Kierkegaard's edifying discourses; he returns to it many times, at every possible occasion, and even without occasion. And it is necessary to dwell on it with particular attentiveness, because it presents to us, although in a negative fashion, one of the most burdensome and tormenting preoccupations of his mind. After what I have already said in the preceding chapters, there can hardly be any doubt of the source of Kierkegaard's idea that the relationship of man to God is regulated by duty. We have seen that all "you must's," no matter how much they would like to be considered independent and without limitations (i.e., uncreated, or, like man as seen by the Pelagians, liberated from God), are basically inseparable from ideas of the rule of Necessity in the world. When Necessity proclaims its "impossible," ethics hastens to its aid with its own "you must." The more absolute and invincible the "impossible," the more threatening and implacable the "obliged." We have witnessed how Kierkegaard's indignation was aroused by the sarcastic observation about honor made by Shakespeare's Falstaff. It stung him in his most sensitive spot, and he answered the man, who ought, properly speaking, not to have been admitted at all to a discussion of philosophical problems, with all the thunders at his disposal—as if that man were not Falstaff, but Hegel himself. He could not help admitting that the ethical is powerless to return a man's arm or leg; nevertheless the ethical retains

* VIII, 109.

a certain power: it can mutilate the human soul as the
most vicious torturer could never mutilate the human
body. And so it appears that the ethical with its "you must"
is the only possible regulator of "man's relationship to
God." It is obvious that somewhere in the depths of Kierkegaard's soul there remained alive a firm conviction that
the world contains "impossible's" which neither God nor
man can overcome, and which are inescapably accompanied by all those threatening "you must's." Moreover, in
Kierkegaard's work these impossibilities turn out, as always, to be connected, not with any universally historic
events—that would not be so "paradoxical"—but with
that same boring and ridiculous story which he has already
dinned into our ears: his break with Regina Olsen. He
remarks in his journal: "Let us suppose that someone does
possess the enormous courage which is necessary in order
for him to believe that God literally will forgive all his
sins . . . What then? All is forgiven. He has become a new
man. But can it be that the past has left no traces? To put
it another way: is it possible that such a man could begin
life anew as carefree as a youth? Impossible! . . . How
could a man who believes in the forgiveness of sins become once again young enough to experience erotic love!"
What could seem more proper and natural than this question? And yet it reveals with singular clarity that "thorn
in the flesh" of which Kierkegaard speaks both in his
journals and in his other works.* "Is it possible?" he asks.
But to whom is this question directed? Who decides, who
has the right to decide, where the realm of the possible
ends and the realm of the impossible begins? For God,

* A particularly forceful and intense article by Kierkegaard is entitled
"The Thorn in the Flesh."

Kierkegaard

Kierkegaard tells us again and again, nothing is impossible. Consequently, someone different, something different, not the power of God, has taken possession of Kierkegaard's thought. Is it not that Nothingness with which we are already familiar, fear of which was implanted in the first man and, through him, in all mankind by the Biblical serpent rejected by Kierkegaard? The fact cannot be disputed: Kierkegaard was unshakably convinced that, even if God Himself had forgiven his sins, youth and the carefree quality of youth would never have returned to him. But—where he got this unshakable conviction, he does not tell us. He does not even question it, he cannot make up his mind to question it. But, as a matter of fact, he need only have recalled his own words from *The Sickness Unto Death* in order to realize that this question cannot be avoided. As he himself said: "For God everything is possible; God signifies for man that everything is possible. For the fatalist, everything is the result of necessity; his God is necessity. This means that for him there is no God." * But, if there is no God where there is necessity, and if forgiveness of sins is necessarily accompanied by a loss of youth and youth's freedom from care (perhaps it is also, just as necessarily, accompanied by other, even more terrible, losses!), then forgiveness of sins does not come from God, but from the source whence theoretical philosophy draws its metaphysical consolations. The "mad struggle for possibility" has ended in complete failure; the master of the world of the "finite" turns out to be, not the knight of faith, but necessity, and the full realization of the human ideal is to be found in the knight of resignation. The poor youth will never get the king's daughter, Job will

* VIII, 37.

not see his children again, Abraham will slaughter Isaac, and people will make fun of Kierkegaard himself, as though he were a crank, a half-wit. Moreover, it will be demanded of us that we recognize this state of affairs as natural and desirable, and even see in it the fulfillment of a wise design planned by some primordial principle. "It is madness," writes Kierkegaard, "(and, from the point of view of esthetics, comical) that a creature for whom eternity is waiting should make every effort to possess the transitory and keep it unchanged." And, at another point in the same book: "To desire the finite absolutely is a contradiction, for the finite must have an end." * It is fruitless to argue with all these self-evident truths, as long as we remain on the plane of rational thinking. However, Kierkegaard has summoned us to the Absurd, which cannot be fitted into a plane of two dimensions, and which presupposes as a condition for grasping the truth a new third dimension—faith, of which it has been said: "If ye have faith as a grain of mustard seed . . . nothing shall be impossible unto you . . . (οὐδὲν ἀδυνατήσει ὑμτν). The children of Job, and Abraham's Isaac, and the king's daughter, and Regina Olsen—all these are "finite." It is inconsistent, and, therefore, ridiculous and mad, to strive, and strive with infinite passion, for something that must have an end.† If we ask ourselves where Kierkegaard got this truth, we hardly need hesitate over the answer: it came to

---

* VII, 105 and 81.
† Cf. *ibid.*, 231, where Kierkegaard, inspired by the pathos of the "Absurd," which he extols in the preceding pages without fear of inconsistency or comicality, both of which he uses as snares when necessary, says: "It is incomprehensible to the thinking that something which was not eternal could become eternal." This is one of many striking examples of how thinking, when it finds a new dimension, rises above truths that seem to the ordinary man insuperable.

him from Socrates, the wisest and best of men up to the time of, and outside the realm of, Holy Scripture; and its proper place was in the work of Socrates. Socrates knew only Zeus, and Zeus himself was in the power of natural, uncreated reason; for him, not everything was possible. The law of birth and destruction of everything that is born was superior to him and stronger than he was. Everything that has a beginning must also have an end. We cannot imagine it otherwise: "It is incomprehensible to the thinking that something which was not eternal could become eternal." But is a thing which the thinking cannot grasp the same as a thing which cannot exist in reality? Kierkegaard told us that in order to achieve faith, one must renounce thinking. And then the ridiculous and the mad will cease to be ridiculous and mad, and the infinitely passionate striving for the finite will be justified. And, on the other hand, if thinking, Socratic thinking, i.e., two-dimensional thinking in which *intelligere* has crushed *ridere, lugere et detestari,* triumphs; if reason with its "impossible" and morality with its "obliged" turn out to be primordial and are triumphant; then faith, which arises from *lugere et detestari,* together with an infinite striving for the finite, will turn out to be mad, useless, and ridiculous. And Holy Scripture will consequently have to be systematically amended and interpreted, in order that it not turn out to be mad and ridiculous also.

As strange as it may seem, Kierkegaard kept to both paths at once, and this was probably the best, or indeed the only, possible way for him to deal at all with the overpowering questions which continually threw him off the ordinary course of human existence.

We know that he felt obliged to eliminate the serpent

from the Biblical story of the Fall. The serpent did not fit in with, and even insulted, our religious-ethical ideals. Sin, as human beings understand it, cannot and must not enter the soul from without. Kierkegaard also was not able to reconcile himself to the words of Holy Scripture that the sun rises for sinners and righteous men alike. Every time something reminded him of this, he became indignant, and resolutely protested; in our world, the material world, things are really like that, but in the world of the spirit there is another "law." There "the man who does not work does not eat"; there the sun does not rise for evil men, but only for the good. He speaks of this more than once even in his early works: *Either/Or* and *The Concept of Dread.* And it must be admitted that he observes strict consistency on this point. If it becomes necessary to eliminate the serpent from the story of the Fall in order to satisfy the ethical, then under no circumstances can one retain the words of Jesus in the New Testament which say that the sun rises for sinners as well as righteous men. Sinners are an evil, and the ethical will never admit that what it condemns is not also condemned by God. If God Himself, i.e., the religious, opposes the ethical, it will condemn even Him. It is the ethical alone, and only the ethical, that decides what is good and what is evil, what is sin and what is righteousness. Socrates taught that the gods have no power over the ethical; the holy is not holy because the gods love it; the gods love the holy because it is holy. For Socrates, good, like reason, is primordial, uncreated, and completely independent of God, Who created the world. For him, therefore, it would be the supreme blasphemy to assume that sin had its origin in the tree of knowledge. On the contrary: all sins come from ignorance.

Kierkegaard

There is also no doubt that sin calls for retribution; the sun must not shine on the sinner, and the rain must not give him its refreshing coolness. Sinners will fall prey to the absolute power of the ethical. The ethical cannot give back a man's severed leg, his lost children, his beloved. But it can punish him: Kierkegaard's reply to Falstaff is comment enough on this.

XII

The Power of Knowledge

Superstition attributes the power of Medusa's head to objectivity, which turns subjectivity to stone, and the absence of freedom deprives man of any possibility of breaking the spell.

KIERKEGAARD

The primordial, uncreated "ethical" can give man nothing, but it can make demands of him. And what is more: the less it is able to give, the more it demands. If Kierkegaard had wanted in this case as well to "go on to the end," he would have had to answer the words of the Gospel that say that the sun rises for both righteous men and sinners alike in the same way that he answered Falstaff. Although the words are different, this is, in effect, the meaning of the impassioned "edifying discourses" assembled in his book *Life and Works of Love*. This book is entirely devoted to a development of the thesis that the essence of man's relationship to God is defined in the words of the Prophet: "thou shalt love." *You must* love God, *you must* love your neighbor, *you must* love the sufferings and the horrors of life, you must, you must, you must. When Kierkegaard begins to speak on the subject of "you must," he is inexhaustible. The idea that the moment of "you must" can be eliminated from the relationship of man to God is painful and simply monstrous to him. He is not afraid to declare straightforwardly: "The hideous time of slavery is past; now humanity thinks that it will be making another step forward if it abolishes the dependence of men upon God, to Whom each of us belongs (not by birth, but be‑ cause we were created out of nothing) more surely than any slave ever belonged to his earthly master." * Kierke‑ gaard could not have found this in Holy Scripture. There it is said: "Ye are gods; and all of you are children of the most High"—and this is repeated in the Gospel of St. John (10:34): θεοί ἐστε. If we recall that Kierkegaard had pre‑ viously written: "Ethics regards every man as its slave," then we will be able to guess without difficulty the origin of his persistent idea of identifying the relationship of man to God with the relationship of slave to master. And this is, in its own way, the strictest sort of consistency: the re‑ lationship of man to the commandments of the ethical is, like his relationship to the "laws" of reason, a relationship of unconditional, slavish dependency, all the more terrible and destructive to him because morality and reason them‑ selves can yield nothing in their demands; for they have no will. Kierkegaard is wrong only in his assertion that men have expunged the ethical "you must" from their relationship to God. Just the opposite: of all that men have associated with the idea of God, only "you must" has

* *Edifying Discourses,* III, 121; cf. *ibid.,* p. 114: "Every man is in bond‑ age to God."

survived intact for contemporary man. God Himself long ago ceased to exist for many people, but "you must" has outlived even God. Kierkegaard was able to attack Falstaff by using a "you must" of his own, with such authority in his voice that one would think even the fat knight might have heard it. In any case, Falstaff would have found Kierkegaard and his threatening "eternity" which engulfs all that is transitory easier to believe than the tales in Holy Scripture about a God without Whose will not even a hair can fall from a man's head. For both "experience" and "understanding" repeatedly assure Falstaff that there exists in the world some kind of force that indifferently takes from men what is most precious to them, but that there is no force capable of returning what has been taken. Of course, it is impossible to convince Falstaff that the Absurd can offer any opposition to understanding and experience. He may not have read Plato, but he is perceptive enough to understand that the greatest misfortune for man is to become a μισόλογος and entrust his fate to the Absurd. Like any intelligent man, he sees clearly that a struggle with objective truth can come to nothing, and that objective truth is maintained by the power of uncreated, unyielding Necessity. With a certain amount of education in philosophy, Falstaff would easily discern the inherent connection between the necessary and the ethical, for this connection is established by reason, all the benefits of which he valued highly in the course of his long life. But Kierkegaard ridiculed objectivity. "Superstition attributes the power of Medusa's head to objectivity, which turns subjectivity to stone, and the absence of freedom deprives man of any possibility of breaking the spell," * he said in *Fear and*

* V, 139.

Trembling. It was he who assured us that "only the conclusions of passion—they alone are the only ones on which we can rely." * How often and how inspiredly he spoke of this! And yet the ethical tempted him—tempted him with exactly that against which he had put himself on guard, and had warned others: his objectivity, his soberness. The ethical's absolute "you must," unlimited by any conditions or considerations, conceals the same immutable, implacable "law," binding upon all, which upholds the impossibilities proclaimed by reason. Kant, who found a synthetic a priori judgment in theoretical reason, provided practical reason with categorical imperatives which fully satisfy all the needs of the "ethical" whose praises Kierkegaard has sung. Only through a misunderstanding (and perhaps not a completely unintentional one) could Kierkegaard, who was quite familiar with Kant, complain that philosophy has eliminated the ethical. On the contrary, nowhere has the ethical been given so reasonable and honorable a reception as in those fields to which the power of theoretical philosophy has spread. Even Nietzsche, the "immoralist," bears witness to this: the ethical has only to nod its head, he says, and it will win over to its side the "freest" of thinkers. And here I must emphasize once more: the fascination of the ethical is maintained solely and exclusively by its connection with Necessity. As long as, and insofar as, Kierkegaard felt that his youth would never return to him and that even though God could forgive and forget sins, He could not make the existent nonexistent—as we have seen, this state of mind overwhelmed him more than once—he forgot Abraham and Job and the poor youth who loved the

* III, 95.

king's daughter, dashed headlong back to Socrates, and misinterpreted Holy Scripture in such a way that it would have offended neither the reason nor the conscience of the wisest of men. God cannot make something which once existed nonexistent, and there is much else that He cannot do: eternal truths are stronger than God. God, like His Apostles, has no power, but only authority: they can only threaten and demand, or, at best, exhort. In one of his edifying discourses on the subject of love and charity, Kierkegaard quotes the beginning of the third chapter of Acts: "Once when the Apostle Peter was going to the temple, he met a lame man who asked him for alms. And Peter said to him: Silver and gold have I none; but such as I have give I thee: In the name of Jesus of Nazareth rise up and walk. And immediately his feet and ankle bones received strength. And he leaping up stood and walked." After citing this passage, he "explains": "Who can doubt that this was a charitable deed? And yet there was a miracle here. The miracle draws all our attention to itself and distracts our attention from the charity, which is never revealed so distinctly as in those cases where it can do nothing: only then are we not prevented from seeing clearly and distinctly what charity is." * Perhaps, upon reading these lines, some people might involuntarily say to themselves: *timeo Danaos et dona ferentes*. But still, here again there is strict internal consistency. Here, above all, there is evident that "sublimeness" to which we are committed by the ethical, which tries, in spite of everything, to root out all "concern" from the human soul. Not just Socrates, not just Kant—but Hegel, too, would have saluted Kierke-

* *Life and Works of Love,* 337.

gaard. Hegel went even further; he completely rejected the miracles of the Gospels, and was angered by them, thinking them to be a "violation of the spirit." And, indeed, this is true: the miracle described in Acts is capable of obscuring completely, and making us forget, all the edifying discourses ever uttered by men. Is this not offensive? And would it not have been better if the Apostle Peter had limited himself simply to words of love and comfort, instead of healing a lame man, as Jesus of Nazareth himself had once done? Or if the lame man himself, rising to those heights where the ethical dwells, had said to the Apostle: I have no need of your miracles, I seek only love and charity, for, although I am no Hegel, I do know for certain that miracles are a violation of the spirit. And so once again it becomes necessary to amend or misinterpret Holy Scripture—to fit it into our ideas of "the sublime and the obligatory," which keep within the limits of the "possible." The idea of God held by ignorant carpenters and fishermen is too crude and naïve, in fact, one might say, primitive. It inclines them to the miraculous, inclines them to a God for Whom everything is possible. Before accepting their truths, we must sift them through the strict thinking of Socrates, through his "possible" and the ethical connected with the "possible," i.e., through his κάθαρσις. And we must, above all, turn our attention away from the miracle; this can be done only by pure, disinterested love. It, of course, is powerless; it cannot set the lame man on his feet. With a strange persistence, as if he were drumming it into our heads, Kierkegaard repeats on every page: charity can accomplish nothing. He repeats it at such length and so insistently that he finally achieves his aim: the reader's attention is wholly distracted from the miracle, and it begins to seem that the passage from Acts quoted by him was taken, not from the Bible, but from the writings of Epictetus, or the words of Socrates; and that the Apostle Peter had the authority necessary to teach, but not the power to help men. Eternity, inflexible and invincible, stands above the Prince of Apostles, as it stands above the wisest of men—exactly as the wisdom of the Hellenes had already represented it. The god of Socrates is just as weak and powerless in the face of eternity as Socrates himself. He has at his disposal only virtue and wisdom, which he willingly shares with mortals, as befits a most benevolent being. But the world and all that is in it are not subject to him, and it is not he who commands the world. For this reason he has "humbled himself," and has taught men humility, attempting to distract their attention from miracles which no one has the power to bring about, and trying to instill in them a taste for love, charity, and conversations about the sublime, in which they find out that the ethical is their only source of help, that it alone has any value in heaven, and ought to be the only thing valued on earth. Socrates "knew" that the highest good for men, both here on earth, and in the other world, if the other world turns out to be, not the fruit of our imagination, but a reality, amounts entirely to holding edifying conversations. Spinoza, too, constructed his ethic upon this: *beatitudo non est praemium virtutis, sed ipsa virtus* ("happiness is not the reward of virtue, but virtue itself").

Now we must ask ourselves: in what order did the thinking of Socrates and Spinoza proceed? Were they first of all convinced that there are limits to both the abilities of men and the abilities of the gods, limits which they cannot escape, and then, convinced of this limitation on the abili-

169

ties of all living creatures, did they begin to look for a higher happiness in virtue, which is as helpless as they are themselves; or did they, without making any preliminary inquiries, become enamored of powerless virtue, just because it is valuable for its own sake, and only then discover that it can do nothing for men? In other words, did the impossible precede the obligatory, or the obligatory, the impossible? I think that there cannot be two answers to this question. Kierkegaard admitted to us that the "possible" and the "impossible" have no regard for our estimations of value, and that even the forgiveness of sins cannot give a man back the freshness and spontaneity of youth. The fate of virtue is decided in the council of powers which are entirely indifferent to human needs. There is a mysterious "dialectic of being" which develops according to its own laws (not only Hegel, but the mystically minded Jakob Böhme as well spoke of *Selbstbewegung*—self-movement), drawing to itself and grinding to bits all that exists in the universe—both the living and the dead. And there is only one way to save oneself from it, which Zeus recommended to Chryssip: to leave the world of the finite or the "real" for the ideal world. Love, charity, and all the other virtues have an intrinsic value, completely independent of the course of events in the outside world, in which they cannot, and do not wish to, change anything. Even if all mankind, all living creatures should vanish from their presence—love and charity and the whole multitude of virtues surrounding them would not be moved or disturbed in their self-sufficient and self-satisfied existence.

All the sermons, all the edifying discourses of Kierkegaard—what do they glorify? Again I must say: they glorify the fruit of the tree of knowledge of good and evil.

How did this happen—for he has assured us that the ethical is not supreme, that if the ethical is supreme, then Abraham is lost. Now it turns out that Socrates knew the truth, that the ethical is supreme. And the biblical serpent with his *eritis sicut dei scientes bonum et malum* ("ye shall be as gods, knowing good and evil") knew the truth. The father of faith was an abominable murderer!

"My severity is not of my own making," wrote Kierkegaard. There is no doubt that it was not of his own making: if it had been for him to decide, he would never have condemned a suffering man to still greater suffering. But who is the source of that severity? Who dares to say a suffering man must be made to suffer even more? Kierkegaard answers: it is Christianity that says it. Is this so? Is Christianity really preoccupied with adding to the number of human afflictions, which are hard enough to bear as it is? And does Holy Scripture really not know a milder word? Peter healed a lame man; Jesus of Nazareth not only healed the sick, but raised the dead. And, obviously not foreseeing the critique of practical reason, he even said, in the simplicity of his heart, that it is "greater" to heal a sick man than to forgive his sins; but then, he was the incarnation of love and charity. Well then, why did he indeed distract our attention from charity by showing us a miracle, and thereby commit an offense against the ethical? Let this question be answered for us by Dostoyevsky, a writer who is one of the closest and most congenial to Kierkegaard. "I maintain," he says, "that awareness of your inability to help or to bring any benefit or relief whatever to suffering mankind, at the same time that you are fully convinced of the suffering of mankind, can turn the love in your heart for mankind to hatred for it." Weak, powerless,

Kierkegaard

helpless love reduced Dostoyevsky to horror. But then, Kierkegaard himself was horrified by it. And did the friends of Job, against whom he rose up in anger, declare anything more than powerless love? They could not help Job— and they offered him what they had to give—words of charity. Only when Job laid bare their "stubbornness," and their "obstinacy," and rejected their "moral" and "metaphysical" consolations, did they attack him with their reproaches, justifiably seeing this as "rebellion" and "mutiny" against the ethical. And they were right: the ethical does the same thing itself and orders all its knights and servants to do likewise. It is powerless to return Job's children to to him, but it is able to strike at his soul with anathemas that are more painful than physical torture. Job is guilty before his friends and before the ethical because he scorned the gift of love and charity, and demanded "repetition," *in integrum restitutio* of what had been taken from him. And Kierkegaard was on Job's side. The ethical and its "gifts" are not supreme. In the face of the horrors that befell Job, helpless love and powerless charity must themselves understand their own insignificance and appeal to another principle. Job's friends are guilty of the greatest of sins: the desire to deal in their own pitiful human way with a matter that awaits, and calls for, a different comforter. If the ethical is supreme, then Job is not only a lost man, but also a condemned one. And, on the other hand, if Job is justified, if Job is saved, it means that there is a higher principle in the world, and that the "ethical" must take its humble place and submit to the religious. This is the meaning of the words by Dostoyevsky quoted above, and—at present this will seem surprising, to say the least, but I hope further explanation will bear it out—it is also the meaning of Kierkegaard's edifying discourses, and of all that unprecedented and extreme cruelty or, as he himself called it, savagery which he sought and found or, more probably, inserted, not in Christianity, which had, in his opinion, abolished Christ, but in the actual words of Christ Himself. As we shall see, it is precisely here that Kierkegaard's method of "indirect communication," which I have already mentioned, has been carried out with special persistence.

XIII

Logic and Thunders

Lament, implore. The Lord will not be afraid. Speak, raise your voice, cry out. God can speak even louder: all the thunder is at His disposal. And thunder is the answer, it is the explanation: firm, trustworthy, primordial. God's answer, even if it smashes man to pieces, is superior to all the chattering by human wisdom and human cowardice about divine justice.

KIERKEGAARD

All Kierkegaard's edifying discourses—and he wrote an immense number of them—are one continual fiery, unrestrained, ecstatic hymn to horrors and suffering. And although he emphasizes many times, with extraordinary persistence, that he possesses no authority and that he presents his edifying discourses as a private individual (for this reason he never calls his discourses sermons)—he speaks in the name of Christianity, refers to its good tidings. "My severity is not of my own making—it comes from Christianity." He repeats this in his later works, especially *The Sickness Unto Death* and *Training in Christianity*. He takes great pains to prove to us that the mildness of Christianity's teachings is simply an illusion; that the good tidings they bring amount to the same thing as Spinoza's statement that "happiness is not a reward for virtue, but virtue itself"; and that Christian happiness is, in human estimation, more terrible than the most grievous misfortune. In the intensity and gloomy pathos with which he depicts the horrors of human existence, and the merciless severity with which in the name of Christianity he preaches of cruelty, he does not yield to, and perhaps even surpasses, Nietzsche, who so astonished our age with his words about "love for the far-off." On every occasion, and even without occasion, Kierkegaard reminds us of Christ's earthly sufferings and, in the name of Christ, declares almost word for word what Nietzsche declared in the name of the superman, or Zarathustra: "Do you think that I have come here to make things more comfortable for the suffering? Or to show you who have lost your bearings and taken the wrong road an easier way? No, more and more frequently the best of you will perish, for it will become harder and harder for you." There is no need to enlarge upon the "severity" of Nietzsche's doctrine. It is true that people have become used to hearing it and are accustomed to it, and there are few whom it disturbs—but everyone knows it well enough. I remind you only that Nietzsche, like Kierkegaard, felt constantly obliged to avow that his severity was not of his own making. But then—whence did it come to him? Was it also from Christianity? Or does some other force stand behind the Christianity of Kierkegaard, as behind the superman of Nietzsche? Nietzsche at long last did reveal his secret: he had not chosen cruelty, cruelty had chosen him. His *"amor fati"* had as its source the invincibility of fate: it was the totally devoted, totally altruistic, totally unlimited love of one helpless in the face of destiny. If we pay close attention to the discourses of Kierkegaard, we will discover the same thing in them . . . They all contain an indirect but nevertheless evident recognition of the invincibility of destiny. "The life of Christ," he says, "is a unique kind of unhappy love: he loved by virtue of the divine concept of love, he loved all mankind . . . Christ's love was not sacrificial in the human sense of the word—by no means was it that: he did not make himself unhappy in order to make his followers happy. No, he made himself and his followers as unhappy as was humanly possible . . . He offered himself as a sacrifice only in order to make those whom he loved just as unhappy as he was himself." * And like Nietzsche and Kierkegaard, he did this entirely against his will. He, too, could have cried out: My severity is not of my own making! But if it does not come from Christ, does not come from God—then who is its source? Nietzsche attributed it to fate, Kierkegaard to Christianity. To whom would Christ attribute it, to whom would God attribute it, that God for Whom "nothing is impossible"? Or must we once again return to the Hellenic concept of a God Whose possibilities are limited by the very structure of existence? Is there something which binds God Himself, and does our reason reveal a principle or principles above God, independent of Him, uncreated by Him, which set limits to His will and compel Him to be satisfied with what is possi-

* *Life and Works of Love*, 116 ff.

ble? Confronted by these principles, God is just as powerless as mortals: He possesses only love and charity, which
can do nothing. Kierkegaard firmly declares: "You must
love. It is only the duty, only the obligation to love that
secures love against any changes, makes it eternally free
in blessed independence, guarantees it happiness forever,
keeps it from despair." * And again he says: "Only when
love is a duty is it secure for eternity." The further he ad-
vances his "you must," the more abruptly and insistently
he does it; not with that serene, disinterested lack of passion with which *The Critique of Practical Reason* speaks of
duty (Kierkegaard never mentions *The Critique of Practical Reason*, although he was quite familiar with Kant), †
but with a tension and violent lack of restraint unusual
even in his works. One can find in his writings still more
words of the sort I have just quoted, that deserve—I
almost said, imperiously demand, which would seem more
accurate—to be repeated at once: "Christ's love was not
self-sacrifice in the human sense, least of all can it be called
self-sacrifice: he did not condemn himself, in the human
sense, to unhappiness in order to make his followers happy.
No, he made himself and his followers as unhappy as was
humanly possible . . . He offered himself as a sacrifice in
order to make those whom he loved just as unhappy as he
was himself . . ."

"My severity is not of my own making," Kierkegaard

---

* *Ibid.*, 31.
† Cf. XII, 1: "Real seriousness begins when a man, armed with the necessary strength, feels that something higher obliges him to work in spite
of his own inclinations, i.e., if I may say, to direct all his abilities against
his inclinations." This sounds exactly like a translation from *The Critique
of Practical Reason*, yet it was written in the last year of Kierkegaard's
life.

tells us as justification when he says that in his opinion there is only one way to console those who suffer: to heap still more horrors and suffering upon them. And Zeus justified himself in the same way to Chryssip: he would have been kinder to men if he could have done as he pleased. Christ's position is no better: he, too, has no power of choice—whether he wishes to or not, he is forced to condemn both himself and men to unbearable torment. He *must* love, only love, love in spite of everything, without being able to foretell what his love will bring to him and those he loves. Whence came the "severity" of this "must" to Christ, Christ who—and Kierkegaard never forgets this—is the incarnation of charity, gentleness itself? Kierkegaard's writings do not throw any light on this question. But his depiction of the horrors which accompany the gentle doctrine known as Christianity is all the more brilliant and powerful. If I had wished to quote every relevant passage from the works of Kierkegaard, I would have had to fill many hundreds of pages; nearly half of Kierkegaard's books are devoted to recounting the horrors reserved by Christ for those who accept his good tidings. Whenever he mentions the words of Christ, he does it only to demonstrate once more all the inhuman cruelty, or, as he prefers to call it, all the savagery of the evangelical commandments. He lingers with particular attention, not to say fondness, over the famous passage from the Gospel of St. Luke: if you do not hate your father, mother, and so on, Christ, Christ himself demands that you hate your father, mother, wife, children. This alone can reconcile Kierkegaard; only reaching this paradoxical limit of cruelty can "set his mind at rest," if the phrase "set one's mind at rest"

can in any sense be applied to Kierkegaard. * It would be
better to say that he stopped at this: one can go no further.
And perhaps there is no need to. The "dialectic of unhappy
love" † has accomplished its lofty aim. Love, which can
do nothing, love, which is condemned to powerlessness, is
transformed, as Dostoyevsky predicted, into massive, ago-
nizing, irreconcilable hatred. And this is evidently Kierkegaard's intention. Here is how he "interprets" the words of
Christ: "Come unto me, all ye that labor and are heavy
laden, and I will give you rest," in his book *Training in
Christianity:* "If you who are the unhappiest of the unhappy want to be helped in such a way that you will become even more unhappy, then go to Him: He will help
you" (IX, 50). And in order that there be no doubt of
what he understands the power and mission of Christ to
be, a few pages later he again remarks sarcastically: "To
go to a man who is dying of hunger and say to him: I
bring you word of the beneficent forgiveness of sins, is
simply shocking! This is almost laughable, but it is too serious to laugh about" (IX, 55). Thus, Christ taught men
to rise above the finite, just as the ancients taught and the
sages of today teach. Kierkegaard reproaches Hegel:
"Some have found immortality in the writings of Hegel,
but I have not found it there" (VI, 23). But if, as he writes
in another part of the same book: "Immortality and eternal life are found only in the ethical" (VI, 218)—then

---

* Kierkegaard did not know it, but Epictetus, in Chapter XIV of his *Discourses,* also calls for renunciation of father, mother, etc., in the name of
"you must."
† As early as *Stages on Life's Way,* Kierkegaard wrote, not in reference
to Christ, but to a character in his story: "Unhappy love has its own
dialectic, not within itself, but outside it" (IV, 374).

Kierkegaard's reproach is unjustified. In this respect Hegel kept pace with Spinoza; but then his work is in general thoroughly imbued with the spirit of Spinoza—he always speculates *sub specie aeternitatis.* He probably would have subscribed to the famous words of the Dutch recluse: *sentimus experimurque nos aeternos esse.* Kierkegaard, of course, was familiar with what the Gospels say about the life and works of Christ: He fed the hungry, healed the sick, gave back sight to the blind, and even raised the dead. Kierkegaard certainly could not forget how Christ answered the messengers sent by John the Baptist: "Go your way and tell John what things ye have seen and heard; how that the blind can see, the lame walk, the lepers are cleansed, the deaf hear, the dead are raised, to the poor the gospel is preached" (Luke 7:22; cf. Isaiah 35: 5, 6). No more could he forget what follows immediately after these words: "Blessed is he, whosoever shall not be offended in me"—he considered this the fundamental precept of Christianity and never took his eyes from it. But strangely enough he seems to have been afraid to associate "offense" with the idea it is associated with in the Scriptures. Just as in his interpretation of the passage from Acts quoted above, Kierkegaard directs all his energies to "distracting" our attention from everything "miraculous" described in the Gospels about the life and works of Christ, and to turning our attention wholly toward edification concerning the virtues, which can do nothing, but then are not supposed to do anything. Christ, too, finds *summum bonum* in the ethical; the earthly sufferings of men do not interest him—he does not wish to, and cannot, fight against them. Kierkegaard even becomes incensed when he hears of a pastor comforting a person in distress with quotations from the Scriptures. "If a bereaved person comes to him, the pastor is ready with words about Abraham and Isaac. What sort of nonsense is that? Can it be that to be bereaved means to sacrifice, etc., etc." Kierkegaard is annoyed, not because the pastor confuses "bereavement" with "sacrifice," but because he does not want anyone to look to Scripture for consolation; the purpose of Scripture is not to console people—we have already heard enough on this subject.

Why is this? Why should one not seek consolation in the Scriptures? Why is Kierkegaard so careful to weed out—both for his readers and for himself—all the miracles related in the Scriptures? It surely cannot be said that he did not realize what he was doing. For a "miracle" means that for God everything is possible. It is possible for the person consoled by the pastor to regain what he has lost, just as it was possible for Job's children to be returned to him, Isaac to be returned to Abraham, etc.—as Kierkegaard has already assured us. And then all of a sudden it seems that it is necessary to "distract attention from this" and concentrate solely on contemplation of charity and love and their powerlessness. Has Kierkegaard forgotten his own words: God signifies that everything is possible?

No, he has not forgotten. When he is composing his hymns to the cruelty of God and the powerlessness of virtue, as if in self-oblivion, precisely then is he most mindful of Job, and Abraham, and the lovesick youth, and his own Regina Olsen. When he rejects the miraculous, he is thinking of nothing but the miraculous. It is as though he were making a desperate and terrible experiment on himself and others: what will happen if one not only rejects the miraculous, but strikes it from life entirely, as the intellec-

tual scrupulosity of a thinking man demands; if God Himself is placed within the limits of what is possible according to our experience and our understanding; and if the
"ethical" thus finally and forever becomes "supreme." In
his early book *Repetition* he mentions the Greek philosopher Hegesias, known as the πεισιθάνατος because of his
passionate glorification of death, and, evidently foreseeing
that he could not escape the necessity of carrying his experiment through to completion, he ends the first half,
which constitutes something of an extended introduction
to the subject of this book, with these words: "Why has
none of the dead ever returned? Because life does not
know how to be as persuasive as death. Yes, death is so
thoroughly persuasive that no one has been able to devise
any objection to its arguments, no one has ever been
tempted by the enticements which life can muster in opposition to it. Oh, death—you *know how* to persuade; and
was not your most eloquent champion the πεισιθάνατος, who
used your own persuasiveness in speaking of you?" * Even
when Kierkegaard was still a child, his father noticed the
stille Verzweiflung, the quiet despair, which had established itself in his soul, and which originated in his sense
of "powerlessness" before the inescapable.† Through the
years this sense of powerlessness grew and intensified, and
began to take on in his eyes the dimensions of a universally

* III, 164.
† Cf. what Kierkegaard says in *Fear and Trembling* (III, 41) about infinite resignation: "Infinite resignation is the shirt described in the old
folk tale: the thread is spun with tears, the cloth is bleached with tears,
the shirt is sewn with tears; and yet it is a better protection than iron
and steel." This emphasizes very clearly that Kierkegaard sought in the
lugere et detestari rejected by Spinoza what *intelligere* should have given
him. That is why he said despair is the beginning of philosophy. It can
be rendered in the words of the Psalm: *De profundis ad te, Domine,
clamavi*, as a dimension of thought hidden from theoretical thinking.

historic event. In his journals he repeats more than once that he will never call by its true name that which hurled him beyond the boundaries of normal existence, and sternly forbids his future biographers to try to find out about it, even warning that he has made every effort to baffle those who are too inquisitive. Biographers and commentators would usually consider themselves obligated to honor a wish so explicitly stated, and not try to pry into his secret. But Kierkegaard's literary legacy—both his books and his journals—imperatively demands something different of us: he says that he wants to carry his secret to the grave, but he does everything to insure that it will remain on earth. "If I had had faith—I would not have had to leave Regina" and the "repetition" which "must give him back the ability to be a husband"—these statements alone are more than enough to establish the concrete fact about which he has forbidden us to inquire. He repudiated faith in order to gain knowledge; he repeated what our forefather had done—and the result was the last thing he could have expected—powerlessness. Knowledge turned out to be a gift similar to the one requested of the gods by the mythical Midas: everything was changed into gold, but then it all either died or was transformed into a lovely phantom, a shadow, an image of reality, just as Regina Olsen became for Kierkegaard a shadow or phantom. This is why he made a connection between all his observations and original sin, and why sin has such central significance, and is so indissolubly linked with faith, in his existential philosophy. Only faith can pave man's way to the tree of life—but in order to attain faith one must lose reason. And then, only then, in the light or the shadow of the Absurd, will the miracle of "repetition" take place: the phantoms and shadows will become living beings and man will be cured of his powerlessness before what knowledge calls the "impossible" or the "necessary." For the opposite of sin is freedom. Kierkegaard felt the burden of "sin" in everything—but at the same time he also felt that only the idea of sin as it exists in Holy Scripture can inspire man and raise him above those self-evidencies on whose plane our thinking wanders, to the sphere where divine possibilities dawn for man. In contrast to theoretical philosophy, which tries to forget, or, more precisely, tries to make us forget, about sin and the horrors of sinful life on earth, and therefore aims at fitting even original sin into moral categories, i.e., disposing of it as oppressive and foolish nonsense, existential philosophy sees it as a revelation of what is most needful for us. With an enthusiasm which will probably bring a shudder to more than one soul among the educated readers of today, in *Repetition,* the same book in which he bears witness to his own powerlessness and the powerlessness of every man who has exchanged the fruit of the tree of life for the fruit of the tree of knowledge, that powerlessness which was so unexpectedly and vividly revealed to him when he suddenly became convinced that the woman he loved had, without apparent cause, turned into a shadow, Kierkegaard writes, again referring to Job: "I need you: I need a man whose voice truly cries out to heaven where God and Satan are forging their terrible plots against man. Lament, implore. The Lord will not be afraid . . . Speak, raise your voice, cry out. God can speak even louder: for all the thunder is at His disposal. And thunder is the answer, it is the explanation: firm, trustworthy, primordial. God's answer, even if it smashes man to pieces, is superior to all the chattering by human wis-

dom and human cowardice about divine justice." * Even
Kierkegaard was rarely able to find such original words to
express the position in which the human soul finds itself
which it touches upon the secret of Holy Scripture: God's
thunder is the answer to human wisdom, to our logic, to
our truths. It breaks to bits, not man, but the "impossibilities" placed by human wisdom—which is at the same time
human cowardice—between itself and the Creator. Everything "terrible" in Scripture is not terrible, for it is of God.
On the contrary: the "terrible" in Scripture is irresistibly
attractive to Kierkegaard. As is well known, Kierkegaard's
father, driven to despair by poverty and the cruelty of
those whose servant he was as a child, cursed God when
he was still only a boy.† The old man could not or would
not conceal from his children this horrifying event of his
own childhood—and young Sören was compelled throughout his life to remember his father's sin as if it were his
own. Not only did he not protest about this to God, Who
had held him responsible for an act he did not commit, but
he would not even admit the possibility of such a protest.
"Life," he writes, "vociferously confirms the teaching of
the Scriptures that God visits the iniquity of the fathers
upon the children unto the third and fourth generation.
And it is useless to try to get rid of what is horrible in this
by passing it off as a Jewish doctrine. Christianity has
never maintained that it put man in the privileged position of being able to start from the very beginning in all

* III, 182.
† In his journal (I, 238) Kierkegaard describes in these words what his
father told him: "A terrible thing happened to a man who, as a little
boy, herded sheep on a heath in Jutland, endured much, went hungry,
and, reduced to complete misery, ran to the top of a hill and cursed God:
and that man could not forget about it even when he was eighty-two
years old."

external matters." * It is always thus in his writings: the point at which common sense and "natural justice" become indignant over the "terrible" and the "thunders of God" described in the pages of Holy Scripture is where Kierkegaard's thinking always finds what it, what man, needs most of all, "the one thing that is needful." Of course, it is very tempting to dismiss Kierkegaard and all his insights by citing the exaggerated and unusual sensibility which always accompanies a nervous disorder. And, if we approach the thinking of Kierkegaard with our usual criteria, there will be little left of it. All the horrors he suffered can then be easily challenged. He said himself that men cannot bear what madness and death have to tell them. It may be that in a certain sense, i.e., "practically speaking," men are right: but they have not the strength to reduce madness and death to silence. Madness and death can be driven away temporarily, but they will return, and, having returned, will carry out their purpose: they will ask man questions which he would rather forget forever. Kierkegaard was aware of all this; in *Stages on Life's Way* he wrote: "The bustling parsons and their advisors from the laity, who wish to deliver man from fear of the terrible, are opposed to me. It is true that anyone who wants to attain anything in this life would be better off forgetting about the terrible. But anyone who sets himself problems of a religious nature must open his soul to the terrible." †

And it cannot be disputed that the "religious" and the terrible are bound together by mysterious ties. This was no secret to the Greeks: Plato even defined philosophy

* V, 69.
† IV, 341.

as μελέτη θανάτου, training for death, and the enigmatic πεισιθάνατος mentioned by Kierkegaard was far closer to Plato than one might think; Kierkegaard even considered him a precursor of St. Bernard of Clairvaux. But—here we once again return to the basic question: what can man do when confronted with the horrors of existence? The Greeks sought salvation in κάθαρσις: in liberation from attachment to the transitory and the finite, which are by their very nature doomed to destruction. Any attempt to revolt against Necessity, to which even the gods must submit, was considered madness by the Greeks. Their wisdom led to renunciation; other than that they saw no escape for man. Greek wisdom was unacceptable to Kierkegaard. He wanted to think, he wanted everyone to think, that for God there is no Necessity. And yet in the name of Christianity he summons us to the bliss of κάθαρσις, purification. But strangely enough, in contrast to the Greeks and an overwhelming majority of Christian preachers, he paints such a shockingly dismal picture of the "bliss" of those who have experienced purification that it would reduce even the most ardent of his supporters to fear and trembling—moreover, a fear by no means full of awe, but instead ordinary, almost animal. Kierkegaard could not remain in the middle, among the "more or less's" within which men are accustomed to hide themselves from the summonses and secrets of existence. If Necessity is primordial, uncreated, if there is no justice higher than it, then not only is the bliss reserved for men by Christianity worse than the most horrible torment imaginable—so, too, is the bliss of God.

The life of Christ is one uninterrupted failure of love, like the life of Sören Kierkegaard. "Quiet despair" had also made its home in Christ, the only begotten Son of God, and over him there hung the same curse that hangs over man: he was powerless; he wanted to, but could not, stretch forth his hand to the tree of life; instead he plucked the fruit of the tree of knowledge and all reality turned into a shadow that continually slipped from his grasp. There is no other way out than to accept man's powerlessness and the powerlessness of God, and to regard this as bliss. One must not become embittered by the horrors of life, but seek them out just as God, Who became incarnate in human form for that very purpose, sought them. Immortality and eternal life exist in the ethical. The idea of voluntary sacrifice reigns supreme. Not sacrifice of the sort that directed Abraham's hand when he raised the knife to Isaac; Abraham believed that even if he should kill his son, he would regain him: for God nothing is impossible. This kind of sacrifice is pleasing to God, but unacceptable to the ethical. The ethical, which takes pride in its own powerlessness, forbids man to entertain thoughts of a God for Whom everything is possible. Abraham must offer his son in sacrifice to a God for Whom, as for man, the return of the dead to life is an absolute impossibility. God can shed tears, can grieve—but can accomplish nothing. However, this is all that is necessary, for love and charity are revealed in all their spotless purity only when they are doomed to inaction. In his journal for 1854—that is to say, in the final year of his life—Kierkegaard wrote: "When Christ cried out: My God, My God, why hast thou forsaken me?—this was terrible for Christ, and so it has usually been described. But it seems to me that it was still more terrible for God to hear. It is terrible to be so inflexible! But this is still not what is most terrible:

the most horrible thing is to be so inflexible and at the same time to be love: this is endless, profound, abysmal suffering! Alas, I, too, unhappy man that I am, have experienced something of this sort, have experienced this conflict—not to be in a position to alter my course, and, at the same time, to love—and what I have experienced helps me to form, from a great distance, of course, a very great distance, a faint idea of the suffering of divine love." *

When God hears the cries of His tormented, exhausted Son, He cannot even answer him, just as Kierkegaard could not answer Regina Olsen. Above Him stands the ethical, deaf and therefore indifferent to all, with its implacable "you must": you must be inflexible. And one cannot even ask: whence came this unlimited power of the ethical? The only thing left for us to do is to imitate God and the Son of God incarnate in man: without asking any questions, to bear the horrors which descend upon us and find our bliss in that. We must suppose that even God Himself felt bliss at having delivered His Son to torment: He had gratified the ethical. And this, Kierkegaard informs us, is the content of the good tidings Christianity has brought men: Christianity's aim is the realization on earth of the "ethical." But then how is Christianity different from the wisdom of the Greeks? The Greeks also taught that a virtuous man will be blissful even in the bull of Phalaris. For the Greeks, philosophy was not yet mere theoretical speculation, but a kind of action. Plato's κάθαρσις, as we have seen, is still an action, but the Platonically minded Epictetus unmasked with almost Socratic candor and sarcasm those philosophers who, instead of following the example of

* *Journal*, II, 364.

Kierkegaard

Zeno and Chryssip, memorized and commented upon excerpts from their works. If existential philosophy has not thought of anything different, then what is the reason for forsaking Socrates and exchanging Hellenic wisdom for Biblical revelation? Why should anyone turn his back on Athens and place his hopes in Jerusalem?

However, the surprising thing is that Pascal, who was so sincerely well-disposed toward Epictetus, whose austerity of life and indifference to earthly blessings even today impress everyone favorably, still felt the existence in Epictetus of something extremely hostile to him, something he could not accept, which he expressed in the words *superbe diabolique*. Even Kierkegaard himself inexplicably draws back from Epictetus and calls him a slave. He never gave any reason for this harsh judgment, but it would hardly be wrong to assume that he, like Pascal, perceived an element of *superbe diabolique* in Epictetus' soul. Epictetus, like Socrates, considered the "ethical" supreme and himself in bondage to the ethical, and, as a dutiful bondman, he compelled himself to live in those categories in which he thought; in this "philosophical" life he found, and commanded others to find, the happiness to which a rational being can aspire. As he read Epictetus, Kierkegaard must have recalled the words of the Apostle Paul: all that is not of faith is sin (no doubt Pascal, too, remembered them.) Or his own reflections on the father of faith: if the ethical is supreme, then Abraham is lost. Lost—for the ethical would maim him as no torturer has ever maimed his victim, if he did not forget his Isaac. What disturbed Kierkegaard most in Epictetus was that Epictetus unquestionably did live in the categories in which he thought, and found that sort of life completely satisfying.

The more consistent Epictetus was and the more his life conformed to the decrees of the rational and the ethical, the stronger Kierkegaard's exasperation and suspicion became. We hardly ever find Spinoza mentioned in Kierkegaard's writings—although it is known that he had in his library all the works of Spinoza and was very familiar with them. But in all likelihood Kierkegaard was inwardly provoked and offended by Spinoza even more than by Epictetus. *Acquiescentia in se ipso ex ratione oriri potest et ea acquiescentia qua ex ratione oritur maxima est quae dari potest* ("Inward peace can be born of reason and the peace which is born of reason is the greatest gift it can give")—these words by Spinoza, as well as the words which crown his ethic: *Beatitudo non est praemium virtutis, sed ipsa virtus* ("Happiness is not the reward of virtue, but virtue itself"), must have sounded to Kierkegaard like a sentence of death. All human hopes rest on virtue and reason, which is at the same time free will; in Spinoza's work the ethical rejoices in its complete victory. I repeat, Kierkegaard very seldom speaks of Spinoza, but he does not venture to attack him—perhaps in part because Schleiermacher, whom Kierkegaard held in high regard, positively worshipped Spinoza, and also perhaps because he himself was impressed in spite of everything by the profound thinking and detachment of the Dutch recluse who scorned all that men think valuable (*divitiae, honores, libidines*—riches, honors, passions—according to Spinoza, this is what all ordinary human interests amount to) for the sake of *amor dei intellectualis* (intellectual love of God). But there is no doubt that Spinoza, with his *acquiescentia* and *beatitudo,* troubled Kierkegaard's heart much more than Epictetus. If there was any man, at least in modern times, who came close to realizing that most difficult of commandments: thou shalt love the Lord thy God, certainly that man was Spinoza, and he was also first among those for whom virtue itself meant happiness. But it is for precisely that reason that he horrified Kierkegaard even more than Epictetus had horrified Pascal, for the more perfect he was, in the human sense, the more evident was his *superbe diabolique*. He was truly capable of bearing, and bore with tranquil and serene heart, *utramque faciem fortunae*. Everything took second place and lost its significance *sub specie aeternitatis,* with the exception of spiritual love of God and a similarly spiritual joy in virtue. The greatest genius is, at the same time, the greatest sinner: it is "hard" to admit this, as Kierkegaard makes clear to us, but one cannot remain silent about it. Socrates and Spinoza, and even the modest Epictetus, were not righteous men, as we have been accustomed to think, but sinners who by their righteousness concealed from themselves and from others the powerlessness of unbelief. I repeat once more that perhaps they are the sinners over whom, it is said, there will be more rejoicing in heaven than over dozens and hundreds of righteous men—but then, the passage from Scripture which tells of this is just as incomprehensible and enigmatic to us as the passage in which it is said that the sun rises for good men and evil alike, or the passage about Cana in Galilee, which is intended to persuade us that God can concern Himself with such trifles as the entertainment of guests at someone's wedding. Hegel, in speaking of Cana, purposely mentioned Voltaire's most malicious and blasphemous gibes at the Bible, and Socrates, Epictetus, and Spinoza would all have sided with Hegel. Hegel was not speaking for Himself: he was speaking in the name of reason and ethics, in the name of wisdom. Is wisdom then the expression of *superbe diabolique?* That is, of the greatest sin, of which it is written: *initium omnis peccati superbia?* ("Pride is the beginning of every sin.")

XIV

The Autonomy of the Ethical

*Both of you died and one attained the
same bliss as the other (the witness for
the truth). Think about that—and then
see if you do not say the same thing as
I: what sort of crying injustice is this,
that we have attained equal bliss.*

KIERKEGAARD

"My severity is not of my own making," Kierkegaard
tells us. But whence came the severity of Socrates, of Epictetus, of Spinoza? And—the time has come to ask one
more question which is perhaps, in its own way, even more
important: why did the Greek sages, who glorified virtue,
elaborate so little and, as it seems, only lightly upon the
difficulties to be found in the way of the righteous, while
Kierkegaard's journals and his other writings are filled to
overflowing with weeping and wailing about these horrors? Kierkegaard asked that men imitate Christ in their
own lives, and seek from life, not joy, but sorrow. The
Greek κάθαρσις could be summed up, without exaggera-

194

tion, as an imitation of Socrates, and the Greeks taught of
the wise man's bliss in the bull of Phalaris. And even what
Kierkegaard says about the poverty, humiliations, etc.,
willingly accepted by Christians finds a parallel in the
teachings of the school of the Cynics, which derived from
Socrates. There is a well-known saying, attributed to An-
tisthenes: μανείην μᾶλλον ἢ ἡσθείην ("I would rather go mad
than experience pleasure"). But no matter how stern the
demands of the wise men of Greece were, not one of them,
with the exception of Hegesias, ever thought it necessary
to depict the difficulties and horrors of a virtuous existence
in the painstaking manner of Kierkegaard—they all preferred to speak of the beauty and sublimeness of the just
life. No one ever heard Socrates complain, and he certainly had reason to complain. He drank the cup of poison
brought to him by his jailer as if it were a healing potion:
how movingly was this story told, in the words of the disciples who were present at his death, by the divine Plato
for the edification of posterity! The same may be said of
Spinoza: he, too, knew want and sickness, suffered persecution, died young—but this left no outward traces visible
in his philosophy. Like Socrates, he truly was not dis-
tressed that fate had given him, not an easy and happy
life, but a difficult and sorrowful one. His virtue would
have been consolation enough for him even if everything
described in the books and journals of Kierkegaard had
fallen to his lot; it would have defended him against *'lugere et detestari'* and the despair which accompanies *lugere et detestari*. Wisdom itself was speaking through the
voice of Epictetus when he asserted that, had Socrates
been in the position of Priam or Oedipus, he would have
remained calm, would have said serenely: if it pleases the

gods, let it be so. Socrates never heard of Job; but had he been able to meet Job, he would have tried to cure him in his usual manner: with dialectic and irony. Kierkegaard's books and journals would have evoked great indignation from him and inspired him with unfeigned disgust. How could anyone think that Job was right, not when he said: God gave, God has taken away, but when, deaf to reason, he wailed and cursed senselessly! A rational man must *aequo animo utramque faciem fortunae ferre:* everything in the world is given to man as a loan, not as a possession, and it can always be taken back again. And Socrates would have been even more disturbed by Kierkegaard's assurances that each man decides for himself what his Isaac is to be, for this is free will, the truest, most genuine free will, an orgy of free will. Not only man, but the gods themselves cannot, as they imagine, decide what is important and what is not: it is not because something is holy that the gods love it; the gods can and must love only what is holy. Bliss, for both mortals and immortals, is not to be found in the "finite," in transitory joys and the absence of equally transitory sorrows, but in "good," which has no connection with either our joys or our sorrows, and which is made of an entirely different stuff from that which men usually prize, or love. This is why, even in Epictetus, "you must" towers above and dominates every "I want." But it does not tower as it does in Kierkegaard's work. Epictetus, like Socrates, would never have dreamed of saying that the bliss promised by his philosophy is worse, in human estimation, than any misfortune we may suffer. Philosophy does not even pay any attention to the "general estimation" and what people consider to be their misfortunes; if it does, by any chance, think of them, it is only to dismiss them as worthless, petty, and futile. Even Abraham's sacrifice would not have perplexed the sage of Greece: "if it pleases the gods, let it be so," he would have said. Anyone who is unable to ascend to such heights of intellectual vision is not worthy to be called a man; he is a miserable slave, chained by mean and despicable attachments to the transitory. The free man rises above all this, sets out for the pure realm of the ethical and the eternal where the noise and tumult of earth cannot be heard. Freedom is by no means the possibility Kierkegaard declares it to be, citing Holy Scripture; freedom is the possibility, granted to men by the gods, of choice between good and evil. And this possibility, which makes us equal to the immortals, has been given to every man. Socrates wanted to be free, and he was free; he sought the "sublime"—and only the sublime—in life, and found it. His philosophy was the exercise of freedom in the pursuit of the sublime. Anyone who wishes to enter the Kingdom of God must follow the example of Socrates. And it makes no difference at all whether a man happens to suffer greatly in life, whether he is persecuted or not. If Socrates had enjoyed general respect, and had died a natural death, nothing would have been essentially changed by this; his successes in life would have detracted as little from his worth as his failures had added to it. The wise man takes neither the one nor the other into account. This is why he proudly proclaims his independence even from almighty fate: everything that is not within our power ($\tau\grave{\alpha}$ $o\mathring{v}\kappa$ $\dot{\epsilon}\phi$' $\mathring{\eta}\mu\hat{\imath}\nu$) is a matter of indifference to us. No one, not even the gods, can punish or reward him. The keen mind of Pascal, of course, correctly saw in this lofty "independence" of the Greek sage from God, which so impresses everyone, that *superbe diabolique,* that pride of which Holy Scripture speaks; and perhaps no one has been able to expose for us the nature of pride, both human and diabolic, as clearly as Epictetus. Indeed, Epictetus himself, who could not and did not wish to conceal anything, gives us a hint of the required "explanation." In his words, "philosophy has its beginning in the helplessness of man and in his awareness of his own powerlessness before Necessity." Pride, as Holy Scripture represents it, or what Epictetus calls the freedom and independence of man, is only a shell, only a façade, behind which he hides his powerlessness before necessity. And can there really be any doubt of the origin of this pride? Can there be any question that Pascal was right when he discerned *superbe diabolique* in the wisdom of that remote spiritual descendant of Socrates? But Kierkegaard was even more deeply aware of it. For him, the ethical of Socrates and Epictetus offered the greatest offense. When the horrors of reality advanced upon him, He turned his eyes to the God of the Bible, for Whom nothing is impossible. And at times it seemed to him that God answered him, that God had answered his prayers and would free him from the nightmarish and senseless idea, which had become rooted in his being, that in the Absurd of faith the "immutable" truths obtained by our forefather from the tree of knowledge would disappear without trace and the way to the tree of life would be laid open. But the years went by and the nightmare did not vanish, but grew and grew. And then he forced himself to turn his attention away from the impossible and concentrate wholly upon the possible. Even in the healing of the sick he made himself see, not a miraculous vanquishing of powerlessness— powerlessness cannot be vanquished—but only the love

and charity of the Apostle. He would have preferred it if
Peter had limited himself to a mere word of consolation,
in order to put an end once and for all to his futile and
tormenting hopes that for God everything is possible, that
by God's word the blind will see, the deaf hear, the lepers
be cleansed, the dead be raised. Socrates dispensed with
that sort of God. He knew for certain, through human reason, that the impossible does not exist, that the impossible
is impossible for that very reason, that it has never existed
anywhere and never will, and that all must therefore come
to a halt before impossibility. He was no less certain that
reason does not deceive us and there are no magic formu-
las in the world which can free man from the power of
rational truths; that, on the contrary, man has a will which
commands him to love these truths and obey them. The
fundamental thesis—not of Biblical revelation, as Kierkegaard sometimes maintained in moments of doubt, but of
Greek wisdom—was that sin is the result of the obstinacy
and stubbornness of the will. Alcibiades himself did not
deny that, if he had wanted to, he could have followed the
example of Socrates in everything and become a model of
every virtue. He could have, but he did not wish to; he
was attracted by the good things of this world—*divitiae,
honores, libidines*—and wallowed in the filth of vices. He
became a sinner for whom there was no salvation either in
this world or the next, for, as Plato explained to us, the
man who devotes himself, not to philosophy, but to his
desires, will never attain the salvation which is reserved
for the righteous and the righteous alone. In our finite existence, as experience shows, the sun rises for good men
and evil alike. Here it often happens that the man who
does not work eats, and the man who works has nothing to

eat. Here the lilies of the field, which think of nothing and do not worry about the future, are clothed more richly than King Solomon. Here the fowls of the air sow not, neither do they reap, nor gather into barns—and they have all that they need. All this is as the Scriptures tell us. Socrates tells us that this is a "crying injustice." He even "knows" that "there," there is another law: he who does not work (κάθαρσις is work) does not eat. "There" the ethical keeps step with the rational. Whenever Kierkegaard feels obliged to "turn his attention" away from the "miraculous," to forget that for God nothing is impossible, it is not within his power, indeed he has no desire, to contend with Socrates and his "ethical!" What if God does forgive sins —man can still never regain his innocence. Forgiveness is only forgiveness, only oblivion; even God cannot abolish, destroy, extirpate the sin which runs through existence —*quod factum est infectum esse nequit*—there is no escape, either for God or for men, from the horrors of existence. But, if this is so, if these horrors are so inextricably bound up with existence—then not only must they not be hidden away, they must not even be covered over; they must be brought to view, and must not be avoided, but sought out, not only accepted, but given our blessing. The pagans taught that the wise man can be blissful even in the Bull of Phalaris; Christianity, transforming itself into the ethical, "goes further"—but in the same direction: only in the Bull of Phalaris will man find true bliss. A man who "imitates" Socrates will not fear the bull of Phalaris, but he who "imitates" Christ will be dismayed at escaping it . . . . Pascal saw *superbe diabolique* in Epictetus. But Epictetus wanted only to emulate Socrates, who was the wisest of men, but nevertheless a man. What should we call the desire to become equal to Christ, i.e., God, by imitating him?

Once again it must be said that Kierkegaard was astute enough to see the difficulty concealed here. In one of his edifying discourses he proposes this question: is it right for a man, in defense of the truth, to run the risk of having those near to him tear him limb from limb and thereby take upon themselves the most grievous of sins? And he answers: it is not right, even though Christ himself did this. Christ was able to do it because he has the power to forgive all, to forgive even those who crucified him—but a man who does not possess this power must not, even in bearing witness for the truth, overstep the limits set for him. And yet, although Kierkegaard plainly realizes that man must not wish to become God's equal, he sings his passionate hymns to suffering as ecstatically as ever, both in his edifying discourses and his other writings, and imperiously demands that men seek out martyrdom in their earthly lives. The older he grows, the more violent and unrestrained his frenzied preaching becomes. He does not venture to attack Luther openly, but at times Luther's *sola fide* drives him into a rage. "Picture two believers," *

he says, addressing the reader; "one of them has passed his life on earth happily, without knowing poverty or sickness, has enjoyed general respect, and been a happy family man. The other man, on the contrary, has suffered persecution during his entire life in defense of the truth. Both of them are Christians and both of them hope for bliss in the next life. I have no authority," he continues, "and I am

---

* We would not go wrong in assuming that these two believers are Bishop Mynster and Kierkegaard himself; the details of Kierkegaard's thinking on this subject give clear enough evidence of that.

not about to take exception to this, although if you should come across a man who does possess authority, he would probably have something quite different to say to you, and you would realize to your horror that your Christianity is only a word, and that hell awaits you. I am far from considering this view an exaggeration, but I have no authority and it would not be right for me to say that I believe you will find bliss, as if I were a genuine witness for the truth or a hero of faith. But I do say to you: remember how you have lived and how he has lived. Remember what he had to sacrifice, he who renounced everything: both that which seems at first glance hardest of all to give up, and that which is all the harder to give up with the passage of time. Think of how he suffered—how painfully, how long! And at the same time you were living happily in the bosom of your family, your wife loved you with all her heart, your children were a joy to you—only think what a comfort it is to live your life in such peace and tranquility—and this was your life for all your days on earth . . . and then think of the witness for the truth. You did not live in idleness (I do not think that), but your work did not consume all your time: you were able to rest and refresh yourself; you may not have lived in luxury, but you did not know want . . . In short, your life was passed in quiet joy, but his—alas!—was hard work and suffering day in and day out. And now you have both attained bliss; you have attained what he has." Further on Kierkegaard tells us more specifically what the "witness for the truth" had to bear, how he was driven and persecuted, and after that he concludes: "Then both of you died and one attained the same bliss as the other. Think about that and then see if you do not say the same thing as I: what sort of "crying injustice" is this, that we have attained equal bliss." * I hope that the reader will not complain because I have quoted such a long passage. It gives us an extremely vivid description of what the religious becomes when it yields to the temptation of the "ethical," or, if you prefer, it shows us the devices to which the ethical can resort when it finds it necessary to "distract our attention" from the religious. Kierkegaard, who composed such fiery hymns to suffering, Kierkegaard, who scornfully rejected earthly joys, even in the other world cannot settle his dispute with Mynster regarding these joys and sufferings. Even in the other world where eternal bliss has fallen to his lot, the "witness for the truth" does not forget the insults he received on earth, which he himself had sought, or the joys he "willingly" rejected. Neither immortality, nor bliss, nor eternity can erase the memories of the ignominy he experienced in his finite existence, and even less can they replace the joys of which he was deprived. It is as if he were repeating the words of Lermontov's Demon: I involuntarily envied imperfect human joy. This imperfect joy is better than immortality, better than eternity, better than the heavenly bliss reserved for us by the ethical. One step further, and he would be saying: it is better to be a day laborer on earth than a king in the world of shadows. The only thing that can reassure him is his confidence that even "there" the ethical will retain its power. Of course, even there it will not be able to add anything to his bliss, nor to the bliss of his companion. The fruit of the tree of life is beyond his reach; only the fruit of the tree of knowledge is available to him. We found out long ago from Falstaff that the ethical cannot

* XI, 15, 16.

reward; it can only punish. And, even if the Almighty Himself does open the gates of paradise "impartially" to the one that bore witness for the truth and the one that did not, the ethical will not give up its prerogatives. It will poison the "bliss" of the man who did not work, it will turn heaven into hell for him, so that the witness for the truth will be able to say in all sincerity, as he looks upon his unhappy companion in bliss: "I thank You, Lord, that I am not as that publican." To be sure, even Kierkegaard does not speak as harshly as this. But still, when he mentions the parable of the Pharisee and the publican, in passing, it is true, he cannot help putting in a kind word for the Pharisee. It could hardly be otherwise: Christ, in this parable, did "overstate" his love for sinners all too far. Once the ethical intervenes, it must decide the fates of men itself. Most men would not venture to revise this parable as Kierkegaard did—but nevertheless virtue always collects its tribute. After reading about the publican, a man says to himself: "I thank You, Lord, that I am not as that Pharisee." And, in fact, if the way to bliss passes through the ethical, if bliss comes from the tree of knowledge and not from the tree of life, if it was not God, but the serpent that revealed the truth to the first man—then there is no other way out; man not only can, but must, save himself by his own powers, as the ancients taught. This is the only real salvation. And so once again it becomes necessary to amend the Scriptures: where it is said: *initium peccati superbia,* we shall say: the beginning of righteousness is *superbe diabolique.*

XV

The Enslaved Will

*Who would hesitate between choosing
to trust in God and not choosing to do
so? But my choice is not a free one. I am
hardly aware of my own freedom, for I
am wholly in the power of Necessity. I
do not choose the path to God, for the
choice is not mine.*

KIERKEGAARD

"My severity is not of my own making." We have gradu-
ally begun to understand where it does originate. "Look
out over the field of battle"—the most hardened foe does
not deal with the vanquished as mercilessly as the ethical.
But we must not forget that, although it carefully guards
this secret from the eyes of outsiders, the "ethical" did not
itself invent its stony "you must's," but took them ready-
made from its master, Necessity. Kant told us: "you must,
therefore you can"; he derived the ethical from freedom,
intelligible freedom, it is true, but freedom nonetheless.
However, closer attention reveals something different. The

statement should be: "you cannot, therefore you must not." The source of moral imperatives is not freedom, but Necessity. That severity is certainly not of Kierkegaard's making, but neither does it come from the ethical. If the ethical does not clearly understand this, it is only because it wants to be autonomous, to have its own laws, to be the supreme and ultimate principle, bound by no other laws, and the equal of reason, which also and for the same reasons conceals from all the fact that it is in bondage to Necessity. Only here can we find out why Kierkegaard demanded so insistently that the knight of faith pass through the stage of resignation; why, at the same time, he saw sin as the swoon of freedom; and, moreover, why he simultaneously determined that the opposite of sin is not virtue, but freedom. It is true that in so doing he was citing "dialectic," but we will be closer to him if we leave dialectic to the Greeks and Hegel, and begin to seek other sources for Kierkegaard's insight. However much we may expound upon "dialectic," in the last analysis, as I have already indicated, it always presupposes a certain self-movement: even Jakob Böhme "eagerly strove" to find a dialectical process in the world and in life, and, as is well known, it was chiefly this that made him attractive to the authors of German idealism. At times it even seems—although at first glance this appears paradoxical—that the German idealists, by the whim or the malicious intent of history, felt almost involuntarily obliged to demonstrate a retrospective influence upon the inflexible Böhme and drive him into the orbit of their own ideas. But when Kierkegaard freely and skillfully employs dialectic to show us the process by which the knight of resignation becomes the knight of daring, who is also the knight of faith, he is not at all interested in making us see this change of appearance as comprehensible, that is, natural in its regularity and continuity. In his work, dialectic always accompanies entirely different movements of the mind, which by their very nature neither demand nor seek explanations, but are rather directed at proclaiming the uselessness and futility of all explanations. And indeed, what sort of explanations can there be where, according to the testimony of our reason and experience, all possibilities come to an end, and there arises the truly mad problem of breaking through to a God for Whom nothing is impossible? And here Kierkegaard summons up his "severity," his ethical, his Necessity, and leads the knight of resignation to them. God, in concert with Satan, thought to "tempt" man: He sent Job's misfortunes upon him, He demanded Abraham's son. What is temptation? For reason, our knowledge, and our ethics, there is no answer to that question. Therefore, with characteristic confidence, they reject it: temptation is the fruit of idle fancy and, in fact, neither God nor the devil tempts man. Job lost his livestock and his children—this happened naturally; Abraham killed, or attempted to kill, his son—that, too, happened naturally, in a fit of mental derangement. This meaningless word must be dropped from the vocabulary of the enlightened man; Job must be left on his dunghill, and Abraham before the body of the son he murdered. The knight of resignation is definitely sure that there is no escape from the reality he sees, and no appeal from it. What has happened has happened; one must accept and submit to it. Hegel "deified reality," but we cannot deify it, if, having subjugated man, it is itself no longer subject to anything! Hegel demanded that our thinking draw its truths from reality and add nothing of itself, and he was right; only such truths can withstand experience and time and eternity. But if reality is rational, if we can derive truth only from reality, then elementary consistency demands of us that we pass Biblical revelation through the filter of the truths obtained from reality. And, conversely, if revelation receives the sanction of truth, it must wear the halter of reality. Zeus himself told Chryssip this many hundreds of years before Hegel, as we have already mentioned more than once. Plato, too—I shall repeat this once again, as it cannot be said too often—saw with all possible clarity and distinctness the existence in the world of Necessity, which is indifferent to everything, and is the source of all the wrongs and hardships which fall to the lot of men. Can we properly draw an opposite conclusion, and say that Necessity is always perceptible behind the severity? If that is correct, then, are not Kierkegaard's discourses on the incomparable and boundless ferocity of the Gospels evidence of how he struggled against Necessity and realized that he was ultimately powerless to overcome it? The more insistently, impulsively, and, in their own way, inspiredly his words ring out, the more we are convinced that here before us is one of the most important and significant of his "indirect communications," although it may be unintentional. He cannot openly say that the power of Necessity is intolerable to him; this would appear to everyone a banal and ridiculous truism. It is still harder for him to admit that he is helpless to throw off that power. Regardless of the fact that Necessity, like the ghost of Banquo, although immensely effective, is illusory, fate chose to give such a revolting and shameful form to Kierkegaard's powerlessness that even he did not have enough courage to speak directly of what was for him the most important thing in the world. He even avoided using the word "powerlessness," justifiably afraid that by doing so he might betray his secret. But, on the other hand, he could not remain silent about this, or, to be more precise, he could not talk about anything else but the powerlessness of man before Necessity—precisely because even those who call themselves Christians try with all their might to forget about "Necessity," to hush it up, as if they felt instinctively that before Necessity everything, even their faith, must retreat and bow low. From this came his "indirect communications"; at times he hides behind his pseudonyms (the majority of his books are signed, not with his own name, but with the most varied pseudonyms) or behind the plots of the stories he invented, which always tell about a struggle between a living man and an infinitely powerful and completely indifferent force; at other times he sings the praises of a Christianity which is just as destructive and merciless as Necessity itself. And this is again an expression of the strict internal consistency in Kierkegaard's writings; if a Christian must and can "turn his attention away from the miracle" in Biblical revelation (i.e., from the idea that for God everything is possible, that even Necessity has no authority over God), and see as its essence the preaching of a love that can do nothing, then the more highly we interpret Christianity, the closer it comes to theoretical philosophy. In other words, if Christianity is only a doctrine, only edification, then it has in no way "surpassed Socrates," whose spiritual demands answer the strictest requirements of morality.

But then, what is it that makes Kierkegaard "turn his attention" from the miraculous and summon us to power-

less love? We have already come up against this question
more than once; for Kierkegaard it is the basic question
to which he persistently returns, since it is the *articulus
stantis et cadentis* of existential philosophy. To turn your
attention away from the miraculous means to admit the
existence of *veritates aeternae*—which are also *veritates
emancipatae a Deo*—truths independent of God, truths to
which God is subordinate; it means to admit that for God
not everything is possible. And to admit that for God
not everything is possible is equivalent to admitting—as
Kierkegaard himself has told us—that there is no God.
Moreover, the Christianity which amounts to a doctrine,
although an extraordinarily sublime one, of *veritates
aeternae* is a denial of God, and the sublimeness of its
doctrine is in direct proportion to the obstinacy and persistence of its denial. How often Kierkegaard himself said
that Christianity is not a "doctrine," and warned against
the "Dozenten" who turn the word of God into a rigid
system of regulations, arranged in sections, chapters, and
paragraphs! And yet at the same time we read in his
Journal: "They would like to convince us that objections
to Christianity come from doubt. This is a pure misunderstanding. Objections to Christianity have as their source
insubordination, unwillingness to obey, rebellion against
all authority. Consequently, until now, those who have
fought doubt with intellectual weapons, instead of com-
batting that insurrection ethically, have fought in vain." *
At first glance it seems that the "ethical struggle" with
unwillingness to obey can in fact be contrasted with what
Kierkegaard calls an intellectual struggle with doubt; that
in the sphere of the religious only the first kind of struggle

* *Journal*, I, 313.

is appropriate; and that this is the task of existential philosophy. But has he not told us: "To believe that what, for human reason, lies beyond the limits of the possible is possible for God: this is the most decisive provocation to offense"? * We have more than once before considered this enigmatic moment in the history of Kierkegaard's spiritual struggles. It is perfectly obvious that in his case there can be no talk of "insurrection," of unwillingness to obey. More than anything else in the world, he needed faith in a God for Whom that which, according to human reason, lies beyond the limits of the possible, is possible. He continually asserted: "If I had had faith—I would not have had to part from Regina." But he just as invariably repeated: "I cannot make the movement of faith." Why not? Was it because of "unwillingness to obey"? Because of pride? It may have been because of pride, but not the *superbe diabolique* which we discovered in the most humble Epictetus and that wisest of men, Socrates, and which—as we shall presently see—has nothing in common with the usual conception of pride. "Who would hesitate," testifies Kierkegaard, "between choosing to trust in God and not choosing to do so? But my choice is not a free one. I am hardly aware of my own freedom, for I am wholly in the power of Necessity. I do not choose the path to God, for the choice is not mine." † The inhuman and terrifying feeling of anguish which accompanied Kierkegaard's awareness that man cannot choose his own path is expressed with even greater force in his short essay "The Thorn in the Flesh." I shall quote it in German, in order

---

* *Ibid.*, VIII, 115.
† IV, 319. Cf. III, 48: "It is completely impossible for me to make the final movement, the paradoxical movement of faith, whether or not I am obliged to make it, and even though I am more than willing to make it."

not to weaken by a second translation the original, which has probably already been somewhat weakened by its first:

Wenn man geängstigt wird, geht die Zeit langsam; und wenn man viel geängstigt wird, da ist selbst ein Augenblick langsam mordend; und wenn man zu Tode geängstigt wird, da steht die Zeit zuletzt stille. Laufen zu wollen schneller als je, und da nicht einen Fuss rücken zu können; den Augenblick kaufen zu wollen mit Aufopferung alles andern, und da zu lernen, dass er nicht feil ist, weil es nicht liegt an Jemands Wollen oder Laufen, sondern an Gottes Erbarmen.

He seeks God with all his soul, and upon the question of whether or not he will find God hangs his own fate and the fates of humanity and the universe—but he cannot make the "movement of faith," cannot stir even a limb; it is as if he were bewitched and his will paralyzed, or, as he himself said, in a swoon. And he clearly realizes this; he feels that he is in the power of Necessity, a power which he considers monstrous, hostile, and immensely hateful—but he has not the strength to overcome it. Can there be any talk here of insurrection, of rebellion—of unwillingness to "obey" God? To fling back the provocation to offense would have meant salvation for him. To believe that for God there is nothing impossible would mean salvation for all men. But he does not make, and cannot make, this movement, nor can anyone else in the world; Necessity has cast its spell over them all, and even Kierkegaard consults a doctor about the "truth," not daring to raise his eyes to the promised οὐδὲν ἀδυνατῆσει ὑμῖν (nothing shall be impossible unto you.)

Now we are at last able to ask: whence came this Necessity, and who or what gave it such boundless power over man? Kierkegaard has told us of stubbornness, inveteracy, insurrection, unwillingness to obey, etc.—but we have seen that the matter does not lie here. Kierkegaard quotes Scripture to prove that he is right, but we have also seen that he could not have found any support for himself in Scripture, and that the source of his "insight" was not Scripture, but Greek wisdom—he felt obliged to amend Scripture continually in order to adapt it, in some measure at least, to his own interpretations. And his severity increased in proportion to his revision of Scripture, so that Christian doctrine, which everyone had thought to be gentle, became in his hands a doctrine of infinite "ferocity." I have already quoted a number of passages from the entries in his journals and from his other writings which are evidence of this. I do not think it would be superfluous to add a few more, so that the reader may obtain a graphic picture of the incandescent atmosphere in which Kierkegaard's life was passed: only then will he see the connection between Kierkegaard's "severity" and existential philosophy. In one of his "Christian discourses" we read: "For, in truth, Christian doctrine inspires greater despair than the most grievous earthly suffering or the greatest misfortune." And in the same discourse he says: "Only through torture can a confession be extracted from a man (i.e., a confession of the truth of Christian doctrine): natural man will not willingly submit to that." * In his journal for 1850 he makes this entry: "Perfect love consists of loving that which makes us unhappy. Man cannot rightfully demand this. But God can, and there is something infinitely sublime in that. It must be said of the man

* *Christian Discourses*, 81.

213

who is religious in the strict sense of the word that, in loving God, he loves that which, even though it makes him blissful, makes him unhappy in this life." Strangely enough, he hastens to add here: "I have not the strength to understand this; moreover I am greatly afraid that in so doing I would become entangled in the most dangerous of the snares which have been set for us, which is to begin to believe in our own merits. But the man who is in the strictest sense religious is equal to this danger." * And, finally, in the last year of his life, he writes in the little magazine, *The Instant*, which he published himself and to which he was the only contributor: "God is so terrible (humanly speaking) in his love; it is so terrible (humanly speaking) to be loved by God. For as complement to the proposition: God is love, there is another proposition: He is your mortal enemy." †

The persistence with which Kierkegaard, throughout his writings, invariably returns to the theme of the horrors brought into the world by Christianity, and the miserly restraint of his language on the subject of the blessings reserved for witnesses for the truth, remind one of those righteous men who, in thundering against vice, endlessly describe its charms, and only in conclusion, hurriedly, as if discharging a tedious duty, add that atonement will have to be made eventually for the joys provided by vice. Kierkegaard portrays the horrors of Christianity with stunning power, but he paints no vivid pictures of its blessings. It is as though he wished to say: what possible blessings can there be in a world where the "religious-

* *Journal*, II, 163. Cf. 204, 261, 277, and still other entries made after 1850, in which the same subject is mentioned.
† XII, 54.

ethical" rules! He clearly has no desire to lead the way to
Christianity as it is understood by contemporary man,
who is obliged to turn his attention away from the miracle
(i.e., the idea that for God everything is possible) and be
content with a faith that has justified itself before the
court of reason. This is why he, for once in complete
agreement with Holy Scripture, never fails to remind us
that the greatest offense for man lies in the words: "for
God everything is possible." This means that the rational
and the ethical are not supreme, as Socrates had taught;
neither the immense number of "you cannot's" dictated by
reason, nor the even greater number of "you must's" imperiously set before man by the "ethical," can lead us to
the supreme principle, the ultimate source of being. It is
with this principle that "doubt" is waging its struggle to
the death, and only through a misunderstanding, as Kierkegaard has told us, can one see in this doubt an obstacle
to the faith which is basic to Biblical revelation and all
that Biblical revelation presupposes. As long as we rely
upon the guidance of reason, faith and the ability, given
us by faith, to see that for God everything is possible will
appear to be inconsistent with the truth. To say that for
God everything is possible means to offer a final and
decisive challenge to reason, which cannot tolerate any
other power as its equal and is therefore always trying to
undermine the strength of faith. Reason clearly, distinctly,
and definitely sees where possibilities come to an end;
it does not accept a faith which considers its claim to be
omniscient and all-seeing completely nonexistent and
looks for the truth to a living God Who is not bound to, or
limited by, anything. Kierkegaard himself has said to us
that faith begins where all possibilities end for reason. But

men do not want to think about this; they do not even want to glance in the direction where the fire of faith, which for some unknown reason they think to be sinister, has begun to burn with a flame that is destined to reduce reason to ashes. We have seen that, although they are very dissimilar in all else, Bonaventura and Hegel are in agreement on this; they both have confidence, the former in religion, the latter in philosophy and reason. It is different with Kierkegaard; he feels with his whole being that reason, by its very nature, strives to render faith defenseless, to suck it dry of its vital juices. He is sure that faith begins where reason ceases to be of service to man. Of course, he knows that men refuse to enter the realm in which reason can no longer guide them; the commonplace cannot bear what madness and death have to tell it. But it is for precisely that reason that Kierkegaard summons man from theoretical to existential philosophy, as if he wanted to force our thinking in the very direction toward which it is least inclined to go. It is not enough to say that the wise man will be blissful in the Bull of Phalaris—one must arrange one's entire life so that its substance will be exhausted by that bliss. We will recall that Kierkegaard not only remained aloof from Hegel and theoretical philosophy, but also drew a line between himself and the mystics; we would hardly be wrong in saying that what repelled him most of all in the mystics was the very thing that makes them so attractive to most people, even educated persons of our own time: their earthly bliss, humanly attainable right here on earth. Nowhere does he say this directly, but it seems that the more triumphantly and inspiredly a mystic conveys his joy at union with God, the more gloomy and impatient Kierkegaard becomes.

The mystic has already received his reward, and he has achieved it for himself by his own powers; is this not that *superbe diabolique* we have met before, which always conceals human powerlessness? In other words, have not the mystics, like the wise men of old, exchanged the fruit of the tree of life, which is inaccessible to them, for the fruit of the tree of knowledge, which after the fall of the first man became accessible to all? But if the fruit of the tree of knowledge is truly more valuable than the fruit of the tree of life, then why do the mystics so assiduously avoid the horrors of existence? They know that Socrates and Plato were convinced there is no higher principle than reason, which is why it is said that the greatest misfortune for man is to become a μισόλογος. But they also know that not everything is possible for reason, that it shares its power with Necessity. Why are they silent about the chaos with which Necessity fills the world—and why do they continue with their praises as if there had never been any Necessity at all? The mystics extol the bliss of the man who has renounced finite attachments—Kierkegaard speaks of the horrors of such an existence. The mystics, like theoretical philosophy, have a final and definitive answer for every question asked by the man who has been left to himself and his reason; existential philosophy subjects these answers and their finality to a new test. The virtues—and the highest of divine and human virtues is love—will be confronted with the horrors of earthly existence; could philosophical or mystical bliss endure such a trial? Beneath the "bliss" of mysticism, as beneath Spinoza's *beatitudo non est praemium virtutis sed ipsa virtus*, is there not visible the ancient *eritis sicut dei scientes bonum et malum*? Christian mysticism and philosophy, the enemy of faith, are equally incapable of hearing what "madness and death have to tell" them. Their promised "blessings" are an expression of *superbe diabolique,* which suffices to elevate poetic creativity to dizzying heights, but is powerless and helpless to restore anything to a Job who has been crushed by the hammer of God. The "miserable comforters," who do not know themselves what they are saying, are those that, like the friends of Job with their rational, human considerations, venture into the presence of a man whom the Lord is testing with His horrors.

XVI

God is Love

*God is love . . . You cannot even re-
motely imagine how He suffers. For He
knows how difficult and painful it is for
you. But He can change nothing of it,
since otherwise He Himself would have
to become something different, something other than love.*

KIERKEGAARD

We have made an exhaustive study of "existential philosophy," as represented in the sermons and Edifying Discourses of Kierkegaard, in our attempt to explore its true
meaning and significance. We have discovered that it
expresses—in indirect form—the most tormenting, but
also what I would call the most cherished and original, of
Kierkegaard's thoughts: the imitation of Socrates led the
wise men of pagan times inevitably to the Bull of Phalaris;
the imitation of Christ led to quiet despair for those in
whom Biblical revelation had been refracted through Hellenic wisdom. Both the former and the latter men ac-

cepted only that "bliss" which they had created by themselves. Where, so far as even the most perceptive could see, the slightest confusion existed, *superbe diabolique* unexpectedly emerged. And now it becomes clear why Kierkegaard insists that the beginning of existential philosophy is despair, why he demanded that the knight of faith first of all pass through the stage of resignation, and what precisely he understood by the knight of resignation. The knight of resignation is the man who has "turned his attention away from the miraculous." He knows that eternal bliss—the only sort which living creatures can attain—lies in "conquering his own inclinations," and scrupulously carrying out all the "you must's" addressed to him by a higher power. A few months before his death, Kierkegaard wrote: "There is only one permissible relationship to revealed truth: faith in it. What a man believes can be demonstrated in only one way: by his readiness to suffer for his faith; and the extent of his faith can be told only by the extent of his readiness to suffer for it." * These words are tempting in the extreme—who would venture to "dispute" them? But is not the knight of resignation a good example of this? Did he renounce suffering? Were not Socrates, and Epictetus, too, embodiments in this respect of the proclaimed ideal of the faithful? What then is the purpose of revealed truth? Kierkegaard could upbraid Hegel for not making his philosophy the guide of his own life and seeking more tangible blessings than those which were appropriate for him as philosopher of the spirit, but even the worst enemies of Socrates or Epictetus could not reproach them in the same way. And

* XII, 152.

among modern philosophers one could name more than a
few who are in this regard above all suspicion: Spinoza
was prepared to undergo, and did undergo, the greatest
suffering for his convictions; Giordano Bruno was burned
at the stake; Campanella spent his life in prison, and was
not broken by the tortures of his inquisitors, to whom he
staunchly retorted that he had burned more oil in his
lamps—the symbol of toil and wakefulness by night—
than they had ever drunk of wine. I could also cite men
who are remote from any philosophical doctrines: Mucius
Scaevola or Regulus, whom St. Augustine so often referred
to as Stoics who lived before Stoicism. We are, of course,
entitled to assess their incomparable courage and other
spiritual qualities as highly as we please—but faith and
revealed truth have nothing to do with that. Quite the
opposite—both in their lives and in their opinions, these
men defied revealed truth and faith (I have in mind, of
course, not the Roman heroes, but Bruno and Spinoza.)
St. Augustine always spoke of Mucius Scaevola and Regulus with unconcealed irritation. And yet, if we keep to the
criteria set forth by Kierkegaard, we must see them as
witnesses for the truth, even men of faith; for they proved
their faith by their suffering and the courage with which
they accepted and bore that suffering. Not only did the
"ethical" not take them under its protection; it held them
up as an example to those who are not willing to distinguish themselves in its service. Their absolute "disinterestedness"—for they did not count on "bliss," either in
this life or the next—guaranteed complete triumph for
the ethical, which is powerless to give us anything but
praise; disinterestedness has put man in bondage, i.e., it
has fulfilled that *conditio sine qua non* which alone makes

it possible for the ethical to gain absolute control over the world.

Kierkegaard never mentions the names of these men; but if he had, he would scarcely have taken their part against St. Augustine. Rather, he would have reminded us of the well-known saying: *virtutes gentium splendida vitia sunt* ("The virtues of the pagans are splendid vices"), which even to this day has been attributed to St. Augustine, and would have countered their "disinterestedness" with the same indignant words he let fly when faced by those speculative philosophers who take pride in their readiness to "accept" objective truth, whatever it may bring with it. No sufferings, no sacrifices, not even voluntary ones, could have justified these original martyrs to the ethical in Kierkegaard's eyes. Their faith, faith in the ethical which has once and for all rejected the miraculous, would have seemed to him monstrous, the ultimate in lack of faith. And this would only have emphasized again that Kierkegaard's edifying discourses must be understood as "indirect communication," and that existential philosophy, insofar as it glorifies the eternal truths of reason and morality, liberated from God and therefore petrified, is merely preparation, merely the first step toward the great and final struggle to which he dedicated his brief life. Kierkegaard never raised the question of whether Luther was a "witness for the truth." It is true that more than once he expressed his regret that Luther had not managed to end his life in martyrdom,* and it is also true that Luther's *Table Talk* inspired him with extreme annoyance and even indignation, but nevertheless he did not venture to say

* *Journal*, II, 336 . . . from 1854, and, therefore, a year before his death: "Luther did immeasurable harm by not becoming a martyr."

that Luther was not a witness for the truth (as he had said of Bishop Mynster, after the latter's death). And if he had been asked whose was the true faith, that of Mucius Scaevola and Regulus, who "proved" by voluntary martyrdom their readiness to carry out what they considered their duty, or that of Luther, whom history gave no opportunity of offering such "proof," he would hardly have hesitated over his answer. Faith is not proved by martyrdom or sacrifices. Faith is not proved at all; it does not require proofs and has no need of them. And existential philosophy, which is so closely united with faith that only in the presence of and through faith can it do its work, finds in faith that new dimension which sets it apart from theoretical philosophy. Faith dwells beyond proofs, as it dwells, to use Kierkegaard's words, beyond death. When all possibilities come to an end for man's thinking, new possibilities are "revealed" for faith. An example from elementary geometry can serve to make somewhat clearer to us, or at least give us an approximation of, the way in which Kierkegaard perceived faith. It is impossible to draw more than one perpendicular to a straight line from a point on a two-dimensional plane. And if any line occupies the place of the perpendicular, that privileged position is forever unattainable by all the other innumerable straight lines at large in the universe; the laws of contradiction, of the excluded third, etc., keep that fortunate and privileged line safe from all other pretenders' temptation to become its equal. But what is impossible on a two-dimensional plane suddenly becomes possible when we pass from plane to solid geometry; when, enriched by a new dimension, we transform a flat surface into three-dimensional space: an infinite number of perpendiculars can be drawn to a line from one and the same point, and the smallest, most insignificant line, forgotten by all, almost forgotten by itself, is equal in "value" to that "one" line which enjoyed the enviable and seemingly inalienable right of forming two equal and adjacent angles with a given straight line, of being the geometrical location of fixed points, and so on and so forth. Every kind of understanding, every kind of knowledge, every *intelligere* takes place on a plane surface, is by its very nature in conflict with the new dimension, and tries with all its might to compress and flatten the human—all too human, in its estimation—*ridere, lugere et detestari* into this plane. And conversely, the latter break away from the plane where *intelligere* has pressed them down, toward a freedom which does not know how to, and cannot, coexist with *intelligere*. This is why existential philosophy, as we have seen, abandoned Hegel and the greek symposium for Job and Abraham. And yet, more precisely: for that very reason we cannot justifiably turn our backs on Kierkegaard's "severe" Christianity. And this is in spite of the fact that, in the last year of his life, in *The Instant,* where he published his vehement phillipics against married pastors, complacent theologians, and the laity who had turned Biblical revelation into a comprehensible and tolerable, even advantageous, moral system, and in which he declared that Christian man had abolished Christ, Kierkegaard frankly admitted that he did not even consider himself equal to the demands made upon him by Christianity. After repeating for the hundredth time his fundamental idea: "The truth is that to be a Christian means to be unhappy in this life and you will be (humanly speaking) all the more unhappy and will suffer all the more in this life, the more you devote yourself to God and the more God loves you," he adds, immediately afterward: "To the weak man this idea appears terrible and destructive, demanding a superhuman straining of all his powers. I know this from twofold experience. First of all— *I myself cannot endure it* [italics mine] and can only observe from a distance, only get a hint of, this truly Christian idea of Christianity . . . secondly, the peculiar circumstances of my existence have riveted my attention upon it; otherwise I would never have concentrated on it, and would be even less capable of bearing its burden." * In a footnote he provides an even more detailed explanation: "Therefore," he writes, "I do not even consider myself a Christian—I am far from that. But in one respect I have an advantage over official Christianity: when I speak of Christianity, I am talking about the real Christianity and not adulterating it, and I speak in the same way of my relationship to Christianity." This unusually valuable admission (of a sort which, incidentally, is not uncommon in his journals and other writings) sheds new light and aids us in discovering what inspired his "indirect communications" and why "existential philosophy" needs them and cannot do without them. Kierkegaard himself could not endure his own "severity" and his "ferocious" Christianity, and I think it would not even be a distortion of the formal text for us to say that there is not a soul alive who could endure the severity of Kierkegaard's Christianity. It remains only to ask: could God Himself endure this sort of Christianity? There can be no doubt that this question lies hidden beneath all Kierkegaard's edifying discourses and that all of them have only one aim: to

* XII, 82.

pose this question. Human cowardice, as Kierkegaard said more than once, cannot endure what madness and death have to tell us. But madness and death have no regard for human endurance and continue to spin out their endless narrative; the works of Kierkegaard are nothing other than this narrative, more or less systematized and put into order. But if human cowardice cannot endure it—could divine courage? It would not be amiss to mention at this point that by "sufferings" Kierkegaard does not mean the usual hardships, however considerable, which men must overcome, and do overcome to a greater or less degree, together and separately, guided by the counsel of their reason and supported by their moral strength. When Kierkegaard speaks of "sufferings," he means the hopelessness and gloom from which even reason and virtue flee as from the plague. In the presence of Job, wallowing in filth, in the presence of Abraham, raising the knife above his son, the wise and truly sublime words of the friends of Job seem like the salt that has lost its savor. And here we ask: could even God endure horrors such as these? There is, at the same time, another question: who or what is it that inflicts these horrors upon mortals and immortals alike? And if there is something in the world that does inflict us with these horrors, then is it strictly necessary to accept and endure them? Are acceptance and endurance man's only possible answer to the horrors of life?

Kierkegaard has just told us that he could not endure true Christianity, or what he, in his works, calls true Christianity, and that he could not realize in his own life what Christianity demands of man; he could only set forth, without any alteration or falsification, what he had learned from Holy Scripture. But this is exactly what is rejected and forbidden in the most decisive way by existential philosophy. Existential philosophy requires, not the exposition, however accurate, of any doctrine, but its carrying out in life, its realization. Even Epictetus knew this; a man can in no way justify himself by honestly and humbly admitting his weakness and inability to rise to the proper level of morality. "I cannot's" of any sort discredit not just the man, but the philosophy, too, in the eyes of existential philosophy (which is why it is existential, and not theoretical, philosophy).

In the very middle of the eighteen-fifties, that is, just at the height of Kierkegaard's battle with the official Christianity that had abolished Christ, he became acquainted with the works of Schopenhauer, who was already at that time coming to be well known in Germany. They made a great impression upon him. "In spite of my complete difference of opinion with him," he remarks in his journal, "I was amazed to find a writer who resembled me so closely." * And then he rebukes Schopenhauer for "developing an ethical doctrine that does not have the power to compel its teacher to manifest it in his own life." However, the same must also be said of Kierkegaard: he cannot in all conscience be excused by his admission that he did not think he could properly call himself a Christian. Schopenhauer is only "honest in that" he does not pretend to be the equal of the righteous men he praises, and does not try to pass himself off as a holy man—Kierkegaard stresses this. And yet he applies the scale of existential philosophy to Schopenhauer; would like to "compel" him to embody his doctrine in his life, although he does not find it necessary or possible to oblige himself to do the

* *Journal*, II, 344.

same; and, after his encounter with Schopenhauer, continues to preach "ferocious" Christianity with an ever-increasing passion. It would, however, be a mistake to see any inconsistency in this. Rather, the opposite is true: I would say that what is expressed here is a complete indifference, even hostility, toward theoretical consistency, as toward everything which smacks of "coercion." Existential philosophy cannot endure coercion; coercion has remained wholly the property of theoretical philosophy. And although Kierkegaard demands that Schopenhauer affront people, not in his books, which may or may not be read, but in public places, in theaters, in churches, it is by no means absolutely necessary that he do so; to be more precise, it is not necessary at all. *Si vis me plere, primum est tibi ipse dolendum* ("If you wish me to weep, you yourself must suffer first"); he feels that Schopenhauer became habituated to his pessimism, accommodated himself to it—and he cannot forgive him this. Schopenhauer ridiculed Leibniz and called his optimism "dishonest." But a pessimism which has "accomodated itself" in life, which can remain calm in the fact of the questions which Kierkegaard sets for philosophy, seems far more dishonest.

In his peculiar way of speaking, Kierkegaard calls his relationship to Christianity "simultaneousness": for him the horrors of Christ's earthly life exist not in the past, but in the present; they are not ended, but continue. And he sees this as "crucial." Moreover, although he has admitted that he can do no more than set forth Christian doctrine, and can never put it into practice, he unhesitatingly declares: "This [simultaneousness] is crucial. This idea has been the idea of my entire life. I can truly say that I have felt honored to suffer for proclaiming it. I would gladly

die for it, infinitely grateful to Providence for having given
me the opportunity of fixing my attention and the attention of others upon it. I am not its author—God forbid
that I should be so presumptuous—this idea was originated long ago; it is stated in the New Testament. But I
was fated, in my suffering, to remind people anew of this
idea which, as rat poison is death to rats, is death to
Dozenten, that miserable scum which is destroying Christianity at its roots, *Dozenten,* those fine fellows who construct tombs for the prophets and *objectively* interpret
their teachings, who objectively (for subjectivity presupposes a morbid affectation; it must be assumed that
they take pride in their objectivity) make use of the suffering and death of better men, while they themselves (always with the aid of their celebrated objectivity) maintain a position outside, and as far away as possible from,
anything that recalls in any way the possibility of their
sharing the suffering of these men . . . Simultaneousness—
this is the crux of the matter. Picture a witness for the
truth, that is, a man who follows an ideal. He has borne
every sort of insult and endured, long endured, all manner
of persecution. In the end he is executed, and the death to
which he is condemned is a terrible one. He is burned,
burned with exquisite cruelty in a slow fire. Picture this to
yourself. Christianity and the seriousness of the case demand that you picture this graphically, as graphically as
if you yourself were a contemporary of that man, and that
you recognize him for what he really is. In this lies the
seriousness of Christianity." * I find it necessary to quote
further passages from Kierkegaard's works in order that we
may come closer to what is not only the central idea of his

* XII, 126.

philosophy, but has been and always will be the object of intense consideration for every living man. Plotinus called this τὸ τιμιώτατον (the most important, most significant), Scripture calls it the one thing that is needful. "We human beings suppose that the main thing is to pass our lives happily in this world. Christianity, however, holds that all horrors are of the next world; the horrors of our world are but child's play in comparison with the horrors of eternity; and therefore the problem is not to live happily in this world, but to achieve through suffering a genuine relationship to eternity. Man lives only once. If at the hour of death you are convinced that you have led a righteous life, i.e., have kept your eyes fixed upon eternity—then praise and thanks be to God for evermore; if not, there is no way to make amends: all is lost. Man lives only once. If you have missed the opportunity of suffering, or avoided it, you will never be able to set matters right. God does not wish to coerce you. Not for anything in the world would the God of love coerce anyone; by doing so He would accomplish an entirely different aim from the one He had intended. How could the God of love even think of demanding love by coercion? . . . God is love. There is not a man whom this thought would not fill with indescribable bliss, especially if he were to give it a concrete, personal interpretation: God is love; this means that God loves you. But as soon as a man comes to the conclusion that to be loved by God means to be doomed to suffering, and becomes convinced that the sufferings will not be trivial—he is horrified. Yes, but this is the result of love. You cannot even remotely imagine how He suffers—for He knows how difficult and painful it is for you. But He can change nothing of it, since otherwise He Himself would have to become something different, something other than love." * God does not wish to coerce man, says Kierkegaard. Well, how could anyone really conceive of God coercing man? And yet coercion remains, notwithstanding the will of God. He can do nothing about it. Power passes from God, Who does not wish to use coercion, Who forever abhors coercion, to eternity, which in this respect is just as unconcerned and indifferent as the ethical; it has the desire and the ability to employ coercion, *sine effusione sanguinis,* of course—but at its disposal are horrors beside which the shedding of blood and all the other terrors of our earthly existence seem mere child's play. It is impossible to prevail upon Eternity, to beseech it, to appeal to its conscience; like the ethical, it has no ears with which to hear. And in this case God has no advantage over mortals: He has no common language with the ethical or with Eternity. God Himself suffers, suffers unbelievably, when He sees how Eternity and the ethical deal with human beings. God is indeed love. And yet He dares not, He cannot, put them to flight, just as the god of the pagans could not oppose the order of existence which he did not establish. Even for Zeus, Eternity was the ultimate judge. Kierkegaard's remark that all is lost for the man who has not gone through suffering during his life is no more than a free translation of Plato's words about κάθαρσις; as we will recall, Plato felt that he who did not philosophize, who did not purify himself in this life, had ruined his soul forever. Kierkegaard only takes us a little further along, but still in the same direction. Plato and Greek philosophy did not venture to threaten the immortals. There is perhaps a certain inconsistency here,

* *Ibid.,* 130.

but their gods somehow avoided κάθαρσις, and even the Greek κάθαρσις, as I have already said, was more eager to display its blessings to men than to point out the horrors conditional upon those blessings. We find no attempt in any of the Greek philosophers to depict graphically and concretely the torments experienced by a sage who had been enclosed within the red-hot brazen bull. In their writings, the Bull of Phalaris acts as a theoretical sluice gate against the dialectical attacks of their opponents: "intellectual vision" is completely engulfed by the contemplation of bliss. Kierkegaard's "Christianity," on the other hand, mentions blessings seldom, and even then reluctantly, as if doubtful that anyone could need them. Are such blessings, then, truly necessary? And can one accept the writings of Kierkegaard without first making an effort to penetrate through them to his actual experiences?

Listen to what he tells us himself, and not even in one of his books, but in his journal: "There is no question that, in the entries made in my journals for 1848 and 1849, I often included material that I invented. It is not easy for a man as productive as I to hold it back. It comes by itself, as soon as I take pen in hand. By myself I am a different man, self-controlled, serene. But as soon as I begin to write, poetic invention gains the upper hand. How very strange this is! I have no desire to put down on paper my religious impressions and thoughts: they have too great a meaning for me. There are only a few of them, but of my writing there is a great deal." * And in another passage from his journal on the same theme, he writes, under the heading "About Myself": "Silence concealed in silence is suspicious and inspires suspicion, and it seems as if some-

* *Journal*, II, 325.

thing were being betrayed; at least it is betrayed that silence is necessary. But the silence concealed beneath brilliant and talented conversation, that is genuine; it is a real silence." * Such admissions are not infrequent in Kierkegaard's writings, and anyone who sets himself the task of getting closer to his true purposes must, whether he wants to or not, make his way through Kierkegaard's "brilliant" talk to his "silence," which alone can make us privy to what he considers important, necessary, and significant. And perhaps an entry from his journal for 1854 which I have quoted before should be included in the little that truly expresses his religious, i.e., his final and decisive, experiences, and that is concealed, not beneath his fascinating, sometimes dazzling, literary works, but beneath his invisible, seemingly nonexistent, silence. Its message is essential, and for that reason I shall quote it once again: "When Christ cried out: My God, my God, why hast Thou forsaken me?—this was terrible for Christ, and so it has usually been described. It seems to me that it was more terrible still for God to hear that. It is terrible to be so inflexible! But no—this is still not the most terrible thing: that is to be so inflexible and, at the same time, to be love; this is profound, endless, unfathomable sorrow." And immediately thereafter he adds, with an audacity which cannot and must not be weakened by any of the reservations which accompany it: "Alas, I, too, unhappy man that I am, have experienced this conflict—not to be in a position to alter my course and yet to love! Alas, my experience helps me to form, from a great distance, from a very great distance, an idea, however feeble, of the sufferings of divine love."

* *Ibid.*, 363.

XVII

Kierkegaard and Luther

> *Quia homo superbit et somniat, se sapere, se sanctum esse, ideo opus est, ut lege humilietur, ut sic bestia ista, opinio justitiae, occidatur, qua non occisa, homo non potest vivere.*
>
> LUTHER

We have witnessed the unlimited proliferation of horrors in Kierkegaard's soul; in this incandescent atmosphere of horrors there arose the immense audacity of a man who had begun to think that he might, "although from a distance, from a very great distance," represent not only the heroes of the Biblical narrative, Job and Abraham, but also the Creator of heaven and earth, to be just as powerless and tormented as he was himself: and at that moment existential philosophy was born. But what are all these horrors to us, what have they in common with philosophy? Were not the Greeks right to turn away from horrors and direct all their attention upon bliss? Is this not the meaning and the task of philosophy, and the final word in wisdom? Kierkegaard does not even pose this question, as if he had completely forgotten that one must ask: were the Greeks right or not? He found himself faced with the unbearable horrors of existence; he was compelled to enter into a final and desperate struggle with them. "My severity is not of my own making," Kierkegaard has told us, taking issue with the usual interpretation of the texts of Holy Scripture. An even more horrifying feeling seizes us when God Himself is compelled to repeat these words in the presence of His beloved Son. But from whom does this severity come? And—most important—from whomever it may come and however terrible may be the horrors prepared in the world for mortals and immortals, what concern are they of philosophy, whether it be called existential or theoretical? Philosophy is the search for truth and truth alone; not for anything in the world will philosophy renounce truth, whether it brings men the greatest bliss or unbearable horrors, for truth is entirely independent of whether or not it pleases men. This is why we speak of the objectivity of knowledge, and if existential philosophy has no regard for this, then for that very reason it ceases to be philosophy and loses its great ability to lead men to the beginnings, the sources, the roots of being. Horrors,—and everyone must realize this—no matter how limitless they may be, have no power to shake the stability and firmness of truths obtained by knowledge. Whatever truth may demand from men or from the gods, it will obtain all and yield to nothing. And truth does not in the least resemble God: truth is not love, truth is truth, and, as truth, it never varies; it does not, and cannot, have any reason to change in any way. When love comes face to face with truth, it is love that must retreat. Truth has at its disposal every

235

"necessity" and every "you must." If anyone does not yield to it willingly, it can coerce him forcibly. God never uses coercion, but, then, truth is not God: it coerces.

It would seem proper to put an end to questions here, to recall Aristotle's tempting ἀνάγκη στῆναι ("It is necessary to stop"). But precisely at this moment Kierkegaard begins his tale of the horrors he experienced when, in fulfilling the "you must's" set before him by truth, he was forced to ruin with his own hands the life of the woman who was dearer to him than anyone else in the world. This, of course, is terrible, much more terrible than it might appear to a man who has never had to undergo such an experience. But he had no choice: his love was helpless before the "you must's" presented to him by truth. And yet even this is not the most terrible thing, Kierkegaard tells us, suppressing with difficulty the triumph which pervades his whole being; more terrible, infinitely more terrible, is what the "good tidings" have imparted to mankind: God hears the cry of His beloved Son and, like Kierkegaard, cannot stir even a finger. His love is also forced to bow before the "you must's" which imperiously demand that He be inflexible. How did this come about? Why has divine love given way before "you must," and not "you must" before divine love? And why does Kierkegaard exult over this?

With respect to himself, Kierkegaard had good reason to say that, in his life, "you must" had won the upper hand over love; that is a fact, and there is no disputing facts; at least, everyone is sure that there is no disputing facts. But what is the source of his confidence that, if God had to choose between love and inflexibility, He would do the same as he, Kierkegaard had done? Had he cared to recall the "relationship to God" of his beloved hero, Abraham, the father of faith, he would have seen that God certainly does not set as much store by His Inflexibility as philosophizing theologians would like Him to: God decided to destroy Sodom and Gomorrah and then renounced His intention, yielding to the persuasions and entreaties of His servant. It is clear that confidence in the absolute inflexibility of God was not suggested to, or, more precisely, in spired in Kierkegaard by Holy Scripture: another power intervened here. It seems evident as well that it was not Scripture that prompted him, apropos of the story from the Acts of the Apostles, to sing the praises of charity, which can do nothing. It is also entirely beyond dispute that when he amended the parable from the Gospel which says that the sun rises for good men and evil alike, and the one concerning the lilies of the field which are arrayed more richly than King Solomon, he was obeying some power which he encountered, or, more probably, which encountered him as he deviated from Holy Scripture. He himself said to us that God does not coerce man. But horrors coerce: the reason, and the only reason, they are horrors is that they coerce, and how they do coerce! We will recall that no torturer can equal the ethical in mercilessness and cruelty. But the ethical is not alone. "Eternity" works at its side: all the scorpions our empirical existence can boast are nothing in comparison with the torments prepared by eternity for those who obey its laws. Now we can "understand" why God did not venture to renounce His Inflexibility and answer the cries of His Son. Even God dares not disobey Eternity. God Himself, of course, does not coerce anyone. But Eternity cares as little about God as it does about men. If He had dared to move an inch

Kierkegaard

from His inflexible position, Eternity would not have seen Him as God; it would have visited all its horrors upon Him —horrors compared with which the agony He felt when He heard His Son's cries would have seemed but child's play. Eternity, like the ethical, is almighty; they alone rule by might, for they have no scruples about "coercion" and, what is more, they have contrived to insinuate to every conscious and living being in the world that "coercion" ought not to be despised. There is nothing that can threaten them; they have no fear of horrors, for horrors are not horrors to them. They present their implacable demands to God and men alike, and as if their demands were not enough, they want both God and men to find bliss in the fulfilling of those demands. Did Kierkegaard prove to have attained the proper height: did he really feel "bliss" when he suppressed his "finite" love for the sake of eternity's "you must"? And did God also feel "bliss" when He turned away from His Son in order to preserve the spotless purity of His Inflexibility?

Few writers in world literature have attempted to portray with such passion the rights of the eternal and the ethical over mortals and immortals. Indeed, even Kierkegaard himself did not dare to speak of this openly: here more than anywhere else he uses "indirect communication," and I do not conceal, either from myself or from the reader, that, in my comparisons of quotations, I have been more concerned to point out his "silences," or, to be more precise, what he was silent about, than to show what he said. However, this was necessary, for the subject on which he is silent, and on which we are all silent, is infinitely more important and significant than that about which all of us, including Kierkegaard, talk. What is this power that compels God, Who is love, to remain deaf to the cries of His Son? What is this Inflexibility that can enfeeble and paralyze divine love? And, finally: how does Kierkegaard "know" that there exists in the world "coercion" that can force even divine love to bow before Inflexibility? He cites his own experience, and does so scrupulously, at least to a certain degree. But can "experience" really provide "general and necessary judgments"? Especially the kind of experience of which he speaks? He loved Regina Olsen more than anyone else in the world. The necessity of breaking with her filled him with boundless horror, so much so that even during the last days of his life, many years after Regina Olson had become the wife of Schlegel, in spite of that accomplished fact and all the evidence that told him over and over that what has once existed cannot become nonexistent, he inwardly continued to try to assert his rights to her. At his death, he did not think about the judgment of eternity, of which he told us in his discourses, but seemed rather to expect that the evidence would give way, dissolve, turn into nothingness, and that behind it he would find a new truth, entirely incomprehensible to reason: that Regina Olsen belonged, not to Schlegel, who was married to her and possessed her, but to Kierkegaard, who had left her and, in this life, could only touch her shadow.

I do not know how those to whom he addressed himself took what he had to say, or what they understood in it; but if what he said had any meaning whatever, then we must admit that such an insignificant, everyday occurrence as Kierkegaard's break with Regina Olsen was indeed an event of universally historic importance, more momentous than the discovery of America or the invention of gunpowder. For if it turns out that, from a standpoint invisible and immaterial to anyone else, Kierkegaard maintained his rights to Regina Olsen in the face of self-evidency, then every basis of our "thinking" is shaken. Philosophy is forced to turn from Hegel to Job, from Socrates to Abraham; forced to turn from reason to the Absurd. Our fundamental, immovable truths become "feathered dreams."

Even as bold and radical a thinker as Duns Scotus, who was not afraid to sweep aside the "ethical" barring his way to divine free will —philosophers and theologians to this day have not been able to forgive him for his presumptuousness—did not venture to think that God has the power to make what has once existed nonexistent, just as he did not venture to dispute the law of contradiction. This, in his opinion, was the beginning of the realm of uncreated truths which depend on no one—and, as a result, we are obliged to see it as the limit of divine omnipotence. But before the "horrors" compiled by Kierkegaard, these truths, too, begin to waver: for God everything is possible, God can make what has once existed nonexistent. God is above the law of contradiction, above all laws. "If I had had faith, I would not have had to forsake Regina," Kierkegaard has repeated to us a countless number of times. Now it may be said that, when faith comes, Regina will return also. And all "doubts" about whether a man can, after the difficult ordeals connected with experiences like those which befell Kierkegaard, love again with a young, careless love—to put it differently, whether the way to the tree of life can ever be made open, through the forgiveness of sins, for a man who has tasted of the fruits of knowledge—all such doubts will vanish by themselves: the "horrors" transmitted from the soul of one individual to the very substance of the universe will explode the foundations upon which rest all our "impossibilities." They have already been shaken by the wails and curses of Job; will they be able to endure a battle with the omnipotence of God? Human cowardice, or, more accurately, human weakness, cannot bear what madness and death have to say. But will God—not the God of Hegel and theoretical philosophy, but the God of Holy Scripture, the God of Abraham, the God of Isaac, the God of Jacob—also reject the cries He hears from people crucified by madness and death?

As we have done more than once before, we must again recall Kierkegaard's words: "My severity is not of my own making." And now we can better understand, if not from where and from whom his severity came, then at least why Kierkegaard spoke with such frenzy and passion about the "savagery" of the "mildest" of teachings. From those "horrors" he forged a fearful weapon against the eternal and unshakable truths of our reason. Not only men, but God Himself is doomed to unendurable torments, if reason is the source of truths and if its confederates, the "ethical" and the "eternal," have the power over existence ascribed to them by the wisest of men. Kierkegaard is no longer content to ask Job's permission to make common cause with him. He feels that he is within his rights to take his case to the Creator Himself. God will understand him; when He had to "sacrifice" His love to Inflexibility, He felt what Kierkegaard felt when he had to break with Regina. He, too, dares not disobey the "ethical," although that is what He would like to do more than anything else in the world. And again—just like Kierkegaard—He is obliged to conceal this; He, too, is keeping a "secret from the ethical": He would rather be love, but acts as if He were Inflexibility. He was as powerless to do anything for His Son as Kierkegaard was powerless to do anything for Regina Olsen. The menacing "you must" strikes at His freedom; He can weep, suffer, despair, and yet, not only can He not respond to the call of His crucified Son, but He must pretend that powerless love and powerless charity are the "one thing that is needful," reserved for both mortals and immortals.

Here we return to the ideas of the Fall and of faith, as Kierkegaard saw them, and, at the same time, we return to existential philosophy in the true sense of the word; the horrors of existence, both human and divine, have led us to that array of problems, the very possibility of which is an affront to the ordinary consciousness. In an enigmatic way, even in his edifying discourses, where he paints a horrifying picture of the wild riot of frenzied beasts, clothed in the splendid vestments of the "ethical" and the "Eternal," who have broken loose from their chains to fall upon helpless man, Kierkegaard does not cease to remind us that man's destruction comes only from sin. And if we compare with this his statements that the opposite of sin is not virtue, but faith; that the opposite of sin is freedom; that, moreover, freedom is not the freedom of choice between good and evil, but "possibility"; and that God signifies that everything is possible—then we will have come close to what Kierkegaard understood by the words "existential philosophy." That philosophy has nothing in common with the legacy of "wisdom" handed down to us by the Greeks. Kierkegaard's "fearless dialectic" perceived diabolic pride beneath the wisdom of Epictetus, and ultimately Socrates was discovered by him to be the sinner κατ' ἐξοχήν ("par excellence"). Their sin lay in the very quality commonly regarded as their virtue and thought by us to be to their immortal credit before men and Heaven: they embodied an ideal, i.e., they lived in the categories in which they thought. But if Kierkegaard was sorely provoked by the discrepancy between the lives of Hegel and Schopenhauer and their philosophy, he found completely unbearable in Socrates and Epictetus the very fact that they embodied their philosophy, not in their teachings, not in words, but in their entire lives. "If the ethical is supreme, then Abraham is lost." And yet, existential philosophy, as the Greeks understood it, and as Kierkegaard himself understood it when he considered Socrates, may be summed up thus: the "ethical" is supreme, there is no principle higher than the ethical. Reason peremptorily demands this, so peremptorily that it is proper, indeed obligatory, for us to add one more "if": "If reason is the source, and the only source, of truth, then the ethical is supreme, then there is no principle higher than the ethical." But what is the principle against which Greek philosophy was so careful to defend its truths? There can be only one answer to this: truth does not want to be subject to the principle of a Creator; truth wants to be uncreated, as uncreated as the Creator Himself. In its estimation, both it and the Creator can only be the better for that. And man will benefit still more: he will be freed from divine arbitrariness, he will himself become like God, knowing truth, knowing the nature of good and evil. But will these truths, emancipated from God, really bring man freedom? Will not just the reverse happen? Does not the truthfulness of truth lie in its being of God, in its having been *created* by God, so that if it is separated from God and left to its own devices, it will turn into its opposite and become, not life-giving, but death-dealing, not freeing, but enslaving? Petrified itself, it will turn to stone all those who look upon it. Theoretical philosophy does not even ask this question. It scorns created truths; "reason eagerly strives," as Kant told us (essentially repeating what Aristotle had said), for general and necessary judgments, i.e., for judgments that have no master, that are themselves masters over all. And man imagines that by sharing reason's "eager striving," by surrendering himself wholly to it, he will partake of truth and good. He does not in the least suspect that immense danger awaits him here, that he is being threatened with destruction from this quarter.

Kierkegaard had, by his own admission, read little of Luther, and, as we will recall, did not particularly like him. But few men have perceived the lack of grace in truths which have broken away from God (*veritates emancipataes a Deo*) as clearly as Luther. This is the origin of his doctrine of *sola fide*. It is also the origin of the sharp contrast he draws between law and grace. Man cannot redeem himself through law; law only degrades man: it has no restorative power. Law can only expose our weakness and our powerlessness, which we conceal in vain by an outward appearance of pride. This is why Luther says, in his commentary on St. Paul's Epistle to the Galatians: *quia homo superbit et somniat, se sapere, se sanctum et justum esse, ideo opus est, ut lege humilietur, ut sic bestia ista, opinio justitiae, occidatur, qua non occisa, non potest homo vivere* ("Because man is full of pride and imagines that he is holy and righteous, it is necessary to humble him by law, so that in this way the wild beast in him which is confident of its own righteousness may be killed, for, until it is killed, man cannot live"). Man's confidence in his "knowledge" and in the possibility of attaining the highest goal by his own powers not only will not save him, it will deliver him into the clutches of that frightful monster which man must kill if he is to live. *Justus ex fide vivit* ("the just shall live by faith"), said the Prophet Amos.* *Justus ex fide vivit,* repeated the Apostle Paul after him. Reason, which eagerly strives for general and necessary truths (*"concupiscentia invincibilis"*) leads to death; the way to life is through faith. Plato's warning against lack of confidence in reason is the greatest offense. Misfortunes lie in wait, not for the man who despises reason (μισόλογος), but the man who loves it. As long as a man submits to reason, as long as he depends upon the virtues which arise from reason, he will remain in the power of a terrible and hostile force, in the power of the monster which must be destroyed if he is to live. The true meaning of Kierkegaardian philosophy is revealed in the words by Luther quoted above: existential philosophy is the great and final struggle of man with the enigmatic and mysterious monster which has managed to convince him that his bliss, both temporal and eternal, depends exclusively upon his readiness to bow before truths emancipated from God—that struggle, the inevitability of which was felt by the last great representative of Greek philosophy, and which he was bold enough to proclaim: ἀγὼν μέγιστος καὶ ἔσχατος ταῖς ψυχαῖς πρόκειται ("A great and final struggle is at hand for the human soul"). The philosophy of Plotinus sought that which is found ἐπέκεινα νοῦ καὶ νοήσεως ("On the far side of reason and knowledge"). He called upon men to "rise above knowledge" (δραμεῖν ὑπὲρ

---

* [This quotation is not from Amos, but from Habakkuk (2:4). Tr.]

τὴν ἐπιστήμην). A thousand years of experience by select
representatives of humanity who had convinced men to
entrust their fate to the truths of reason lay behind Plotinus, and he "suddenly" saw that, where men had hoped
to find freedom, shameful and unendurable slavery
awaited them. Or perhaps he did not "see," but heard the
good tidings conveyed to him? And, having heard them,
he fled blindly from reason, without knowing himself
where he was going.

XVIII

Despair and Nothingness

> *Even in what men consider most beau-*
> *tiful, most attractive: a charming young*
> *girl in whom everything breathes har-*
> *mony, peace, and joy—even there de-*
> *spair is hiding.*
>
> KIERKEGAARD

Homo superbit et somniat, se sapere, se sanctum et jus-
tum esse: the greatest of dangers lies here; this is the
source of all the horrors of existence. But how did it happen that man was seduced, and continues to be seduced,
by knowledge; how did he come to think that his "righteousness" and his "holiness" are *summum bonum, μέγιστον*
ἀγαθόν ("the highest good")? The question seems perfectly natural and legitimate. However, it is precisely this
question that can and should cause a man to suspect for
the first time the futility of such questioning. When Kierkegaard began his inquiries into the meaning of the Biblical story of the Fall, he felt obliged to expunge from that
story all the elements which seemed to him inconsistent

with, or offensive to, the notions of what is possible and proper that he had found ready made in his own consciousness. He could not understand the need for the introduction of the serpent into the Biblical narrative. And, in fact, this is impossible to understand; without the serpent it would have been much more plausible and reasonable. But, surprisingly enough, Kierkegaard's rejection of the serpent was only verbal, or, more precisely, only conditional. In reality, all his reflections on the Fall depend exclusively upon the assumption that it was the result of an external, alien, even hostile force acting on man, and that some sort of mysterious and enigmatic insinuation had taken place. The first sin occurs in man, as Kierkegaard himself disclosed to us, when his freedom is paralyzed—in a "swoon." This means that in the free state man would never exchange the fruit of the tree of life for the fruit of the tree of knowledge. But the serpent of the Bible is only a figurative expression of this concept: the serpent's role is simply to cast a spell over man and restrain his freedom. The same must be said of the connection, entirely incomprehensible to our minds, established in the Bible between sin and the fruit of the tree of knowledge. If we approach this with our customary standards and criteria, we shall have to reject, not only the serpent, but also—and to a much greater degree—the tree of knowledge of good and evil. It is inexplicable and contrary to what we think reasonable and sensible that the serpent, even though he was the cleverest of all creatures, could have deceived man so and played such a fateful role in his destiny. But even less admissible, even more outrageous and repellent to our entire spiritual being, is the idea that the fruit of the tree of knowledge of good and evil was able to poison our forefather's soul and bring it to the Fall. Quite the contrary: the fruit of the tree of knowledge of good and evil should have purified his soul, made it whole, elevated it. All who have dealt with the Biblical story have, as I said before, been prepared to find there anything but what is really said in the Book of Genesis. They have understood the Fall as disobedience to God, or as a surrender to fleshly temptation, but no one has been able or willing to admit that the root of sin, that is, of original sin, is knowledge, and that the ability to distinguish good from evil is *the* Fall, and, moreover, the most terrible, most ruinous Fall conceivable.

But, at the same time, without the story of the Fall, Holy Scripture, both Old and New Testaments, remains for us the Book sealed with seven seals. The words of the Prophet Amos: "The just shall live by faith," * and the inference drawn from them by the Apostle Paul (which is, properly speaking, not an inference, but an amplification): "All that is not of faith is sin," will reveal their enigmatic meaning to us only when we agree to accept the idea that the first man, tempted by the fruit of the tree of knowledge, thereby brought about his own ruin and that of all mankind. We are, of course, within our rights—who could prevent it?—to reject Holy Scripture entirely and place the Bible in the category of books which do not satisfy the demands of today's cultural level. But, according to the Bible, knowledge not only is not and cannot be the source of truth—according to the Bible, truth dwells where knowledge ends, where freedom from knowledge reigns.† Or, to put it another way, knowledge is a heavy

---

* See footnote 1, chapter XVII.
† I do not know whether this reminder is necessary—but, at any rate, I shall say once more that in this case knowledge means those general and necessary truths for which, according to Kant, reason eagerly strives; and not experience, which always irritates reason.

burden which bows man down and does not permit him to stand erect. Plotinus, as I have said, either perceived this himself or was made aware of it by those of his friends who had acquainted him with the writings of the Gnostics. And there is every reason to assume that those very Gnostics, who "amended" Holy Scripture to conform with the "knowledge" they had adopted from the schools of Greek philosophy, were the inspiration for his incessant striving to "soar above knowledge" (δραμεῖν ὑπὲρ τὴν ἐπιστήμην). But, in the course of the long ages of our existence on earth, our minds have become so thoroughly imbued with the truths suggested to us by reason that we cannot even imagine how we could exist without them. Our everyday experience gives continuous and unchanging evidence that every imaginable misfortune awaits the man who renounces the guidance of reason. Everyone knows this, and there is no need to elaborate upon it; even Kierkegaard never tried to conceal from his readers that in our empirical world reason is absolute master. But philosophy attempts to go beyond the limits of empirical being. Plato, who warned us against μισόλογοι, also taught that philosophy is μελέτη θανάτου ("training for death"), and that to philosophize means ἀποθνήσκειν καὶ τεθνάναι (to prepare for death and dying). Can it be that even in the face of death, on the borderline which separates our visible world from the other worlds, reason continues to retain its power and its rights? We have heard Kierkegaard say— and hardly anyone would dispute this—that the rational consciousness cannot bear what madness and death tell it. But, then, why must we be protective and considerate toward reason and pay it the divine honors it demands? If it still will not release us from its clutches, if it still pre-

tends, in spite of its powerlessness, to play the role of over-
seer of human destinies, does this not imply that, instead
of being our benefactor, it is our mortal enemy, the *bellua
qua non occisa homo non potest vivere?* Reason as the enemy of men and gods is the greatest paradox that one can
imagine, and, at the same time, the most terrible and ago-
nizing that could befall lonely, helpless man: *quam aram
parabit sibi qui majestatem rationis laedit!* ("What altar
will the man who has insulted the majesty of reason provide for himself?"—Spinoza). If reason will not guide us,
if reason will not aid us, if it refuses to serve us—where
are we to turn? Kierkegaard was not exaggerating in the
least when he said that to renounce reason is the greatest
martyrdom. I might add only that it would be all but impossible to find even one man willing, on his own initiative, to take upon himself such martyrdom.

It seems likely that the unaccountable fear which Kierkegaard assumed to be present in the first man was in fact
a fear of being deserted by the guidance of reason. The
serpent made use of this fear when he tempted man into
tasting the fruit of the tree of knowledge. Perhaps it would
be more accurate, and closer to Holy Scripture, to say that
this fear was inspired in the first man by the tempter, and
that sin began in fear. Kierkegaard's second thesis, that
this fear is fear of Nothingness, is one of the most profound insights into the mystery of the Fall. The tempter
had at his disposal only pure Nothingness: Nothingness,
from which God, by His act of creation, had made both
the universe and man, but which without God could neither cross over the limits of its state of Nothingness nor
have any meaning in existence. However, if the omnipotence of God was able to create the world out of Nothing-

ness, it was the limited nature of man, and the fear inspired in him by the serpent, that transformed Nothingness into an enormous, all-destroying, all-consuming, annihilating force. Nothingness ceased to be nothingness, ceased to be nonexistent. It became existent and, together with its lack of being, established itself and took root in all that exists—although there was absolutely no need for it to be. Nothingness has turned out to be a mysterious Proteus. Before our eyes it has transformed itself, first into Necessity, then into the Ethical, then into Eternity. And it has fastened its chains, not only upon man, but upon the Creator Himself. It cannot be fought by ordinary means. There is no way to get at it, no way to overcome it—it hides beneath its lack of being whenever it senses the approach of danger. And—from our point of view—God finds it even more difficult to contend with than man does. God abhors coercion. There is nothing that Nothingness abhors. It is maintained by coercion alone, and accomplishes nothing but coercion in its unforeseen and totally superfluous existence.

Nothingness has appropriated for itself (again, without any right) the predicate of being, as if that had in fact always been its inalienable property. And reason, whose duty should have been to prevent this unlawful seizure,—since it has available both the law of contradiction (βεβαιοτάτη τῶν ἀρχῶν: "the most unyielding of all principles," as Aristotle put it) and the no less powerful law of sufficient basis—reason has remained silent; it has not dared, or has not had the strength, to stir. Nothingness has cast a spell over everything and everyone: the world seems asleep, frozen still, even dead. Nothingness has become Something, but a Something permeated by Nothingness. Reason, our human reason, which we have been taught to consider the best that is in us (*pars melior nostra*), which makes us akin to God, having quietly and indifferently watched all this happen, almost automatically went over to the side of Nothingness after its victory (for all that is real is rational) and to this day continues to stand guard over the conquests of Nothingness.

The idea of original sin is entirely unacceptable to our reason. For—and now I hope to make this clear—the power and the sovereign rights of reason are maintained only by sin. If man could, even for a moment, become an embodiment of the truth of Holy Scripture, reason would immediately be deprived of its sovereign rights: it would cease to be an independent giver of laws and would assume the modest role of dutiful executor. But this very "if," so foreign to our way of thinking, conceals the greatest enigma, an almost insurmountable difficulty. Upon what does this "if" depend? Are we free to make a choice? Can we accept Biblical truth if we want to, and reject it if we do not? Kierkegaard, in company with the most intense inner experience of men driven beyond the limits of the "general" with which theoretical philosophy tempts us, answers this question for us: no, we cannot. Everything was decided for us at the Fall of the first man; sin decided everything for us. Our freedom—that freedom which the Creator shared with man when He summoned him to life—is in a swoon, paralyzed. The terrible monster Nothingness holds us in its power. We know, we feel with our whole being, that this is Nothingness, i.e., that there is nothing to it, and yet we cannot fight against it, just as if it were not impotent Nothingness, but omnipotent Something. What is more, by virtue of some senseless and nightmarish dialectic, we do everything to strengthen the power and might of Nothingness. We ourselves have transformed it into Necessity, the Ethical, Eternity, Infinity. Our understanding and our consciences were not captured by it from without, but, as one might say, from within; we are incapable of doubting the lawfulness of its claims, even when it presents us with the most hideous demands; we see a contradiction in doubt, and Nothingness has taught us to think that horrors of any sort are preferable to a contradiction. When Hegel asserted that the serpent did not deceive man, and that the fruit of the tree of knowledge of good and evil was the source of all future philosophy, he was sincere and spoke the truth: our "philosophy" (i.e., theoretical philosophy) begins with the Fall of Adam. We consider the "real," which has been delivered into the power of Nothingness and is permeated with that Nothingness, to be truly "rational" and eternally justified, that is, both unchanging and desirable. We must accept whatever it may bring us, become reconciled to all of it, grow to like it, and see this truce with reality as an expression of the ultimate in wisdom. But why mention only Hegel! Even as cautious, as calm, as sensitive a thinker as Nietzsche "bowed down" before reality. The crown of his philosophy is *amor fati:* it is not enough to accept, he tells us; we must come to love Necessity, which is Necessity for the very reason that it excludes any possibility of conflict. Nietzsche's audacity apparently knew no bounds. His "on the far side of good and evil," his *"Wille zur Macht,"* summoned men to the ultimate liberation—but before the truths of "knowledge" he weakened; he began to humble himself. The fruit of the tree of knowledge, delightful to look at and pleasing to contemplate, cast its spell over his will, and he exchanged the will to power for resignation, love, and a slavish attachment to Necessity. And he even took pride in this. It is just as Luther said: *homo superbit et somniat, se sapere, se sanctum et justum esse.* A man who has surrendered himself to the power of Nothingness thinks that he is knowing, thinks that he is righteous, and does not even suspect that, the more firmly he becomes convinced of his own knowledge and righteousness, the stronger and more unbreakable grow the chains with which Nothingness has bound him.

This absolute trust in knowledge which possesses immutable truths, dependent upon no one, and the accompaniment to this trust, confidence in the possibility of realizing a righteous life by one's own powers simply by having the desire to do so, have, as I said, transformed Nothingness in our eyes, first into Necessity, then into the Ethical, and then into Eternity and Infinity. It is highly significant that Nietzsche was the first man in the entire history of European thought to perceive the decadent in Socrates, i.e., to see him as a fallen man. But the wisdom of Socrates, whom the god of the pagans praised, amounts to *amor fati,* of which Nietzsche was so proud and boastful, considering it his sole merit. The pagan god, who was himself compelled to bow before Necessity, could not help praising Socrates; the power of *fatum,* as we have seen, extends to immortals as well as mortals. Reality no more belongs to the gods than it does to men. It is in the hands of Nothingness, which has no need of it and does not allow those who need it more than anything else to have access to it. Nothingness has arranged matters so that everything flows, everything passes, everything disappears, in accordance with the "law" of γένεσις and φθορά ("birth and de-

255

struction"), sanctioned by even the most ancient "knowledge." Reality is encompassed by time, its only master, in such a way that nothing is left of it for man: the past is no longer, the future is not yet, and the present, confined between a future which has not yet arrived and a past which has already vanished into Lethe, becomes a mirage, a phantom, a shadow, just as Regina Olsen turned into a shadow or, at best, into a poetic device when Kierkegaard tried to approach her. No one in the world can do anything against this age-old "law" of being established by almighty Nothingness: all are powerless, as Soren Kierkegaard was powerless—only no one recognizes or feels horror at his own powerlessness. There is no difference here between the wise and the foolish, between the learned and the ignorant. In fact, the wise and learned prove to be even weaker and more defenseless than the foolish and ignorant. For wisdom and knowledge not only see the perishable and transitory nature of all that exists; they understand that it cannot be otherwise, and that therefore everything will remain as it is forever, whereas the foolish and ignorant do not even suspect this.

That is the basic and unshakable truth achieved by human understanding and demonstrated by human wisdom. Understanding has revealed to us that there is nowhere to flee from Nothingness. Wisdom has given its blessing to the truth revealed to it by understanding; there is no need to flee from this truth, no need to quarrel and contend with it; one must accept it, grow to love it, extol it. Even the heavens sing its praises; man must echo the heavens.

Such was the "existential philosophy" of the Greeks from Socrates to Epictetus. Every school, including the Epicurean, moved in the orbit of the one whom the god at

Delphi recognized as the wisest of men. The ancients were convinced—Plotinus said this, too—that ἐν ἀρχῇ λόγος καὶ πάντα λόγος ("reason is at the beginning and all is reason") and that the greatest misfortune for a man is not to have come to terms with reason. Even Kierkegaard, as I have already mentioned, looked to Socrates each time his strength left him, and when he did so, he was overwhelmed by the mad fear that all his failures were connected with an inability and unwillingness to love and cherish the gifts brought by reason. Of course, it cannot be denied that the "truth" and "wisdom" of Socrates did give him some temporary comfort and a kind of consolation. Socrates was his defense, so to speak, against Hegel and theoretical philosophy. Perhaps he had Socrates to thank for his idea that his "failure to understand Hegel" was not such an irredeemable disgrace, since Hegel and his universalism (later on Kierkegaard was to speak caustically of the incompletely universal universalism of the Hegelian system) would probably have been received just as severely by Socrates as the philosophical structures of the Sophists had been. Socrates also defended him against Mynster; neither Mynster's life nor his preaching would have been able to withstand the Socratic irony. And even in his conflict with Regina Olsen, it seems evident that Socrates would have taken his side. For she, like Mynster and like Hegel, was not guided in life by the truth revealed by reason or the good that follows truth. If Socrates was not its inspiration, then at least he provided support and reinforcement for Kierkegaard's idea that even beneath the merry unconcern and lightheartedness of youth there is always hidden a slumbering despair which an experienced man with a certain cunning can easily awaken.* All of Kierkegaard's edifying discourses, with which the reader has become familiar in the preceding chapters, are based on Socrates and his "knowledge." Whenever some force compelled Kierkegaard, in his reading of Holy Scripture, to "turn his attention away from the miraculous" and concentrate on "truth" and "good"—just as, in Genesis, the serpent persuaded Adam to "turn his attention" from the tree of life and rest his hopes on the tree of knowledge—he consciously or unconsciously sought help from the man who "up to the time of Christianity was the most remarkable phenomenon in the history of the world." Socrates was indispensable to him; he could not think or live without Socrates. But neither could he live with Socrates. Can there be any doubt that it was during one of the moments when he was completely under the spell of Socrates that the despairing cry escaped his soul: "What force is this that has taken from me my honor and my pride? Is it possible that I have been deprived of

---

* I shall quote this passage *in extenso*, because, apart from its shedding some light on Kierkegaard's relationship to Regina Olsen, it gives additional evidence of the nature of the fruit of the tree of knowledge offered him by the maieutic method of Socrates. "Even in what men consider most beautiful, most attractive—a charming young girl in whom everything breathes harmony, peace, and joy—even there despair is hiding. Outwardly there appears to be happiness; but far, far inside, in the depths, within a shell which happiness has not penetrated, lives fear, i.e., despair. Despair prefers above all to conceal itself there, beneath happiness. Happiness is not spiritual; it is immediacy, and all immediacy, even though it may be accompanied by what seems to be complete serenity and unconcern, is fear, and, certainly, in large part, fear of Nothingness. Therefore, you can never frighten immediacy as much by terrible descriptions of horrors as you can by cleverly, almost casually, but with carefully calculated aim, hinting offhandedly and obscurely that immediacy knows what you are talking about. Of course, it does not know this. But reflection's prey is never so surely guaranteed it as when it makes its snare out of Nothingness. And reflection never expresses itself as completely as when it is itself Nothingness. Immense reflection, or, more correctly, great faith, is necessary if one is to have the strength to endure reflection upon Nothingness, i.e., infinite reflection" (VIII, 22).

the protection of the laws?" He could not, of course, stop at this. His "dialectical fearlessness," or what he called his dialectical fearlessness, drove him on; he arrived at a point from which he could see that his experience extended not just to human beings, but to God as well; God, too, had His honor and His pride taken from Him; God, too, was deprived of the protection of the laws; He looked upon His martyred Son, but, chained by Inflexibility, was unable to stir. What force is this that has taken away God's honor and pride? He is all love, all charity, and yet, like any ordinary mortal, He can only watch the horrors unfolding before Him—and grow numb.

XIX

Freedom

> *The possibility of freedom is not that we can choose between good and evil. Such nonsense is no more compatible with Scripture than with thinking. Possibility—is that we can.*
>
> KIERKEGAARD

It has become clear to us now, I think, what Luther had in mind when he spoke of the *bellua qua non occisa homo non potest vivere*. In these words, as if in embryo, is contained all of existential philosophy as distinct from theoretical philosophy: its *ultima ratio* is not "laws," which deny man protection, but *homo non potest vivere,* and conflict is its method of seeking the truth. Now we will also be able to understand Luther's violent hatred of human wisdom and human knowledge, a hatred which was nurtured and sustained in him by the Apostle Paul's teaching about love and grace. I shall cite two passages from Luther's commentary on the Epistle to the Galatians; they will enable us to come closer still to the sources of Kierkegaard's existential philosophy, and to see for ourselves the abyss which separates it from the existential philosophy of the Greeks. Luther writes: *Ergo omnia dona quae habes, spiritualia et corporalia, qualia sunt sapientia, justitia, eloquentia, potentia, pulchritudo, divitiae, instrumenta et arma sunt ipsius tyrannidis infernalis (h. e. peccati), hisque omnibus cogeris servire diabolo, regnum ejus commovere et augere* ("All the gifts you enjoy—wisdom, righteousness, eloquence, strength, beauty, wealth—all these are the tools and weapons of the infernal tyrant (i.e., sin) and they all compel you to serve the devil, to secure and increase his kingdom"). And in another passage, with even greater force and emphasis: *Nihil fortius adversatur fidei quam lex et ratio, neque illa duo sine magno conatu et labore superari possunt, quae tamen superanda sunt, si modo salvari velis. Ideo, cum conscientia perterrefit lege et luctatur cum judicio Dei, nec rationem, nec legem consulas, sed sola gratia ac verbo consolationis nitaris. Ibi omnino sic te geras, quasi nunquam de lege Dei quidquam audieris, sed ascendas in tenebras, ubi nec lex, nec ratio lucet, sed solum aenigma fidei, quae certo statuat te salvari extra et ultra legem, in Christo. Ita extra et supra lucem legis et rationis ducit nos evangelium in tenebras fidei, ubi lex et ratio nihil habent negotii. Est lex audienda, sed suo loco et tempore. Moses in monte existens, ubi facie ad faciem cum Deo loquitur, non condit, non administrat legem, descendens vero de monte legislator est et populum lege gubernat* (*Ibid.*, 169: "Nothing conflicts with faith more than law and reason, and it is impossible to overcome them without immense effort and labor—but nevertheless they must be overcome if you wish to be saved. Therefore, when your conscience, terrified by law, struggles against the judgment of God, do not consult reason or law, but rely wholly upon the grace and Word of divine consolation. Hold fast to this, as though you had never heard of law, and enter the darkness where neither law nor reason lights your way, but only the mystery of faith, which gives you assurance that you will be saved apart from and beyond the law, in Christ. Thus, the Gospel leads us beyond—and above—the light of law, into the darkness of faith, where there is no room for reason or law. Law must be heard—but at its own time and in its own place. When Moses was on the mountain, where he spoke face to face with God, he knew no law, and did not rule by law; when he descended from the mountain, he became a lawgiver, and ruled his people through law"). I have already mentioned that Kierkegaard had read little of Luther. But Luther's *sola fide,* which inspired his commentary on Galatians, as well as his other writings, completely dominated Kierkegaard's thinking. As long as philosophy has its source in wonder, it finds its fulfillment in "understanding." But what can "understanding" offer man when philosophy is approached by despair, with its questions made from *lugere et detestari?* All the "gifts" of which reason customarily boasts—wisdom, righteousness, eloquence—are helpless against despair, which signifies in itself the end of all possibilities, the ultimate inevitability. What is more, these gifts are found to be, not allies, but merciless enemies—the servants of "a tyrant that compels man to serve the devil." The truths of reason—and the laws ordained by it—which are, at their own time and in their own place, both useful and necessary, cease to be truths when they become autonomous, liberated from God (*veritates emancipatae a Deo*), when they clothe themselves in the vestments of eternity and changelessness. Having become petrified themselves, they turn to stone all those who look upon them. The ordinary consciousness thinks this is madness. Perhaps it is madness: how could anyone exchange light for darkness? Not only to Bonaventura, but to all of us, it seems self-evident, and absolutely indisputable in its self-evidency, that faith is upheld by truths; that, consequently, faith can be defended by the same means which serve to attack it; and that, if we deny this, we discredit faith forever. But the Scriptures revealed something entirely different to Luther: when Moses stood face to face with God, all truths, all laws vanished in an instant, evaporated as if they had never been. Moses was defenseless. And only then did he become a prophet and share the power of God. All the fears, all the apprehensions which force man to seek support, protection, assistance were suddenly dispelled as if by the wave of a magic wand. The light of reason grew dim, the bonds of law were loosed, and in this primeval "darkness," this limitless freedom, man once again found himself in contact with the fundamental *valde bonum* ("very good") which filled the world before our forefather's disastrous Fall. And only in this "darkness of faith" does man's original freedom return to him: not the freedom which Socrates knew and described to men, freedom of choice between good and evil, but the freedom which, to use Kierkegaard's words, is possibility. For if man must choose between good and evil, this means that freedom has already been lost; evil has entered the world and become the equal of God's *valde bonum*. Man has, must have, an immeasurably greater and qualitatively different freedom: not the freedom of choosing between good and evil, but that of rid-ding the world of evil. Man cannot have any sort of dealings with evil; as long as evil exists, there is no freedom, and all that man has called freedom so far is an illusion, a fraud. Freedom is not the choice between good and evil; it destroys evil, turns it into Nothingness—and not the menacing Nothingness of which we have been speaking until now, a Nothingness which in some strange way assumed immense power to ruin, destroy, annihilate everything in its path, and thus took its place beside, and even above, the Existing and gained exclusive control over the predicate of Being—but Nothingness as it was when, weak and powerless, it was transformed according to the word of the Creator into *valde bonum.* As long as Nothingness has not been decisively destroyed, man cannot even dream of freedom. On the contrary, true freedom, which was lost to us at the moment when our forefather, under an incomprehensible and mysterious spell, turned from the tree of life and tasted the fruit of the tree of knowledge, will return only when knowledge loses its power over man, when he finally sees that the "eager striving of reason for general and necessary truths," i.e., for *veritates emancipatae a Deo,* is the *concupiscentia invincibilis* (unconquerable craving) through which sin came into the world. We will recall that even Kierkegaard thought that ignorance is the sleep of the mind. In the midst of many other eternal truths, this one appears to us to be the unshakable and self-evident truth par excellence. However, it is not a truth, but a delusion, the deepest of sleeps, very nearly the death of the mind. Knowledge enslaves human will, making it subordinate to eternal truths which by their very nature are hostile to everything that lives and is at all capable of demonstrating its independence, and which cannot bear to have even God as their equal.

The "swoon of freedom" * which Kierkegaard connects with the Fall of man is also the prerequisite for the possibility of the existence of knowledge, which *The Critique of Pure Reason* actually could not, and would not, take into consideration. And, conversely, the state of ignorance, the state of freedom from knowledge is the source of man's liberation. Ignorance is not something negative, some sort of lack, some sort of deficiency, just as freedom is not insufficiency and negation, but an affirmation of great worth. Innocence has no desire for knowledge; it is above knowledge (let me remind you once more of the words of Plotinus: δραμεῖν ὑπὲρ τὴν ἐπιστήμην), just as the will of the One Who created man in His own image and likeness is above knowledge. Kierkegaard himself gives us the best evidence of this. "Fear is the swoon of freedom," he tells us. "Psychologically speaking, the Fall always takes place in a swoon." And he goes on to explain: "The Nothingness of fear is a complex of misgivings to which the individual comes ever nearer, even though they have essentially no significance in the fear; however, this is not a Nothingness to which the individual has no relationship, but a Nothingness which has a vital mutual relationship with the ignorance of innocence." The first step of knowledge is this: Nothingness, which is supposed to be Nothingness, and which is only Nothingness, breaks its way into the soul of man and begins to take charge there, as if it were in fact

* "The swoon of freedom" is a free translation of Luther's *"de servo arbitrio"*—the enslaved will, i.e., the will which seeks truth, not through faith, but through reason.

the master. Kierkegaard has confirmed this for us: *crede experto*—which means, do not ask the old, ask the experienced. His testimony has such great significance that I feel obliged to reproduce it again in full, as it is only by going through the experience of Kierkegaard and of minds akin to his that one can become at all free of the fatal temptation which attracts us to the tree of knowledge, and begin to ponder seriously the story of Genesis. "If we ask what the object of fear is, there will be only one answer: Nothingness. Nothingness and fear accompany each other. But as soon as the real freedom of the mind is disclosed, fear disappears. What, upon closer scrutiny, is Nothingness as the pagans feared it? It is called fate . . . Fate is the Nothingness of fear . . . The greatest genius has no power to vanquish the idea of fate. On the contrary, the genius reveals fate everywhere, understanding it all the more profoundly, as he himself is more profound . . . This precisely describes the real power of the genius, that he reveals fate, but this is also his weakness. This seems nonsense to the ordinary consciousness—but in fact something great is concealed here, for no man is born with the idea of providence. . . . The existence of such genius is, in spite of its brilliance, its beauty, and its great historical significance, a sin. It takes courage to understand this, but it is so." * There is no doubt that it takes courage —great courage, immense courage—to understand this and to dare to say such a thing aloud. For then it must be admitted that in ignorance the mind is wide-awake and that knowledge induces lethargy and sleep in man. The Biblical narrative must not be "amended"; the Fall was the beginning of knowledge, or, to be more exact, sin and

* V, 93, 96, 99.

knowledge are only different words to denote one and the
same "subject"! The man who knows, the man who is not
satisfied with experience, the man "who is irritated by
experience" and who "eagerly strives to assure himself
that what is *must necessarily* be thus (as it is), and not
otherwise"—reveals a Fate which does not exist.* For man
in the state of ignorance, Fate does not exist, and Fate has
no way to make him yield as long as he continues in ignorance. But then a new light dawns for us in the person of
the serpent, whom we "knowing" men regard as an irrele-
vant appendage to the Biblical story. The renunciation of
the "ignorance of innocence" is a great enigma. Of what
use was knowledge to the first man when he was entrusted
with the power to give names to all things? Of what use
was it for him to exchange the divine *valde bonum,* in
which there was no room for evil, for a world in which
both good and evil exist, and where one must be able to
tell good from evil? We have no doubt that the ability to
distinguish between good and evil improves man and represents the progress and growth of his mind. Even Kierkegaard, in paying tribute to this human, all too human,
notion of good and evil, shifts back and forth from Socrates
to the Bible and from the Bible to Socrates, and feels
obliged to admit that the first man, before the Fall, i.e.,
before he tasted the fruit of the forbidden tree, was somehow not quite complete, not a real man, precisely because
he did not know how to distinguish good from evil. One
might almost say that the sleep of the mind, which was,
according to Kierkegaard, the state of existence of the

* The words in quotation marks are taken, as the reader will probably
recall, from *The Critique of Pure Reason.* —I have italicized only the
words "must necessarily."

first man, really means that he was not yet able to distinguish between good and evil. And so it turns out that the serpent did not deceive man—the Fall was by no means a Fall, but only a necessary moment in the dialectical development of the spirit, as Hegel has told us. Of course, Kierkegaard does not mean this—and yet, when he denies the presence of freedom in man in the state of innocence, he automatically connects this with his inability to distinguish good from evil. And this is the same Kierkegaard who so passionately assured us that freedom is not the possibility of choosing between good and evil, that such an interpretation of freedom is nonsense, that freedom is possibility.*

And, in fact, this is the problem: if freedom were the freedom of choice between good and evil, then this freedom would have to be inherent in the Creator Himself, as the free Being par excellence. And, therefore, it would be quite possible to assume that, having a choice between good and evil, the Creator would prefer evil. This question was the real *crux interpretuum* for medieval philosophic thought. It was impossible to reject the idea that freedom is the freedom of choice between good and evil: the Middle Ages, limited by Hellenic speculation, could not, dared not, separate the religious point of view from the ethical. Neither was it possible to think that God has a "right" to prefer evil over good.

From this "irreconcilable contradiction"—which symbolized the age-old opposition between Biblical revelation and speculative philosophy—arose the "paradoxical"

---

* V, 44. "The possibility of freedom is not that we can choose between good and evil. Such nonsense is no more compatible with Scripture than with thinking. Possibility is that we can."

teaching of Duns Scotus, who overturned all the traditional principles upon which his predecessors had constructed the Christian ethic. He was the first who ventured to utter those terrible words which the rational understanding cannot endure and which even devout philosophers have been careful to avoid: free will. God is free will; there is no principle above God, no law. Whatever He accepts is good. Whatever He rejects is evil. God does not, as Plato thought, choose between good and evil, bestowing His love upon good and hating evil; on the contrary: what He loves is good and what He does not love is evil. God created both good and evil out of Nothingness, which offered Him no resistance, just as He made the whole world out of nothing. The Scholastic philosopher William of Ockham, who followed Duns Scotus, developed the same thesis with even greater clarity. There can be no question that the theories of Duns Scotus and Ockham are in complete accord with both the spirit and the letter of Holy Scripture. But to speculative philosophy, free will and totally unlimited freedom, even though they are God's, sound like a sentence of death. Speculative philosophy cannot construct anything upon "free will"; it loses its footing. And, indeed, Ockham and Duns Scotus are the last independent thinkers of the Middle Ages; after them the "decline of Scholasticism" begins, just as a further development of Hellenic philosophy was impossible after Plotinus and his δραμεῖν ὑπὲρ τὴν ἐπιστήμην. It is necessary either to "soar" above knowledge, "soar" above the ethical, or, if such soaring is not within a man's power, or is actually impossible for him, to renounce "revelation" forever, renounce Him Who appears in revelation, and humbly take up the burden of eternal truths and uncreated laws. Modern philosophy has chosen the second path —where it leads will be shown presently—but the Middle Ages dreaded eternal truths and uncreated laws no less than divine free will. They guessed almost intuitively that truth and law, like man, do not gain their meaning, significance, and worth from their uncreatedness and their independence from God; that uncreatedness and independence from God not only do not add anything of value to them, but take away their very essence. All that is uncreated is also lacking in grace, disadvantaged, and, accordingly, condemned to an illusory existence. All that is "liberated" from God surrenders itself to the power of Nothingness. "Dependence" upon God is freedom from Nothingness, which, because it is uncreated, sucks the blood from everything living, like a vampire. Kierkegaard's account of how Inflexibility had paralyzed not only him, a weak human being, but even the Creator Himself, shows us quite vividly what truth and principles become when they forget their subsidiary function and try to assume sovereign rights. However, in the interests of both historical truth and the problems which occupy us here, I must say that the Middle Ages were not as monolithic in their formulation and resolution of basic religious questions as some would like us to think, and they were not always so subordinate to Greek influence. In its principal course, medieval philosophy, which was very closely linked with patristic philosophy, on the whole simply kept to the legacy of Hellenism, and, even in the person of its most outstanding representatives, dared not and would not break with Hellenism. It is possible and usual, without offending reality, to describe its broad mainstream as leading from Origen and Clement of Alexandria, on the one hand, and St. Augustine, on the other, down to the beginning of the fourteenth century. But in the middle of that century another current appeared, faint and far away, to be sure, which reflected an awareness of the impossibility and uselessness of reconciling Biblical revelation with the rational truths of Greek philosophy. Even Tertullian, whom we rightly consider to be, to a certain degree, Kierkegaard's inspiration and his spiritual father—we have already mentioned this, and will now do so again—even Tertullian realized what a fathomless abyss separates Jerusalem and Athens. However, a particularly brilliant example of this trend was Peter Damian, who in his writings (especially in the book *De omnipotentia Dei*) rebelled, almost four centuries before Duns Scotus and Ockham, with a boldness that amazes us even now, against attempts to interpret Holy Scripture with the help of and on the basis of Hellenic philosophy. He was horrified at the "Necessity" of acknowledging any kind of limit to the omnipotence of God. In the presence of God every Necessity reveals its true nature and is exposed as vain and empty Nothingness. Even the assumption that the law of contradiction or the principle: *quod factum est infectum esse nequit* ("what has once existed cannot become nonexistent") could in any sense bind God or oblige Him at all seemed to him to be a repudiation, a defiance of Holy Scripture and the greatest offense: *cupiditas scientiae,* which led man to the Fall. *Qui vitiorum omnium catervas moliebatur inducere, cupiditatem scientiae quasi ducem exercitus posuit, sique per eam infelici mundo cunctas iniquitatum turmas invexit* ("He who introduced the swarm of vices placed at their head, like a leader of troops, the thirst for knowledge, and thus condemned the unhappy world to an immense number of misfortunes"). What Kant's "critique" regarded as the natural function of "pure reason," what theologians have seen, and see to this day, as *partem meliorem nostram*—the thirst for knowledge, which tells us that what exists must necessarily exist thus (as it does exist) and not otherwise—was in the eyes of the medieval monk original sin, from which his entire soul shrank as from the corrupt breath of death and destruction. There is no principle, ideal or real, that could have existed before God, that could be above God. All power in the universe belongs to God; God always commands, never obeys. Every attempt to place anything whatever above God—regardless, I repeat, of whether it be ideal or material—leads to an "abomination of desolation." That is why Christ, when asked what the first commandment was, answered by repeating the thunderous *audi Israel,* which demolishes both the knowledge of pure reason and all the necessities on which the knowledge of pure reason is based. Tertullian, from whom Kierkegaard borrowed his idea of the Absurd, also took Scripture as a declaration that for God everything is possible. It is true that Tertullian did not say *credo quia absurdum*—words ascribed to him by Kierkegaard and most of his contemporaries. But in his *De carne Christi* we find the same idea even more defiantly expressed. I have mentioned it before, but in view of the close connection between Kierkegaard's theory of the Absurd and Tertullian's approach to Biblical revelation, I feel that at this point I must once again quote these lines, which are unique even in theological literature: *Crucifixus est Dei filius; non pudet, quia pudendum est. Et mortuus est Dei filius; prorsus credibile quia ineptum est. Et sepultus resurrexit; certum est, quia impossible* ("The son of God was crucified; it is no cause for shame, because it is shameful. And the son of God died; it is credible, because it is absurd. And, having been buried, he rose again; it is certain, because it is impossible"). The meaning of the Biblical "Hear, O Israel" is revealed here with a sharpness and intensity that mortal men can hardly bear. Discard your notions of what is shameful, absurd, impossible; forget your eternal truths: they all come from the Evil One, from the fruit of the forbidden tree. The more you rely on your "knowledge" of good and evil, of rational and irrational, of possible and impossible, the further you will be from the source of life and the stronger will be the power of Nothingness over you. The greatest genius, the most virtuous man, is the most terrible sinner. Between Athens and Jerusalem there is no peace, nor should there be. Rational truth comes from Athens; revelation, from Jerusalem. There is no room for revelation within the limits of rational truths; it breaks through such limits. And revelation is not afraid of rational truths: to all their *pudendum, ineptum et impossibile* it replies with its authoritative *non pudet, prorsus credibile* and, crowning all, its *certum;* and the ordinary categories of thinking begin to seem like a dense fog enveloping Nothingness, which, though weak and helpless, appears to everyone to be menacing and invincible.

Neither Tertullian, nor Peter Damian, nor all the others who came with them and after them, were triumphant in history. —But I will ask again: is not the ultimate and most necessary truth to be found in the very voices that so infrequently reach our ears? And do not our *pudet,*

Kierkegaard

ineptum, impossibile, which history takes such pains to defend, conceal the presence of that *bellua, qua non occisa homo non potest vivere?*

Kierkegaard, in venturing to declare that for God everything is possible, departed from the broad road along which thinking humanity, even Christianly thinking humanity, is moving. For him, "triumphant," "victorious," recognized Christianity was a Christianity that had abolished Christ, i.e., God. But on paths unknown to anyone, in wildernesses where no one had even made paths, his ears caught the silent voices of men unknown and unnecessary to anyone: men with the "courage" to look at what madness and death reveal to us. They have seen and heard things that no one has ever heard and seen before. That is why they have nothing, not even language, in common with all the others; these are men who have "withdrawn from the general," as Kierkegaard puts it.*

* "The knight of faith knows how beautiful and joyous it is to belong to the general. He knows how soothing it is to be an individual who adapts himself to the general, and, so to speak, publishes a second edition of himself: neat, pleasing to the eye, without errors, easy for all to read; he knows how good it is to understand yourself in the general, so that you yourself understand the general, and every other person who understands you, understands you in the general, and together with you rejoices in the peace which the general offers the soul. He knows how beautiful it is to be born the sort of man who has the general as his fatherland, for whom the general is an unfailing haven where he will always be received with open arms, where there must be refuge for him. But he knows that a lonely road, narrow and steep, winds above the general; and he knows the horror of being born lonely, of being born outside the general, of being condemned to go through life without meeting a single traveller along the way. He sees very clearly what his relationship is to other people. Humanly speaking, he has gone mad, and cannot make anyone understand him. And yet, "gone mad" is the very mildest expression. If they do not take him to be mad, people will declare him a hypocrite, and the higher he goes on his path, the more he will seem to all an utter hypocrite." (III, 72, 73) And again (*ibid.*, p. 68): "Faith cannot be achieved by means of the general; that would mean abolishing it. Here lies the paradox of faith, and one man cannot understand another in this

Everyone else "rejects" the miraculous, in order to contemplate and rejoice in pure charity, which can do nothing. In our world, where there are no miracles, charity and love are powerless and helpless, and, apart from "spiritual" satisfaction, they have nothing to offer man. In order to return to them the force and power they deserve, one must reject all the "consolations" of ethics, beneath which hide the "impossibilities" of reason, the captive of nonexistent Nothingness. It is difficult, immensely difficult, to renounce reason and the awareness of one's righteousness; for this means to "withdraw from the general." As long as a man goes along with everyone else, he has a sense of stability, of strength, of support—he has a "solid footing." He upholds the rest, but to an even greater extent all the rest uphold him; that is the ultimate and principal temptation of the rational and the ethical. This is why Plato could say that the greatest of all misfortunes is to become a μισόλογος. It is a misfortune, and a terrible one. But surely it is an even greater misfortune to trust in reason and the ethical. They lead us to all-engulfing Nothingness, and Nothingness becomes lord of the universe. And there is no salvation from Nothingness; Nothingness is the very monster *qua non occisa homo non potest vivere.* As long

---

matter. We imagine that if two people are in the same position, they will understand one another. . . . But one knight of faith can in no way help another knight of faith. A man can become a knight of faith only if he will wholeheartedly take upon himself the paradox—otherwise he will never become a knight of faith. Comradeship is unthinkable in this realm. Each man must decide for himself what he understands his own Isaac to be . . . And if anyone should prove to be cowardly and mean enough to wish to become a knight of faith by placing the responsibility for it upon another—it would not matter; nothing would come of it. For only an individual, just as an individual, can become a knight of faith. There is something great in this which I can understand, but not attain. There is also something terrible in it—which I understand even better."

as a man relies upon the support of the "general," as long as he is afraid to lose his footing, as long as he puts his faith in the truths of reason and his own virtues, he is wholly in the power of his worst and most implacable enemy.

XX

God and Coercive Truth

> *For God everything is possible—this*
> *thought is my motto in the most pro-*
> *found sense of the word, and it has ac-*
> *quired a deeper meaning for me than I*
> *could ever have imagined.*
>
> KIERKEGAARD

In the writings of Duns Scotus we find the following admission, which in its own way is remarkably frank: *isti, qui negant aliquod ens contingens, exponendi sunt tormentis quousque concedant, quod possibile est eos non torqueri* ("Those who deny the fortuitousness of anything that exists should be forced to undergo tortures until they admit that it is possible for them not to be tortured"). In itself, this thought is not original: it was a straightforward expression of what all had thought and many had said. It is surprising only that Duns Scotus, whom his contemporaries—not without reason—gave the name of *doctor subtilissimus,* did not perceive that by defending his own position in this way he compromised the entire system of philosophical proofs. Of course, he was right; if a man is subjected to tortures and told that the torture will continue until he admits that it is possible for him not to be tortured, he will almost certainly make the admission demanded of him. If he should turn out to possess the fortitude and courage of a Socrates or an Epictetus, then you would most likely achieve nothing by torturing him; the same would be true if you were dealing with a Regulus or a Mucius Scaevola. There are men over whom torture cannot prevail. What then? Would the argument of the *doctor subtilissimus* retain its power to prove?

On the other hand, men who do not possess sufficient fortitude would under torture admit anything at all to be the truth, if only the torture would stop. If they were asked to admit that it would be possible for them not to be tortured—they would admit that it would be possible for them not to be tortured; if they were asked to admit that it would be impossible not to torture them, they would admit that, too, if only they would be set free. The Apostle Peter denied his master three times, although it was not a question of torture; the threat at hand was only that of a more or less harsh sentence. Therefore, the example given by Duns Scotus is fanciful and contrived. One would have to suppose that as long as the world has existed no one has ever been put to torture in order to extract from him an admission of *aliquod ens contingens*. On the contrary, the opposite constantly takes place before our eyes: life tortures men and continues to torture them from all sides, and for a long time has been wringing from them the admission that what is, not only is as it is, but cannot be otherwise.

However, this is not even the main point. How could

the *doctor subtilissimus,* to whom both will and intellect
were purely spiritual attributes of man, assume that torture, which works on the senses, would play such a decisive role where it is a matter of the truth! When we encounter this kind of thinking in Epictetus, we calmly
overlook it, attributing it to his lack of philosophic insight.
But Duns Scotus is not Epictetus: Duns Scotus is one of
the keenest and most powerful minds, not only of the
Middle Ages, but of all thinking humanity. And he speaks
of torture, of purely physical methods of coercion, as the
ultima ratio of truth. There is something to give us pause
here, especially in connection with what Kierkegaard has
told us about the horrors of human existence. It might
also be appropriate to recall the testimony offered by
Nietzsche. Nietzsche, too, spoke of the "great pain" which
"truth" uses to humble man, and of how truth cuts its way
into us like a knife. The theory of knowledge cannot and
must not remain deaf to such testimony. Whether it wants
to or not, it will have to admit that the purely spiritual
methods of persuasion which it puts at the disposal of
truth for the realization of its sovereign rights are not
going to achieve their aim. Neither the "law" of sufficient
basis, nor the "law" of contradiction, nor intuition with all
its self-evidences can guarantee a man's obedience to the
truth; in the last analysis, it must resort to torture, to force.
God, Kierkegaard has told us, never coerces, but knowledge, with its truths, clearly does not resemble God and
has no wish to; it coerces, it is maintained only by coercion, and the grossest, most repellent coercion at that, and,
as is evident from the example given by Duns Scotus, it
does not even consider it necessary to hide behind the unc-
tuous *sine effusione sanguinis.* The theory of knowledge, in

clearing the way for theoretical philosophy, has ignored this, unwilling to see anything worthy of its attention here. Not only the naive Epictetus, but the keenest of thinkers, like Duns Scotus and Nietzsche, when they inadvertently came upon the methods resorted to by truth when man does not voluntarily agree to submit to it, were not discomfited in the least, as if such things were quite right and proper. Aristotle himself, with almost angelic meekness, tells us of the great philosophers ἀναγκαξόμενοι ὑπ αὐτῆς τῆς ἀληθείας ("coerced by truth itself"). It is true that he was not speaking of torture, having rightly reasoned that there are matters on which it is better to be silent, and that in such cases eloquence is more harmful than helpful. But he has a great deal to say about ἀνάγκη (necessity), which he identifies with force—βία, and its power over human thought. Plato, too, did not mention the tortures to which we are subjected by truth, simply pointing out that the world is ruled by necessity, which even the gods cannot overcome. *Homo superbit et somniat, se sapere, se sanctum et justum esse*—man thinks that if he only closes his eyes to ἀνάγκη (necessity), if he allows knowledge to take over his life, no matter what the price, then holiness and righteousness will follow of themselves. He cannot forget the ancient pronouncement: *eritis sicut dei,* and instead of fighting his powerlessness, he hides from it in his pride. This is why Pascal said, with regard to Epictetus: *superbe diabolique.* Pride is not confidence in one's own power, as we are generally inclined to think—pride is an awareness, banished to the depths of the soul, of one's powerlessness. But, invisible, it is more terrible than when it is visible. Man values this kind of powerlessness, loves and cultivates it in himself. Kierkegaard had to arrive at the frightful awareness that God's love is controlled by His inflexibility, that God is bound and cannot move a finger, that God, too, has been afflicted like us with a "thorn in the flesh," i.e., all the tortures to which the truth subjects man are intended for Him as well—in order for him to dare to oppose theoretical philosophy with existential, to allow himself to ask how truth seized power over God, and to see what is actually manifested in this monstrous device of reason's: the Fall of man and original sin. Even the devout Leibniz, who always spoke in the name of Christianity, was thoroughly convinced that *les vérités éternelles sont dans l'entendement de Dieu indépendamment de sa volonté.* And, again, this idea, like Duns Scotus' idea about the power of torture to prove, is not even his own original idea; the Middle Ages thought the same thing, and so did the Greeks. In the same paragraph of his *Théodicée*, Leibniz himself quotes Plato, who maintained—as the reader will recall—that necessity reigns in the world side by side with reason, but he could have quoted the Scholastics with equal justice, as their general views on the source of evil, which he cites, attest. Perhaps it might therefore be not unprofitable for us to take a closer look at his observations: *On demande d'où vient le mal. Les anciens attribuaient la cause du mal à la matière, qu'ils croyaient incrée et indépendante de Dieu . . . Mais nous qui dérivons tout être de Dieu, où trouvons-nous la source du mal? La réponse est qu'elle doit être cherchée dans la nature idéale de la créature autant que cette créature est renfermée dans les vérités idéales qui sont dans l'entendement de Dieu indépendamment de sa volonté. Car il faut considérer qu'il y a une* imperfection originelle *dans la créature avant le péché, parce que la créature est limitée essentiellement, d'où vient qu'elle ne saurait tout savoir et qu'elle peut se tromper et faire des fautes.* It seemed to Leibniz that only a pagan, far removed from revealed truth, could take for granted the existence of matter which is uncreated and independent of God. But to place ideal truths side by side with and above God, to assume that ideal truths are not created, but eternal, means, as he saw it, to "exalt" God, to glorify Him, to do Him honor. True, he himself admits that all evil in the world arose because uncreated truths, heedless of the will of God, worked their way into His mind—and one would think that this must have troubled him. But not at all: his entire *Théodicée*, i.e., his "justification of God," is based on the idea that God has no power to overcome truths which He did not create. Thus, the *Théodicée* is not a justification of God so much as a justification of evil. Reason, eager to comprehend the existing as something that cannot be other than it is, has had its way. "Experience" no longer irritates, but satisfies; and reason considers the task of philosophy completed. Although it was accomplished by torture, still, God and man have been reduced to obedience. The world must remain imperfect, for it is impossible to destroy evil. Of course, if things had been different, if the truths had not been eternal truths, but created ones, and man had not been created, but eternal, then there would have been no need for evil. Or, if the truths had not succeeded in insinuating themselves into the mind of God without seeking His consent, then, too, evil would have found no place for itself in creation. But Leibniz, or rather, theoretical philosophy, pays no attention to this. Its main concern is to preserve truth—and what happens to man and God is none of its affair. Or worse still: the very essence of theoretical philosophy lies in its absolute rejection of the idea that the power of truth is in any sense limited. This is why Leibniz was so firmly convinced that the act of creation itself already presupposes imperfection, and that man before the Fall, i.e., man as he came from the hands of the Creator, was just as weak and insignificant as all the succeeding generations of Adam. Evil came, not through the Fall, as the Bible says, and not from the Fall, but from the fact that man was *created* by God. And if we taste of the fruit of the forbidden tree and thus allow the possibility of uncreated truths to enter our minds, then we will be as gods, knowing good and evil, and creation as it is will be justified.

Once again we see that the Biblical serpent, a seemingly unnecessary adjunct to the story of Genesis, proves to be the spiritual leader of the best representatives of thinking humanity. Leibniz, following the example of the Scholastic philosophers, saw the act of creation as the source of evil, without even realizing that he was thereby perpetuating evil. Even less did he suspect that by condemning the act of creation he was repudiating Holy Scripture. In fact, Scripture states the opposite: that everything created was *valde bonum* ("very good"). And it was *valde bonum* precisely because it was created by God. Therefore, if Leibniz had really wanted to conform to Holy Scripture, he could have and should have seen, or at least tried to see, that truths uncreated by God, are, for the very reason that they were not created by God, impaired, defective, deprived of that *valde bonum* which, according to the word of the Creator, is shared by everything summoned into being by Him. And, indeed, in spite of all their ideality, eternal truths are just as lacking in spirit and will, just as empty and unreal, as the uncreated matter of the Greeks. They came from Nothingness, and sooner or later will return to it. When Leibniz was still young, barely in his teens, he read Luther's book on the "enslaved will," as well as the *Diatribae de libero arbitrio* by Erasmus of Rotterdam against which it had been written, and, despite his youth, appears to have gained an excellent understanding of the arguments of the disputing sides. But he did not heed Luther's *homo non potest vivere*, even though Luther was not speaking, but thundering. He was thundering specifically against truths which have penetrated, or, more precisely, which think they have penetrated, the will of the Creator, without asking His consent; and against those who, like Erasmus, do not perceive that these eternal truths which have permeated their understanding have also enslaved and paralysed their will. Leibniz in his youth, as in his old age, felt that Luther's *homo non potest vivere* was not an "argument" and could in no way be countered with the "self-evidences" on which eternal truths rest and to which they owe their claim to be independent even of God. And still less, of course, could he admit that our attachment to truths which have penetrated the mind of God independent of His will is in fact the result of the Fall of man described in Scripture; that the curse of sin is upon self-evidences; and that rational or speculative philosophy is just as lacking in grace (i.e., unsanctified by the divine *valde bonum*) as the fruit of the tree of knowledge of good and evil. Original sin, for Leibniz as for theoretical philosophy, was a myth, or, more exactly, a fiction, which ought not to be disputed, out of respect for a book recognized by everyone as holy, but which cannot be taken seriously. However much Luther may thunder, however much the Prophets and Apostles may thunder, the philosopher knows that thunder will not shatter the eternal truths of reason. And even if it should turn out (as Leibniz himself admitted) that all the evil in the world came from eternal truths this would not cause either the eternal truths or the awe felt by philosophy for them to waver. Truth, by its very nature, does not allow hesitation and does not tolerate hesitation in those who look upon it; it has tortures ready for hesitaters. It menacingly demands that it be accepted as it is, and proudly and confidently defends itself from all questions and all criticism by citing its own uncreatedness and independence from the will of any being whatever, even almighty God. And here we plainly find ourselves in an enchanted circle from which a man cannot escape by ordinary means. All the "arguments" are on the side of uncreated truth. It is impossible to quarrel with it; one must fight it, cause it to vanish like an evil spell, like a nightmare. But "reason" will never begin the fight on its own. Reason "eagerly strives" for uncreated truths, not even remotely suspecting that their uncreatedness conceals death and destruction, and that in spite of all their "ideality" they are just as much of a menace to everything living as the "matter" of the ancients. For reason, the divine or Biblical *fiat* ("let there be") is the greatest offense; for reason, life itself is the greatest offense, an offense for the very reason that it bears witness to the Creator's *fiat*, which reason translates into its own tongue as "free will," words hateful to it. That is why *lugere et detestari* are so strictly forbidden man by reason, and why *intelligere* is so peremptorily demanded of him. *Intelligere*

285

means to accept and bless uncreated truths, to wonder at them and glorify them. And yet all man's curses are hurled at the very things accepted and blessed by reason, above all at truths which, imagining that their uncreatedness gives them an advantage, have penetrated, not into the mind of God, as Leibniz assures us, but into the mind of fallen man. And only curses can drive them out of there, only an irreconcilable, ever-ready hatred for the fruit of the tree of knowledge can clear man's way to the tree of life. One must oppose reason and its awe of uncreated truths with the Absurd and its despair before the devastation brought into the world by truths independent of the will of God. Sin came from them—and salvation from sin is not to be found in knowledge of the inevitability of all that comes to pass, or in virtue, which, aware of inevitability, "voluntarily" submits to it, but in faith in God for Whom everything is possible, Who created everything according to His own will, and in Whose presence everything uncreated is only empty and pitiful Nothingness. The Absurd to which Kierkegaard summons us also consists in this, and it is the starting point of existential philosophy, which in contrast to theoretical philosophy is a philosophy of Biblical revelation.

All Kierkegaard's dialectical fearlessness and his unreserved "severity" were needed in order for him to show us the true nature of theoretical philosophy. Theoretical philosophy originated in an immense and inexplicable fear of Nothingness. Fear of Nothingness compels man to search for refuge and protection in knowledge, i.e., in truths which are uncreated, independent of anyone, general and necessary, and, as we think, capable of saving us from the fortuities of free will with which existence is inundated. When Kant says that reason eagerly strives for general and necessary truths, and when he disputes the claims of metaphysics, pointing to the inability of metaphysics to satisfy reason in this respect—he is quite right: metaphysics has no general and necessary truths at its disposal. But Kant does not ask what those general and necessary truths have prepared for man, and why reason is so eager for them. He considers himself a good Christian, he has read Holy Scripture, he knows that the Prophet Amos * proclaimed, and the Apostle Paul repeated after him: *justus ex fide vivit* (the just will live by faith). He also knows the words of the Apostle Paul: "all that is not of faith is sin." It would seem no more than a step from this to guessing, or at least suspecting, that reason's "eager striving" is that *concupiscentia invincibilis* which the Prophet and the Apostle regarded, and have taught us to regard, as the most terrible consequence of the Fall of the first man. Kant boasted that he had suspended knowledge in order to open the way to faith, but what sort of faith is that, if man is striving for general and necessary truths? The Critique of Pure Reason took pains to protect all the necessary truths which in the Critique of Practical Reason duly became imperatives, "you must's." Critical philosophy only proved once again that reason cannot bear and will not tolerate any criticism; the German idealism which grew out of it returned to Spinoza and his testament: *quam aram parabit sibi qui majestatem rationis laedit* (What altar will the man who has insulted the majesty of reason provide for himself)? Luther's efforts to prevail over Aristotle were in vain; history has not recognized them. Even among rather influential Protestant philosophers and

* See footnote 1, chapter XVII.

theologians we will not find anyone who recognized the eager striving of Kantian reason as the *concupiscentia invincibilis* which led the first man to the Fall and saw it as the *bellua qua non occisa homo non potest vivere*. On the contrary: man is so afraid of the freedom proclaimed by Scripture and the divine *fiat* which is not bound by anything that he is prepared to submit to any principle, put himself in bondage to any authority—solely in order not to be left without sure guidance. God coerces no one—this idea seems intolerable to us. And the idea that God is bound by nothing, absolutely nothing is considered to be utter madness. When Kierkegaard approached the threshold of that Holy of Holies where Divine Freedom dwells, his usual courage deserted him and he resorted to indirect communication; if there is any sort of power above God, any principle whatever, whether material or ideal—then even God will not escape all the horrors of existence revealed to us in our experience. Worse yet: God knows horrors, compared with which all the hardships that fall to the lot of mortals seem but child's play. In fact, if God is not the source of truth and the possibilities and impossibilities stipulated by it, if truth stands above God, as it does above man, equally indifferent to God and man, then God is just as defenseless as mortals. His love and charity are helpless and powerless. When God looks upon truth, even He turns to stone; He cannot stir, cannot speak out, cannot answer His crucified Son appealing to Him for help. I have repeated these words by Kierkegaard so many times because they express in a remarkably concrete and vivid form the basic concept of existential philosophy: for God everything is possible. That is also what was meant by his violent attacks on the church. The church and Christianity, by living in peace and harmony with reason, abolish Christ, abolish God. One cannot "live" with reason. *Justus ex fide vivit:* man will live by faith alone, and all that is not of faith is sin, is death. What faith brings with it, it brings without consulting or considering reason. Faith abolishes reason. Faith is given to man, not in order to support reason's claims to sovereignty in the universe, but to make man himself master in the world established for him by the Creator. Faith leads us through what reason rejects as Absurd to what that same reason identifies with the non-existent. Reason teaches man to obey; faith gives him the power to command. Theoretical philosophy condemns us to slavery; the aim of existential philosophy is to break through the self-evidences erected by reason, and reach the freedom in which the impossible becomes reality. As it is written: οὐδὲν ἀδυνατήσει ὑμῖν (nothing shall be impossible unto you).

XXI

The Mystery of Redemption

OMNES PROPHETAE VIDERUNT HOC IN SPI-
RITU, QUOD CHRISTUS FUTURUS ESSET OM-
NIUM MAXIMUS LATRO, ADULTER, FUR,
SACRILEGUS, BLASPHEMUS, ETC. . . . QUO
NULLUS MAJOR NUNQUAM IN MUNDO FUE-
RIT.

Luther

It remains for us to take the final step. Some power has persuaded us of the invincibility of Nothingness, and Nothingness has become lord of the universe. Of all that our experience of life reveals to us, this is the most incomprehensible and enigmatic. Hardly less mysterious is the dull, indifferent resignation with which we all accept the power of Nothingness, as well as our unaccountable and ineradicable fear of it. Rare is the man who pauses and ponders over the extraordinary thing that is happening to him. Pascal sensed the terrible *enchantement et assoupissement surnaturels* here; Luther has told us about the *servo arbitrio*. Kierkegaard repeatedly speaks of the enslaved will. But theoretical philosophy does not choose to recognize this, being unable or unwilling to see that the enslaved will is, in the words of Kant, the prerequisite for the possibility of knowledge. Everyone wants to think that knowledge is the prerequisite for the possibility of freedom, and everyone is also sure that freedom is the freedom of choice between good and evil. The preceding exposition has, I hope, satisfied us that both these assumptions are in fact the prerequisite for the possibility of the existence of theoretical philosophy. In order for theoretical philosophy to exist, the will of man (and of God: Leibniz "demonstrated" this to us) must be subordinated to knowledge, and, subordinated to knowledge, enslaved freedom *ipso facto* becomes freedom of choice between good and evil. Reality, which took form apart from and independent of anyone's will, is presented to man by knowledge as the immediate data of consciousness. In this reality man finds everything ready-made and irrevocably determined; he cannot alter the order of existence, which was established without him. This is the starting point of theoretical philosophy, for which only edification, the source of all wisdom, is left. Philosophy teaches man to understand the "necessary" in the "given" and to "accept" the necessary by adjusting to it, more or less. Philosophy knows, of course, what fateful significance there is in that "more or less." But it obstinately remains silent on this subject, for it, too, cannot bear what "madness and death have to say," which puts an end to all adjustment. In order to emerge with honor from a difficult situation, theoretical philosophy refers us to morality, which has the magic power of turning the inevitable into the obligatory and even the desirable, and thus paralyzes all our ability to resist. The passage quoted earlier from Kierkegaard's *The Thorn in the Flesh* shows us with appalling precision the state of mind of a man who has trusted to "pure reason": he feels, as in a nightmare, that a terrible monster is advancing on him and he cannot move a muscle. What keeps him in this stupor? What has chained and enslaved his will? Kierkegaard answers us: Nothingness. He sees clearly that the power which has defeated him, the power which has defeated us all, is the power of pure Nothingness—but he cannot overcome the fear of Nothingness, cannot find the word or make the gesture that would banish the spell. He is always searching for new "knowledge"; he tries to convince himself through inspirational edifying discourses that our enviable duty lies in a readiness to accept resignedly and even gladly the horrors that fall to our lot; he frantically calls down upon himself new horrors in the hope that they will erase the memory of lost freedom. But neither "dialectic" nor "exhortations" justify the hopes placed in them. On the contrary—the stupor of the soul and the powerlessness of the will continue to grow. Knowledge shows that all possibilities are at an end; exhortations forbid any struggle. The movement of faith, the one thing that could hurl him beyond the limits of the supernaturally bewitched world, he cannot make. Nothingness proceeds with its work of destruction; fear of Nothingness prevents man from doing what could save him.

Does this mean that the end, the final end, has come, that theoretical philosophy with its truths and tortures rules the world, and that the morality of resignation, born of intellectual vision, is all that man can expect?

To whom can a man turn with these questions? Kierke-

gaard rejected the serpent of the Bible, but Pascal did not
hesitate to speak of a supernatural lethargy in man. But if
Kierkegaard was right in thinking that human knowledge
is based on fear of Nothingness alone, then ought we to
strive so persistently to purge Holy Scripture of the "supernatural," and whom are we thus trying to please? Where
do we turn with our questions? Evidently, to that to which
the questions of theoretical philosophy have so far been
addressed—i.e., to Nothingness, fear of which has im-
pelled man to turn from the tree of life and put his trust
in the tree of knowledge. As long as we still ask, we are
wholly in the grip of original sin. We must stop asking,
must renounce objective truth, *must refuse objective truth
the right to decide human fates.* But how is this to be done
by a man whose will is "in a swoon," whose will is enslaved,
paralyzed? Does this not mean to "demand the impossible"? Beyond any doubt, it does mean to demand the
impossible. Even Kierkegaard, who told us so many times
of the swoon of freedom, ventured to say that God signifies
that everything is possible. Or rather: Kierkegaard, the
very man whose experience showed him that the Fall began with the loss of human freedom, that sin is the swoon
of freedom and its powerlessness, the very man who had
to pay such a terrible price for his own powerlessness, was
able to comprehend—even though only in a presentiment
of that which is not yet, and for us powerless, fallen men
has never been—all the immense meaning of the words:
God signifies that everything is possible. God signifies
that the knowledge for which our reason strives so eagerly
and to which it draws us so irresistibly does not exist. God
signifies that there is no evil; there are only the primeval
fiat ("let there be") and the heavenly *valde bonum* ("very

good") before which all our truths, based on the "law" of contradiction, the "law" of sufficient basis, and the other "laws," fade away and become shadows. Man cannot break free from the power of the tempter who revealed Nothingness to him and inspired him with an ineradicable fear of Nothingness. Man cannot stretch forth his hand to the tree of life and is compelled to taste the fruit of the tree of knowledge, even when he is convinced that it brings with it madness and death. But is the human "cannot" really the truth? Is it not simply evidence of powerlessness, evidence which is meaningful only as long as that powerlessness continues? * Let us now hear the words of another man, who, several centuries before Kierkegaard, spoke of the "enslaved will" no less intensely and vehemently than Kierkegaard did of the "swoon of freedom." What attracted Luther most of all in Scripture was the very thing that others find repellent in it. He sought salvation from our clear and precise judgments in *tenebrae fidei* (the "darkness of faith"). The powerlessness and helplessness of our will, which reason takes such pains to conceal from us, rightly perceiving that its might is based on them alone, were felt just as strongly by Luther as by Kierkegaard. Luther was convinced that the enslaved will cannot lead man to that which he needs most of all, and that the enslavement and powerlessness of the will have their source in the truths instilled in us by reason. That is

---

* Cf. the remarkable entry in Kierkegaard's journal for 1848 (I, 379): "For God everything is possible. This thought is my motto in the most profound sense of the word, and it has acquired a deeper meaning for me than I could ever have imagined. Nor for a moment do I allow myself the temerity of thinking that, if I see no way out, this means that there is no way out for God as well. For it is presumptuousness and despair to confuse one's own petty fantasy and so forth with the possibilities at the disposal of God."

why he attacked Scholastic philosophy so violently and rudely, and often unjustly. He took the visible and invisible presence of Aristotle in the systems of the great Scholastics as an insult and a challenge to revealed truth. For him, Aristotle was the embodiment of that *concupiscentia invincibilis,* that *cupiditas scientiae,* which took possession of man after he tasted the fruit of the forbidden tree and which Luther considered the *bellua qua non occisa homo non potest vivere.* Kierkegaard's existential philosophy is the successor to Luther's *sola fide.* Man's task is not to accept and put into practice the truths of reason, but to dispel these truths with the power of faith: in other words, to renounce the tree of knowledge and return to the tree of life. Luther, inspired by Scripture, dared to raise *homo non potest vivere as an objection* to the self-evidences of reason, just as the wails and curses of Job were raised by Kierkegaard *as an objection* to the arguments of theoretical philosophy. Luther's thinking, like Kierkegaard's, was enriched by a new dimension—faith—which the ordinary consciousness regards as a fantastic invention. It is worth noting that Luther's theory has an organic connection with that of the last great Scholastics, Duns Scotus and Ockham, with whom the collapse of Scholastic philosophy begins. The divine free will proclaimed by Duns Scotus exploded the possibility of a philosophy which seeks to unite and reconcile revelation with the truths of reason. After nearly a thousand years of intense spiritual labor, the artificiality, or the unnaturalness, of that mysterious symbiosis of revealed and rational truth which had inspired the works of the most influential representatives of medieval thought was suddenly exposed. If God arbitrarily, regardless of anything, decides what is good and what is evil, then what is to prevent us from going a step further, what is to keep us from asserting, together with Peter Damian and Tertullian, that God just as arbitrarily, unhampered by any laws of thinking or existence, decides what truth is? Perhaps the first proposition is in a way more of a challenge than the second; it might still be possible to come to terms with a God Who does not recognize our logic, but a God Who does not recognize our morality, i.e., an immoral God— what consciousness could find room for that kind of assumption? For Greek philosophy (as for modern) such statements marked the end of any philosophy. Free will as a basic attribute of the divine nature is an abomination of desolation which must repel believer and nonbeliever alike. There is no need to enlarge on this; everyday experience is enough to reveal to us the base and loathsome meaning contained in the concept of "free will." But no matter what everyday experience may have revealed, there is no disputing the fact that medieval philosophy, in the person of its last great representatives (and *immediately* after Thomas Aquinas), patterning itself after the fathers of the church in attempting to "understand" and "explain" revelation, arrived at the idea of divine free will. It is true that the final step was not taken. Even Ockham did not venture to follow the example of Peter Damian; in his writings, too, the law of contradiction had taken over the mind of God. But this does not alter the case. By withdrawing moral sanction from the truths of reason, Duns Scotus and Ockham made it possible for the Absurd to enter into every area of existence. God can overcome the law of contradiction; God, despite the principle of *quod factum est infectum esse nequit*, can, by His power, that *potentia absoluta* which takes precedence over every *potentia ordinata,* make what has once existed into what has never existed, just as He can cause that which has had a beginning to have no end, just as He can give His blessing to the infinitely passionate striving for the finite, even though to our way of thinking this is the same kind of absurdity, the same kind of contradiction, as the concept of a round square, and we are compelled to regard it as an impossibility both for ourselves and for the Creator. To us, the completely unlimited free will of the Creator is an idea as mad as it is terrible. All of us, together with Leibniz, are prepared to wager our souls that the laws of contradiction and sufficient basis alone can offer man the assurance that, when he sets out to search for the truth, he can expect that he will recognize it when he meets it, and never take the truth for a lie, or a lie for the truth. Beginning with Socrates and especially with Aristotle, and down to our own day, human thought has seen these laws and their immutability as an essential bulwark against the errors which besiege us from every side. And then to renounce them! When medieval philosophy encountered the "paradoxes" of Duns Scotus and Ockham, it had to turn its back on its spiritual leader, the *Philosophus,* and accept the fantastic stories of the Bible as the source of truth, or else condemn itself to the miserable existence of casuistic interpretation of the systems created prior to it. There was, of course, a third alternative: to put the Bible in its place, i.e., to stop taking it into account in matters of truth. But this was too heroic an alternative. The outgoing Middle Ages were not prepared to "go so far." Even Descartes did not dare to rely on his own thinking in this manner, or, at any rate, he did not dare to speak of it. Only Spinoza had the courage to raise and resolve the colossal and terrifying problem provided by medieval thinking: if it is necessary to choose between Scripture and reason, between Abraham and Socrates, between the free will of the Creator and eternal, uncreated truths—and impossible not to choose—then one must follow reason and put the Bible away in the museum. Aristotle, as the visible and invisible interpreter of Scripture in the Middle Ages, had done his work; the appearance of Spinoza was the result of his philosophical leadership. Duns Scotus and Ockham uncovered the presence of "free will" in the Biblical concept of the world. Spinoza rejected free will as anarchy, and returned to the idea of knowledge based on proofs, on necessity, that *tertium genus cognitionis, cognitio intuitiva,* which transforms the immediate data of consciousness into unshakable truths. No matter how you search you will not find any laws, any truths in the immediate data of consciousness. They do not contain the law of contradiction, nor the law of sufficient basis. Neither will you find in them the self-evident truth that *quod factum est infectum esse nequit.* It is impossible to "perceive" all this in experience, even through the *oculi mentis* ("intellectual vision") which Spinoza compared to *demonstrationes;* one can only add it to experience. This is the mission of reason, which is only irritated by experience and eagerly strives for general and necessary truths. Only general and necessary truths can make knowledge knowledge. Without them experience is a grotesque, disorderly, undefined succession of events. On all sides the capricious *fiat* lies in wait for us, on all sides we are threatened by the arbitrary unforeseen called into being by *fiat* alone. Knowledge and only knowledge can put an end to arbitrariness. Plato was right; if we renounce reason, if we renounce knowledge, we doom ourselves to the greatest misfortune. He was also right when, anticipating almost prophetically what his remote spiritual descendants, Duns Scotus and Ockham, would find in Scripture, he authoritatively declared in *Euthyphro,* speaking in the name of Socrates, that the idea of good was not created, that it is above the gods, that what is holy is not holy because the gods love it; rather, the gods love and must love the holy because it is holy. Plato realized quite clearly that morality is the guardian of truth and that, if it deserts its post, truth will meet with disaster. Truth and good are uncreated; God has been sentenced to obey the norms of truth and morality, both in His understanding and in His evaluations, to no less a degree than man. *Non ridere, non lugere, neque detestari—sed intelligere* ("do not laugh, do not weep, do not curse, but understand"): this is the first commandment of human and divine thinking, before which all the Biblical commandments must take second place. To be more precise, considering that both the fathers of the church and the Scholastics continually cited Biblical texts, it should be said that Biblical doctrine, refracted through the premises of Aristotelian philosophy, turned into its opposite. The striving to understand, *intelligere,* made and continues to make the most sensitive of people deaf even to Biblical thunderings. Kierkegaard guided us to that appalling moment in history when the love and charity of God conflicted with the inflexibility of uncreated truths—and love was forced to give way; God, like man, is helpless to answer the cry of great despair. Kierkegaard knew what he was doing in sharpening the question thus; never before, even in Kierkegaard's writings, had "indirect communication" been given such terrifying expression as in this conflict. *Intelligere* drained away all God's might, and with it His soul. His will fell in a swoon, became paralyzed, enslaved to some "principle"; God Himself was transformed into a "principle." In other words, God was tempted, God tasted the fruit of the tree against which he had warned man . . . We can go no farther; Kierkegaard has persuaded us that original sin was committed not by man, but by God. Did Kierkegaard persuade us of this? Or was he himself persuaded of it?

This is what brought to my mind Luther's commentary on Galatians. I shall now quote his words, which are also a commentary on those attempts to penetrate to the meaning and significance of the Fall which form the content of Kierkegaard's major works. Having in view, of course, the famous fifty-third chapter of Isaiah, Luther writes: *Omnes prophetae viderunt hoc in spiritu, quod Christus futurus esset omnium maximus latro, adulter, fur, sacrilegus, blasphemus, etc., quo nullus major alius nunquam in mundo fuerit* ("All prophets have seen in spirit that Christ would be the greatest of all robbers, adulterers, thieves, desecrators, blasphemers—greater than any has ever been in the world").

Those are the words of Luther and that is the real meaning of Isaiah 53, so horrifying and destructive to our reason and our morality. And Luther expresses the same idea once more, in words that are even blunter and more intolerable to us: *Deus miserit unigenitum filium suum in mundum ac conferit in eum omnia peccata, dicens: Tu sis Petrus, ille negator, Paulus, ille persecutor, blasphemus et violentus, David ille adulter, peccator ille qui comedit pomum in paradiso, latro ille in cruce, tu sis persona, qui fecerit omnia peccata in mundo* ("God sent His only begotten Son into the world and laid upon Him all sins, saying: You are Peter, the denier, You are Paul, the persecutor and blasphemer, You are David, the adulterer, You are the sinner who ate the apple in paradise, You are the thief on the cross, You have committed all the sins in the world").

XXII

Conclusion

*Kierkegaard's infinitely passionate striv-
ing for the finite—although it contains
an internal contradiction and therefore
seemed, in human estimation, both impossible and senseless—has turned out
to be, in divine estimation, the one thing
that is needful, which is able to triumph
over every "impossible" and "you must."*

L. S.

Dostoyevsky expressed the fundamental ideas of existential philosophy with no less force and passion than
Luther and Kierkegaard; all the years he spent in Siberia
during which he read only one book—Holy Scripture—
were not wasted. It must be assumed that one reads the
Bible differently in confinement than in a writer's study.
In confinement a man learns to ask questions different
from those he asks in freedom, he acquires a boldness of
mind of which he did not even suspect himself capable—
rather, he becomes bold enough to set his mind the sort of

problem he had never dared set it before: the problem of a struggle with the impossible. Dostoyevsky uses almost the same words as Kierkegaard, although he had never even heard Kierkegaard's name. "Men yield at once to impossibility. Impossibility means a stone wall! What stone wall? Why, the laws of nature, of course, mathematics, the conclusions of the natural sciences. For instance, once they have proved to you that you are descended from the ape, it does no good to frown; just accept it as it is. Once they have proved that a single particle of your own fat must actually be worth more to you than a hundred thousand like you . . . , well, accept it, there is nothing to be done about it, for twice two is mathematics. Try to dispute it. For goodness' sake, they will shout at you, no insubordination; twice two is four. Nature does not ask your permission; she is not concerned with your wishes and with whether her laws please you or not. You are obliged to accept her as she is and therefore you must accept all her consequences as well. A wall, then, is a wall, etc., etc." Dostoyevsky has summed up in a few lines what Duns Scotus, Bonaventura, Spinoza, and Leibniz have told us: eternal laws live in the understanding of God and men independent of their will, eternal truths are armed with every imaginable kind of intimidation, and so: *non ridere, non lugere, neque detestari, sed intelligere.* Truth is coercive truth and consequently, whatever its source, it will be truth only if it is able to defend itself by the same means which serve to attack it; for those who will not admit this, tortures have been prepared to force them to make the necessary admission. Dostoyevsky, as is evident from his words which I have just quoted, perceived all this no less clearly than Duns Scotus, Bonaventura, Spi-

noza, and Leibniz. He also knew that our reason eagerly
strives for general and necessary judgments, even though
he had presumably never read Kant. But at the very moment when theoretical philosophy, under the spell of Socrates and Aristotle, was intensifying all its efforts to reduce
revelation to the plane of rational thinking, at the very
moment when Kant was writing his Critiques in order to
justify and exalt the passion for reason, Dostoyevsky waᵉ
seized by a terrible suspicion, or, if you prefer, a magnificent and dazzling suspicion, that this passion for reason
represented the *concupiscentia invincibilis* which took
possession of man after the Fall. I repeat and insist: like
Kierkegaard, Dostoyevsky knew the power that original
sin has over us; but he felt the horror of sin, and in this
horror there dawned an awareness of the illusory nature of
the power appropriated by the truths of reason. Immediately after the words quoted above, which summarize with
such striking conciseness and precision the fundamental
principles of theoretical philosophy regarding coercive
truth, he completely amazes the reader and half amazes
himself by not merely saying, but shouting, in a seeming
transport of self-oblivion (such a thing cannot be said, but
must be "shouted"): "Lord God, what are the laws of nature and arithmetic to me if for some reason I do not like
these laws and this twice two is four? Obviously, I will not
break this wall down with my head if I do not really have
the strength to breach it, but I will not concede to it simply
because it is a stone wall and I lack the strength. As if
such a wall were in fact a reassurance and in fact contained any promise of peace, just because twice two is
four. Oh, absurdity of absurdities! It is far better to understand everything, be aware of everything, all impossibili-

ties and stone walls, and not concede to even one of these impossibilities and stone walls if it disgusts you to concede to them. . . ." Kant "criticized" pure reason; the only truth before which he bowed was rational truth, that is, coercive, compelling truth. The idea that "coercion" is evidence not for, but *against* the truthfulness of a judgment, that all "necessities" must and can disappear in freedom (which he foresightedly transferred to the sphere of *Ding an sich*) was alien to Kant's "critical philosophy" and just as remote from it as from the dogmatic philosophy of Spinoza, Leibniz, and the mystically inclined Scholastics. Dostoyevsky's determination to challenge the power of proofs to prove seemed even stranger to theoretical philosophy, quite outlandish, in fact; how can a man permit himself to take exception to the truth solely because he finds it repugnant! Whatever truth may bring with it, all must be accepted. What is more: man will accept it all, for he is threatened with unprecedented moral and physical tortures if he does not. This is the *articulus stantis et cadentis* of theoretical philosophy, which it has never actually formulated *explicite*, which it has always been at pains to conceal, but which, as we have seen, has always been *implicite* present in it and inspired it. One needs the unlimited audacity of Dostoyevsky, the "fearless dialectic" of Kierkegaard, the sudden insight of Luther, the impetuosity of Tertullian or Peter Damian, in order to recognize in eternal truths the *bellua qua non occisa homo non potest vivere* and, armed with such weapons as *homo non potest vivere*, to take up the fight against the multitude of "proofs" which are the defense of self-evidency. Or, rather, one needs the boundless despair of which Kierkegaard told us, which is the only thing that can lift, catapult man into that dimension of being where coercion ends, and eternal truths with it, or where eternal truths end, and coercion with them.

The powerlessness of God, Who, in Kierkegaard's view, is languishing in the stony grip of Inflexibility, or Luther's God, Who proves to be the greatest sinner the world has ever seen—only he who has survived, and continues to survive, not in words, but in actual experience, all the horror and immense burden of this ultimate enigma of our existence can dare to "turn" his attention away from the "immediate data of consciousness" and expect the truth from a "miracle." And then Kierkegaard hurls his "motto": for God everything is possible; Dostoyevsky launches an attack against stone walls and "twice two is four;" Luther understands that God, not man, plucked the apple from the forbidden tree; Tertullian overturns our age-old *pudet, ineptum et impossibile;* Job sends away his pious friends; Abraham raises the knife to his son; revealed Truth engulfs and destroys all the coercive truths obtained by man from the tree of knowledge and evil.

It is difficult, immensely difficult, for fallen man to grasp the primordial opposition between revelation and the truths of knowledge. It is still more difficult to entertain the thought of truths which are not coercive. Nevertheless, in the very depths of his soul man hates coercive truth, as if sensing that it conceals a sham and a delusion, that it has its origin in empty and powerless Nothingness, fear of which has paralyzed our will. And when they hear the voices of persons who, like Dostoyevsky, Luther, Pascal, and Kierkegaard, remind them of the Fall of the first man, even the most heedless prick up their ears. There is no truth where coercion reigns. It is impossible that coercive truth, which is indifferent to all, should determine the fate of the universe. We have no power to banish the spell of Nothingness, we cannot free ourselves from the supernatural enchantment and stupor that have taken possession of us. To vanquish the supernatural requires supernatural intervention. How it has puzzled men that God permitted the "serpent" to tempt the first man, what devices have they resorted to in order to take the "guilt" of the first Fall from God and transfer it to man! And indeed, who would venture to hold God responsible for the horrors that came into the world with sin? Does this not mean to pass sentence upon God? To our way of thinking, there can be only one answer. Man has sinned and if sin has crushed him—then so must it be. But Luther discovered something different, as does every man who is not afraid to read and listen to Scripture: for God nothing is impossible—*est enim Deus omnipotens ex nihilo creans omnia* ("for He is God Almighty, Who created everything from nothing"). For God there is neither a law of contradiction nor a law of sufficient basis. For Him there are also no eternal, uncreated truths. Man tasted of the tree of knowledge and thereby ruined both himself and all his descendants; the fruit of the tree of life has become inaccessible to him, his existence has become an illusion, has turned into a shadow, like Kierkegaard's love for Regina Olsen. So it has been—Scripture bears witness to that. So it is— Scripture bears witness to that as well, as do our everyday experience and theoretical philosophy. And nevertheless— it was not man, but God that plucked and ate the fruit of the forbidden tree. God, for Whom everything is possible, did this so that what had once existed would become nonexistent, and what had not existed would become existent, even though all the laws of our reason and our morality cry out against this. God did not even stop at "renouncing" His Inflexibility in answer to the cries, not only of His own Son, but of ordinary men as well. The cries of living, although created and finite, men are more audible to God than the demands of stony, although uncreated and eternal, truths. He even created His Sabbath for man and would not allow pedants to sacrifice man for the Sabbath. And for God there is nothing that is impossible. He took upon Himself the sins of all mankind, He became the greatest and most terrible of sinners: it was not Peter, but He Who denied; not David, but He Who committed adultery; not Paul, but He Who persecuted Christ; not Adam, but He Who plucked the apple. But nothing is beyond God's strength. Sin did not crush Him, He crushed sin. God is the sole source of everything; all eternal truths and all laws of morality bow and prostrate themselves before His will. Because God wishes it, good is good. Because he wishes it, truth is truth. It was by God's will that man succumbed to temptation and lost his freedom. It is also by His will—before which Inflexibility, stony like all laws, crumbled to dust when it attempted to resist—that man's freedom will return, that man's freedom has returned; this is the content of Biblical revelation. But the path to revelation is blocked by the truths of our reason and the laws of our morality, which have become petrified in their indifference. The heartless or indifferent power of Nothingness seems terrible to us, but we do not have the strength to partake of the freedom proclaimed in Scripture. We fear it even more than Nothingness. A God bound by nothing, not even truth and good, a God Who created both truth and good by His own will! We take this to be

arbitrariness, we think that the limited certainty of Nothingness is still preferable to the limitlessness of divine possibilities. Kierkegaard, Kierkegaard himself, who
learned well enough from his own experience the destructive effect of uncreated truths, amended Holy Scripture
and rejoiced when Inflexibility stepped between God and
His crucified Son, and "pure" charity, infatuated with
itself, gloried in the knowledge of its helplessness and
powerlessness. We know, of course, that all Kierkegaard's
admissions were forced from him by torture. Nevertheless,
Nothingness, in whose power Kierkegaard and the rest of
us are condemned to drag out our earthly existence, has
somehow or other made fear the inseparable companion
of our thinking. We are afraid of everything, we are even
afraid of God, and dare not trust in Him as long as we
have not been assured in advance that He will not threaten
us in any way. And no "rational" arguments can dispel this
fear; on the contrary, rational arguments foster it.

This is the starting point of the Absurd. It was from the
Absurd, forged by the horrors of existence, that Kierkegaard found out about sin and learned to see sin where
Scripture shows it to be. The opposite of sin is not virtue,
but freedom. Freedom from all fears, freedom from coercion. The opposite of sin—this, too, was revealed to him by
the Absurd—is faith. That is what is hardest of all for us
to accept in Kierkegaard's existential philosophy, and what
was the hardest of all for him to accept. It was for this
reason that he said faith is the mad struggle of man for
the possible. Existential philosophy is the struggle of faith
with reason over the possible, or rather, the impossible.
Kierkegaard does not follow the lead of theoretical philosophy and say: *credo, ut intelligam* ("I believe in order

that I may understand"). He discards our *intelligere* as unnecessary and deadening. He recalls the words of the Prophet: *justus ex fide vivit* (the just shall live by faith), and the words of the Apostle: all that is not of faith is sin. Only faith, regardless of anything, "knowing" nothing and not wanting to know—only faith can be the source of the truths created by God. Faith does not ask questions, does not inquire, makes no investigation. Faith simply invokes the One by Whose will all that is, is. And if theoretical philosophy originates in the given, in self-evidences, and considers them necessary and inevitable, then existential philosophy vanquishes all necessities through faith. "It was by faith that Abraham obeyed the call to go into a country which would be his for posterity, and he went, not knowing himself where he was going." In order to reach the promised land, it is not necessary to have knowledge; the promised land does not exist for the knowing man. The promised land is the place to which the believer has come; it proves to be the promised land *because* the believer has come to it: *certum quia impossibile* ("it is certain—because it is impossible").

Faith is not "trust" in the invisible truths unveiled by reason; it is not even trust in the rules of life proclaimed by teachers or holy books. Such faith is only less complete knowledge and is evidence of the Fall of man, like the *tertium genus cognitionis* (third kind of knowledge) of Spinoza or the uncreated truths of Leibniz. If God signifies that nothing is impossible, then faith means that the end has come for necessity and all the stony "you must's" spawned by necessity. There are no truths; the dawn of freedom has arrived: Hear, O Israel! the Lord our God is one Lord. And there is no sin; God has taken it upon Himself, and destroyed it together with all the evil that came into the world with sin. Theoretical philosophy "explains" evil, but explained evil not only persists, not only remains evil, but justifies its necessity, is accepted, and becomes an eternal principle. Existential philosophy goes beyond the limits of "explanations," existential philosophy sees its own worst enemy in "explanations." It is impossible to explain evil, impossible to "accept" it and come to an understanding with it, just as it is impossible to accept sin and come to an understanding with it; evil can only and must only be destroyed.

Kierkegaard's books, together with his journals, all his direct and indirect communications, are an unbroken narrative of man's desperate, frenzied, convulsive struggle with original sin and the horrors of life which arose from sin. Rational thinking and the morality which stands guard over it—by which men live and with which they are satisfied—brought Kierkegaard to what is most terrible of all: powerlessness. His fate was to experience powerlessness in the most repulsive and shameful form it can take on earth: when he touched his beloved, she turned into a shadow, a phantom. Worse yet—everything he touched turned into a phantom; the fruit of the tree of life became inaccessible to him; the power of death that looms over all men, the despair that lies in wait for all, took possession of his soul even in his youth. Yet this same despair raised him above the plane of ordinary thinking, and it was then that he discovered that his powerlessness was itself an illusion. What is more: the illusory nature of human powerlessness was at times revealed to him even more directly and tangibly than the illusory nature of existence. Powerlessness was and powerlessness was not; it was unmasked

311

as fear of the nonexistent, the uncreated, Nothingness. Nothingness, which does not exist, followed sin into the world and made man its slave. Speculative philosophy, brought into being by original sin and then crushed by it, cannot rid us of Nothingness. On the contrary, it calls upon it and binds it with unbreakable ties to all of existence. And as long as knowledge and intellectual vision are the source of truth for us, Nothingness will remain the master of life.

Kierkegaard experienced all this as directly and agonizingly as few in the world have ever experienced anything; as a result, hardly anyone has been able to give such authentic testimony about sin and the powerlessness of the will as he. In addition, rarely has anyone had the ability and the desire to celebrate so ebulliently, so passionately, so ecstatically the Absurd which paves the way for faith. He could not make the "movement of faith"—his will was paralyzed, "in a swoon." But he despised his powerlessness and cursed it with all the vehemence of which a man is capable. Is this not in fact the first "movement" of faith? Is this not faith itself? Genuine, true faith? He rejected the eternal truths of reason, he shook the unshakable principles of morality. If reason is supreme, if morality is supreme—Abraham is lost, Job is lost, all men are lost; the "Inflexibility" which has permeated uncreated truths will, like a giant python, strangle everything alive, even God Himself, in its terrible embrace.

Ex auditu, from Scripture, there came to Kierkegaard the good tidings that for God everything is possible, that for God there is nothing impossible. And when all possibilities had ended for him, or rather, because all possibilities had ended for him, he hastened to obey the call which had reached his ears. Historical Christianity, which lives in peace and harmony with our reason and our morality, had become for him the monster *qua non occisa homo non potest vivere*. Historical Christianity, which adapts itself to the average conditions of human existence, has forgotten God, has renounced God. It is satisfied with "possibilities," convinced a priori that God, too, must be satisfied with the possible; Christians, as Kierkegaard put it, have abolished Christ.

During Kierkegaard's lifetime no one would listen to him. After his death his books came to be read more and more, and he achieved universal reknown. But is existential philosophy fated to triumph over theoretical philosophy? Will Kierkegaard become a "teacher of mankind"? It makes no difference. Perhaps it is not necessary that he become a "teacher;" most likely it is not necessary. Kierkegaard's voice has been and probably will always remain the voice of one crying in the wilderness. Existential philosophy, which is directed toward God, for Whom everything is possible, tells us that God does not coerce, that His truth attacks no one and is itself defended by nothing, that God Himself is free and created man as free as He is. But the *concupiscentia invincibilis* of fallen man, man who has tasted the fruit of the tree of knowledge, fears divine freedom more than anything else and eagerly strives for general and necessary truths. Can a "rational" man allow himself to think that God, heeding the cries, not of His beloved Son, nor even of Abraham or Job, but of the theology student Sören Kierkegaard, smashed to bits the stony Inflexibility forced upon Him by our thinking, and raised a ridiculous, a petty and ridiculous, incident in Kierkegaard's life to the level of a universally historic event? That He freed Kierkegaard from the spell of the tree of knowledge and gave back to him who was old even in his mother's womb that youthfulness of spirit and that spontaneity which provide access to the tree of life? That Kierkegaard's infinitely passionate striving for the finite— although it contains an internal contradiction, and therefore seemed, in human estimation, both impossible and senseless—has turned out to be, in divine estimation, the "one thing that is needful," which is able to triumph over every "impossible" and "you must"? * There can be only one answer to this question. That is why Kierkegaard turned, not to reason and morality, which demand resignation, but to the Absurd and Faith, which give their sanction to daring. His writings and sermons, raging, frenzied, violent, full of intensity, speak to us of nothing else: a voice crying in the wilderness about the horrors of Nothingness which has enslaved fallen man! A mad struggle for possibility, it is also a mad flight from the god of the philosophers to the God of Abraham, the God of Isaac, the God of Jacob.

* Let us recall Kierkegaard's words once more (V, 46):"And nevertheless it is a wonderful thing to win the king's daughter . . . Only the knight of faith is really happy, only he is master over the finite, while the knight of resignation is a stranger and an outsider."

Kierkegaard 45082

Shestov
Kierkegaard and the existential phil
osophy.

DATE DUE

GAYLORD M-2   PRINTED IN U.S.A.